THE PELICAN LATIN AMERICAN LIBRARY
General Editor: Richard Gott

Servants of God or Masters of Men?

Victor Daniel Bonilla took his degree in philosophy and
letters at the National University of Colombia. He also
studied law at the Externado of Colombia, and sociology
at the University of Paris.

He has been editor of two weekly papers, and
contributed to other daily papers and periodicals.
He was co-founder of the *Gaceta literaria*
published by Tercer Mundo. He has also written
monographs on seven areas of Colombia, five of which
were published in the socio-economic review *Tierra*.

At present he is a member of the Colombian Committee
for the Defence of the Indian; he is also working with
Amazonia autóctona, a new foundation set up to preserve
Indian life while consolidating their cultural inheritance.

Victor Daniel Bonilla

Servants of God or Masters of Men?

The Story of a Capuchin Mission
in Amazonia

Translated from French by
Rosemary Sheed

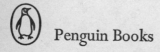 Penguin Books

Penguin Books Ltd, Harmondsworth,
Middlesex, England
Penguin Books Inc., 7110 Ambassador Road,
Baltimore, Maryland 21207, U.S.A.
Penguin Books Australia Ltd, Ringwood,
Victoria, Australia

Published in Pelican Books 1972
Copyright © Victor Daniel Bonilla, 1971
This translation copyright © Rosemary Sheed, 1972

Made and printed in Great Britain by
Cox & Wyman Ltd,
London, Reading and Fakenham
Set in Intertype Lectura

Contents

Note to the Reader

It was the author's decision that this English translation be made from the French of Alain Gheerbrant rather than from the original Spanish, much of which would be of interest to, and perhaps only understood by, Colombian readers. In collaboration with Señor Bonilla, M. Gheerbrant therefore made a number of alterations with European and other readers in view. The English translator has also studied the original Spanish text, and has conferred with Señor Bonilla over doubtful points.

A Prefatory Note

Taken straightforwardly, this book is the account of a Colombian tribe facing a Catholic missionary community; but in a broader sense it is the everlasting story of the West against the Indian. From my own point of view it is also an attempt to contradict the official 'history' of Indian America. It is, if you like, the testament of someone who has a little white blood and a lot of white culture, but does not accept the idealized account of Christian-cum-Western civilization. That civilization, having exploited the Indian for centuries, and having taken a large part of his culture away from him without replacing it with anything at all of value, is still pursuing its work of pillage and destruction. And it always does it in the name of what it holds as its most sacred principles: democracy, progress, 'acculturization' of 'primitives', Christian charity, and the expansion of the reign of God in Indo-America.

VICTOR DANIEL BONILLA

PART ONE

Pax Hispanica – Pax India (1536–1906)

CHAPTER 1

Two Races Meet on the Road to El Dorado

Thus Your Majesty must understand that in these parts there are no Christians, but only demons, no servants of God and the King, but traitors to their law and King.

(Letter from the Bishop of Santa Marta to the King of Spain, 1541)

In the Andes, at what was the northern boundary of the great empire of the Incas, there lies hidden the little valley of Sibundoy. 2,000 metres above sea level, it forms a hollowed-out ellipse of some 8,500 hectares, the edges of which merge into the *páramos** around it: a landscape of contrast, where the mildness of the climate in the valley is very different from the cold on top of the extinct volcanoes which stand, watchman-like, all around it, while ashes from their past eruptions still fertilize its soil. It is for this climate that the valley leaves such lasting memories with anyone who comes upon it after crossing those cloud-capped, wooded peaks.

The attractiveness of the spot and the sense of security it gives must have been what led the pre-Columbian nomads to settle there. The two tribes which live today in the Sibundoy valley are descended from those subjects of the Inca; until the beginning of this century they had it to themselves, and impressed their culture upon it.

But these Indians are now simply a subject and alienated people, forced to submit to the presence of invaders – a situ-

*Those high, cold desert lands to be found nearly everywhere higher than 3,000 metres along the Andean chain are called by the Colombians *páramos*, and the Peruvians *puna*.

...h causes real anguish among those old enough to
...er the time not so long ago when they owned the land
...ere free to organize their own social structure.

...ut it is a long story, and to see in its true context this
little-known episode in which, without a shot being fired, the
colonialist spirit of the West achieved one of its twentieth-
century crusades, we must go back to the days of the original
Spanish conquest.

For the West, the history of the Sibundoy valley starts with
the period when the Spaniards succeeded in conquering the
New World. For the Indians, it goes back to those far more
distant days when they worshipped the Sun and the Moon.[1]

In those days the territory of the Sibundoy extended far
beyond the boundaries of the valley where they live today: it
went from the valleys of the Juanambú river in the north to
the region of La Ensillada in the south, and also contained part
of the high western plateau. It was there that the two races
first met in 1535.

Benalcázar's lieutenants, Ampudia and Añasco, who had
set out on a mission to find El Dorado, attacked the Indians
in order to make them subject to the power of Spain, and
pillaged their wealth. It was their horses and harquebuses
which won the day. On that spot a town was later founded
whose name will recur constantly in our story: 'the Vicious
City of Concepción de Pasto'. Making the most of their
success, they drove the unwilling Indians eastwards, pushing
the Mocoa people, then settled around Lake Guamués, back
towards the Amazon. It was this campaign that brought
them 'half dead' into the Sibundoy valley. There they rested for
three weeks before setting off once more for the north in
search of other regions 'rich in gold'[2]. This further adventure,
notorious for the Spaniards' appalling massacres of Indians
– men, women and children – was ultimately to be their un-
doing: the murderers were destroyed by their victims, and
Añasco himself died at the hands of a woman, the heroic cacique* Gaitana.

*Hereditary chieftain.

The Sibundoy people remember that first encounter only in legend: 'Numbers of them, seeing that they were overrun by the white men, built their own funeral pyres, and went up in smoke to the sky, where the stars are their eyes twinkling down upon us.'[3]

Seven years later, in 1542, Captain Hernán Pérez de Quesada set off from Santa Fe de Bogotá for the south-west, in search of the fabulous treasures of El Dorado, and this was the occasion for the second appearance of white men in the Sibundoy valley.

The conquistador left Bogotá at the head of 240 Spaniards and almost 8,000 Muiska Indians, to explore the eastern ramifications of the Andes. They went as far as the area now called the Putumayo after the huge tributary of the Amazon that flows through it. So disastrous was this venture that he had lost over 7,000 men by the time he arrived to confront the Mocoas who had barely become settled there.

Unfriendly Indians and a harsh climate were not the only causes for his losses – at least if one is to believe some of the accounts of the chronicles: 'A scribe named Francisco García, who must have been something of a glutton, unable to withstand the anguish of intense hunger, so intemperate was he, resolved to bring his life to an end, and all alone, without the help of anyone else, he hanged himself from one of the beams of the hut where he was living.'[4]

Shortly after that incident, two natives captured by the Spaniards spoke of their country in the highlands, with its fertile fields of maize and fruit trees. Captain Pérez immediately sent out a patrol which, after three days' march across mountainous country, 'came out into a valley full of huts and heavily populated, known as Sibundoy'.

As soon as Pérez – who was interminably harassed by the Mocoa attempting to take their revenge for the troubles he had caused them – heard the good news, he at once set off for that valley. The vanguard of his troops arrived in the evening, and settled themselves in 'little huts filled with maize, vegetables and all kinds of edible roots. Their hunger was so ravenous that all night long Spaniards, Indians and even horses refused any exercise save that of their jaws, their hunger so overwhelming as to be apparently insatiable.'[4]

We also learn from the same chronicler that the Sibundoy were 'men of peace'; that there were two of Benalcázar's captains in the valley with a few people from Pasto; and that Hernán Pérez had to sacrifice his few remaining jewels and gold chains in order to purchase enough cattle to 'divide amongst his men to enable them to settle'. After this he allowed his troops 'to go wherever each one wished'.

These accounts prove that despite the seven years of war that had taken place, Pérez de Quesada's men were far from having to conquer an inhospitable jungle to find a living. All the chroniclers agree on the existence of the villages of Putumayo, Manoy and Sibundoy Grande, and their writings are full of fulsome adjectives describing 'this valley full of huts and heavily populated'. Piedrahita boasts of the profits these conquistadors made from their fields of maize after the agonizing hunger of the previous year; Aguado and Cieza de León describe the Indian plantations; and the poet Castellanos speaks glowingly of 'this land so rich in fine food'.

After the slaughter of early times, there followed the *doctrineros**. Historians tell us that it was the Franciscans who got there first. They had begun to Christianize the valley in 1547, launching an attack on the irreligious beliefs of the Indians. Their pious work was marked, among other things, by giving Spanish names to everything: Manoy, Putumayo and Sibundoy were re-christened Santiago, San Andrés and San Pablo, names which were to stand alongside the older ones in all the seventeenth- and eighteenth-century archives. On the other hand, the acceptance of the new religion was enormously facilitated by the fact that most of the Andean Indians identified their Sun God with God the Father, and the Moon and Earth goddesses with the Virgin Mary.

*A *doctrina* was a concession of land granted to the Catholic *doctrineros* to enable them to evangelize the natives. The *doctrinero*, or father of doctrine, was both a spiritual and a civil leader.

The Sibundoy were model catechumens. They readily abandoned their own religious traditions in favour of the doctrines
taught by the priests. Despite such promising results, the Com-
missary General of the order only a few years later decreed 'the
voluntary abandonment of this *doctrina* before the Royal
Court* in Quito which, by a decree of 23 March 1577, entrusted it to the Dominicans from the Pasto friary'. The latter
only stayed for six years, after which they departed, taking
with them the fine statue of Our Lord of Sibundoy, 'to the great
distress of the people'.[5]

The removal of their statue was to become a legend among
the natives, to whom it provided proof positive of the jealousy
felt for them by the white men because God, in the guise of
that statue, had miraculously done what they wished. What is
interesting about the whole story is that it shows how far advanced was their Christianization. Here it is as told by the
chronicler Fray Juan de Santa Gertrudis:

The parish priest of Sibundoy once wanted to remove the village
on to a small plateau, a more convenient situation. The Indians quite
agreed with him, and they built a church and some houses there. In
their old church they had a statue of Christ seated, as in the hall of
Pilate, perfectly proportioned and complete in every way. He had a
brown skin. They set up a chapel for him in the new village, and
finally, when they moved there, they also took their statue; but
during the night it returned to the old church. Three times they
moved it, and three times it went back. Since they thought someone
must be taking it, they ambushed it on the road, armed with wooden
staves to beat the culprit when they caught him. They lay in wait
until dawn; only then did they see the Lord himself walking down
the road. One of them struck his leg with a stave, and as though it

*This is in fact a term for which we have no English equivalent: the
Audiencia real. The Spanish crown, having its colonies so far away, was
anxious to maintain a royal 'presence' on the spot. Thus the Viceroys
and the various *Audiencias* between them could act with full authority
from the King, and men were sent from Spain to fill all the senior posts.
In order that the Viceroys should not become too powerful, the *oidores,* or
judges of the *Audiencias,* carried out certain political and administrative
functions as well as the judicial functions of any high court, while the
Viceroys had correspondingly rather less authority than their title suggests.

were a living leg, the blow made a huge bruise which can be seen there to this day. After being struck, Our Lord turned round and went back to the new church in obedience to the Indians. They told the story to the priest who, in view of its miraculous nature, reported it to his superior. The incident became widely known, and orders were given to take the statue to Quito, where it remains an object of intense veneration, and where it is called the *Zambo* [the word for a Negro-Indian mestizo] because of its brown tint.[6]

Other chroniclers record that the Lord of Sibundoy was transferred not to Quito, but to the Vicious City of Pasto, where its ornaments and worship were enriched with innumerable gifts from legacies.[7] The crucifix which now stands over the altar of the Jesuit Church in Pasto is not like the very precise descriptions we have of that other highly venerated statue, but none the less the Indians continue to this day to visit and venerate this cross, to which they have transferred their former devotion to the 'Lord of Sibundoy'.

Over the passage of the years, though the valley was subject to periodic incursions by conquistadors and *doctrineros*, the daily ritual was in no way affected. Thus the seventeenth century found the place still enjoying the tranquillity that only such isolation made possible, a tranquillity far from the norm in those days. To grasp more clearly just why it was such an exception, we may cast a brief glance over what was taking place at the time around the foot of the Andes.

The area had been made subject to Spanish rule by Don Francisco Pérez de Quesada fourteen years after his brother's ill-fated expedition. He had established two small colonies – Mocoa and Ecija de los Sucumbíos – with the object of exploiting the gold in the rivers with the help of the conquered and enslaved Indians.

This first attempt at colonization was short-lived. The Encabellado* and Cofan Indians set about systematically attacking these settlements to free their fellows; 'so much so that the *doctrinero* had to take refuge behind a stockade, and to

*The word simply means 'hairy', because they wore their hair long, to their waists.

make it safe to say mass, several loaded guns had to be brought into the church'. And, despite the reinforcements of men and weapons that were brought to clear the area, and the capture of several Indian leaders, the colonies finally had to be abandoned.[8]

The underlying cause for these upheavals was the Indians' reaction to the excesses of the *encomenderos**, whose greed knew no bounds in these isolated spots where Spanish law could not easily be enforced. Their abuses were not restricted merely to an outrageous exploitation of native labour, but went beyond the bounds of all human feeling. We find the following edifying example from the memories of one Royal Visitor to the río Orteguaza:

> The aforementioned Doña Juana, because of her jealousy of her husband, would beat and torture the Indian women on the grounds that he, Martín Calderón, was consorting with them; and in the case of one woman named Ana Maria, a serving girl of Doña Juana's who was found to be pregnant, the said Doña Juana put a burning brand and lighted candles into her vagina, so violent was her rage that Martín Calderón should have been having relations with the woman – who died the next day from the punishment inflicted upon her . . .

* The name of *encomenderos*, or beneficiaries of *encomiendas*, was given to the Spanish colonizers who were 'entrusted with' (as the official texts put it) or 'given' (as it was described in common parlance) a certain number of Indians whom they could exploit at will on condition that they ensured their religious training. 'The Spaniards who were entrusted with Indians established with them a relationship not unlike that existing between feudal lords and their vassals' (Salvador de Madariaga). Though the Catholic Queen Isabella had proclaimed the Indians 'free subjects and vassals of Castille', the *encomenderos* were soon behaving like slave-owners. In theory no *encomienda* could last longer than three years; but it soon came to be for a lifetime, and even 'several lifetimes', as the chroniclers said, and as the reader will soon see. This institution – which also brought the Crown a tax of one gold peso per head for every 'entrusted' Indian – was abolished in 1542 by the famous *Leyes Nuevas* of Charles V, as a result of the energetic and persistent complaints of Fray Bartolomé de la Casas, the 'father of the Indians'. But, as will be seen in this book, it took over a century in many cases for the abolition to become fully effective.

And it was heard among the Caguán Indians as a well-known fact that the said Doña Juana had put a 'banana smeared with pepper into the vagina of Juana Mancia, an Indian in her *encomienda*, because of the jealousy she bore her . . .'⁹

This situation was often exacerbated by the insensitivity of certain missionaries who, in their disregard for the mentality and customs of the Indians, created pointless and often irreparable conflicts. It is thus hardly surprising that there were more uprisings some decades later, when the Spaniards returned with their weapons and their Church to the Sucumbíos area.

Fray Bartolomé de Alácano described what happened to the first expedition of Franciscans to the district. In 1635, he says, six Franciscans, accompanied by eighteen soldiers, sixty Indians and beggars, settled in Ecija de los Sucumbíos, where a new colony had been established in 1609 by the Jesuit Father Ferrer. They set about converting the natives in the usual way: massive indoctrination through an Indian interpreter who knew a little Spanish, followed by baptism. The whole thing took place in holy calm, and the chronicler indulges in fervent praises of the Encabellados, stressing their courage and nobility. To read him one would think that Indians and whites alike had forgotten what had happened fifty years before. But, alas, one day . . .

Captain Palacios came to want us to move from that site to another, better and nearer the river, so that we could use our canoes and go fishing. . . . This was done – though it never should have been – and, a few days after we had moved, the Indians did likewise, because of the ill treatment they had received: to us that treatment did not appear terribly serious, but to them it really was so, for they were of such nobility as not to tolerate the slightest blow even from a brother. They also began to withdraw, and no longer came to see us, nor did they bring us food as had been their custom – which was something quite new to us, and exceedingly disturbing. We begged the Lord for help, waiting daily to be attacked, and on the 8 October, the feast of St Bridget, we received information that the Encabellados were armed and advancing upon us. . . . And we came upon so many Indians that it was only by the mercy of God [that they did not slaughter us all].

That day the Spanish captain paid with his life for the outrages inflicted upon the Indians. But the 'seraphic workers'* still saw no reason to modify their behaviour towards their new converts. On their return in 1721 they tried to get them to give up the custom of having more than one wife. And the Indians, Father de Alácano tells us, 'believing that we wanted to subjugate them still further' revolted, with those from all the other villages fighting alongside them. Only two Franciscans, rather the worse for wear, escaped to tell the tale – to which Father Laurentino de la Cruz added that, if later 'the Indians received and treated them well, it was only for fear of the men with harquebuses who came with them'.

But one may note in that violent era one missionary voice which rose in denunciation of the misunderstandings and abuses which caused such bloodshed throughout Amazonia. Fray Francisco Romero said to the king:

If Your Majesty should ask who has destroyed this town [Espíritu Santo de Caguán] . . . I could not in all conscience conceal the truth from you. . . . Know, my Lord, that the guilt is shared between those who have been its temporal and its spiritual rulers. The latter have provided cause for all their parishioners, even the most fervent, to leave in a body, some through the darkest jungles, others to the most uncharted territories where only infidels live.

And to be sure of leaving no possible doubt as to the collusion existing between certain missionaries and the settlers who were blatantly exploiting the Indians, he added:

One of the principal reasons why conversions have become so hated by the infidels, now more than ever, is that they know that to accept our holy faith is to bow their heads and shoulders beneath the intolerable yoke of vassalage to those who are your Majesty's own unworthy vassals.[10]

The clergy of the day did not merely cover up for the behaviour of the colonizers, but actually went so far as to mal-

---

*This is one of the many names the missionaries used of themselves in their chronicles: they were also 'fathers of doctrine', 'bearers of the good news', 'heralds of the gospel', 'servants of God', etc.

treat the Indians themselves, as is quite clear from reading the *Instructions* addressed by the Archbishop of Lima (whose authority extended to the south of Colombia) to the priests authorized to make visitations in his parishes in 1665. In this most humanitarian code, the prelate orders that all food and riding animals provided by the Indians are to be paid for; he forbids his clergy not only to deal dishonestly with the natives, but even to 'play at dice and other forbidden games', all under pain of having to pay back 'two to four times' the amount, and even being suspended from 'every duty and benefice'. Other even more revealing items forbid parish priests 'to punish, wound or strike with their hands any Indian however guilty he may be, or worst of all to shave his head, the penalty for this being three hundred pesos', or 'to prevent the Indians, Negroes and mulattos working for them to marry, or, once married, to stop them from living together'. These wise decrees also include one strictly evangelical rule: 'Everything is to be explained to the Indians in their own language, because it is very important that they understand that the Visitation is made for their good and to improve their situation, even at the temporal level . . .'[11]

But at the foot of the Andes, where even the regulations of the church hierarchy remained a dead letter, uprisings continued during most of the seventeenth century, resulting in the final collapse of the towns of Ecija de los Sucumbíos and Mocoa. The fighting sometimes even extended to the village of Sibundoy Grande itself, which was attacked several times by the Mocoa and Yaguaronjo, as they tried to rally the support of their fellow-Indians in the struggle against the Spanish invader. But few of the Sibundoy would take part; they had been decimated in the first wave of the invasion, and were now well on the way to a daily more evident acculturization.

CHAPTER 2

Three Centuries Safe from the West

And the said lands I leave to my Indian natives from the village of Santiago, and those of the village of Sibundoy Grande, that they may live there and defend them if any threat should come from any ill-intentioned person for such is my will . . .

(From the Testament of CARLOS TAMOABIOY, cacique of the Sibundoy, 15 March 1700)

At the beginning of the seventeenth century the colonial order, as described by so many scholars, already reigned on the high plateaux of the Nariño.

We must recall that during the early decades of the Conquest the Indians of South America had been forced into 'personal service' – in other words, unpaid labour in the homes, plantations and mines of the Spaniards. But in 1520 the Emperor Charles V had *legally* freed them from any such obligation, and at the same time decreed a reform of the *encomiendas*. His successor, Philip II, reinforced these humanitarian measures by establishing the *resguardos* or reserves, to belong communally to the tribes;* this was a further move

---

*It must be understood that the status of the Spanish *resguardos* was very different from that of the reservations in North America, mainly because this was a measure to protect the Indians rather than one of racial segregation, as is clear from the following factors:

(a) these communal holdings were large enough to allow for the population to increase without leaving its traditional habitat;

(b) Indians were not forced to live within the *resguardos*;

(c) those living in the *resguardos* were 'entrusted' (*encomendados*) to Spaniards who were to secure their religious education and acculturization.

towards securing the Indians land of their own, so that they should not have to go on 'dying of emaciation' in the mines and plantations of the Spaniards.

But despite all the good intentions of the kings, most of the measures intended to favour the Indians remained unfulfilled, partly because of a policy of obedience to the letter rather than the spirit, and partly by the institution of *quintos*: this meant that a fifth of the members of every community were forced to *hire* their labour to the Spanish settlers, and though in theory it was designed as a means of protection, in practice it was a way of keeping the natives enslaved.

There was a similar situation on the high plateau of Pasto, where tribes of a considerable size were living. They provided a valuable mine of manpower for *encomenderos* and planters, and, given that economic fact, the *resguardos* set up by the Royal Visitors never really stood a chance of fulfilling their proper function. This we learn from, among other witnesses, the Judge Matías de Peralta, who informed the king that if the wage paid to the *quintos* was twelve pesos, six of that must be handed over in tax, plus another one for the parish priest, while the rest would be given to the Indians in the form of seeds, very often rotten; similarly the shepherds had the value of any dead sheep taken out of their pay, whatever the cause of death. By such methods, the Indians were forced to work for ten or twenty years on end in the vain hope of paying off their debts, 'living without a moment's respite, treated as slaves, lacking even the means to support life'.[1]

This example is enough to show what an advantage it was to the Sibundoy that their valley was so well isolated by its own natural fortifications. For two successive centuries the only whites to visit there regularly were the *encomenderos* collecting tribute, and the *doctrineros*.*[2]

Thus it was a system of a wholly protective and paternalist nature directed to the development of Spanish colonization.

*The long period which this chapter covers so briefly has remained in general somewhat on the fringes of historians' researches. Let me explain that, in order to compile this part of the history of the Sibundoy, I have

Though we have no information about the first *encomenderos* of the valley we do at least know that at the beginning of the seventeenth century Don Martín Díez de Fuenmayor, the military commander, had the 'second lifetime' services of the *encomiendas** of Sibundoy Grande, Santiago and the surrounding areas. We know too that in 1620 one Royal Visitor counted 67 Indians paying tribute in Santiago, and the following year another Visitor, Don Luis de Quiñones, listed 125 in Sibundoy Grande, paying 'each man two pesos, half a pig and a chicken as his tribute, from which would be taken the remuneration of the parish priest, who was the Dominican Fray Alberto de Montenegro, a further fifty-two pesos and fifteen reales for the *camarico*,† two for candles for the Blessed Sacrament, one for the Maundy Thursday altar, and six pesos and six reales for the *corregidor*'.‡[3]

These figures, together with the records of the period, enable us to say two things for certain:

First, that the population of the once 'heavily populated' valley had diminished considerably, as much as a result of massacres as of the epidemics of measles and smallpox brought by the white man;

Second, that the inexactitudes, whether intentional or not, were the fault of the parish priests whose job it was to register all baptisms, marriages and deaths. Their 'errors' were always to the advantage of their purse, or to that of the *encomendero* whose patronage they enjoyed. Don Félix Llano, the Visitor to

had to combine the evidence from various old chronicles, and, in particular, to study the original documents now in the archives of Quito, Pasto and Popayán.

*We may recall that at first the *encomienda* was granted for three years, but soon extended to a lifetime, and later to the son of the *encomendero* for a second lifetime, and sometimes to his grandson as a third lifetime (cf. the note on p. 17).

†The *camarico* was an offering, in theory spontaneous, given to the parish priest in lieu of the old first-fruits – originally it consisted of fruits and animal products. But even as long ago as this it had ceased to be voluntary, and was paid in cash.

‡Office equivalent to that of the American sheriff.

the Province, spoke out in no uncertain terms against 'the falsification of books and records by parish priests, and the exorbitant sums they extort from the Indians'.[4]

From the records of the period there is other information to be gleaned: the speed with which Christianity penetrated the area, the presence of domestic animals, the integration of the Sibundoy into the general financial economy, and the existence among them of a colonial authority. But to return to Don Luis de Quiñones: he took advantage of his visit to rectify the most blatant of the injustices, and in the name of the Spanish Crown 'sold' to the Indians for 400 ounces of silver (*patacones*), the *resguardos* of Aponte and Sibundoy, which did no injustice to the *encomenderos* since they, as we have seen, had the use rather than the ownership of their *encomiendas*. This step on Don Luis's part recorded his name for posterity: the Indians in fact looked upon him as their true protector, because he defined their territory, and gave them the corresponding deeds of possession. This is something the reader must not forget because it is vital to the understanding of what was to happen in the valley at the beginning of this century, when all the official deeds of registration disappeared.

One of the immediate results of the event was that the Indians, now in possession of legal title deeds, thenceforth adopted the legal usages of the white man to defend their holdings, and abandoned the use of force: sixty years later, in 1680, the dispute between the Sibundoy and the Ortiz family over the lands of Aponte provided the first evidence of the value and effectiveness of these new methods. What happened was that Don Luis Narices, cacique of Sibundoy Grande, having sued through the court, received a speedy verdict in favour of his tribe;[5] and this case actually involved a claim against a Spanish captain for his debts to the Sibundoy.[6]

From further somewhat obscure documents we have been able to reconstruct the succession of *encomenderos* established in the area, and the efforts they made to preserve this privilege for their descendants, even going so far as to pay out of their own pockets the tribute owed to the king.[7]

But towards the end of the seventeenth century, the small incidents chronicled here faded into insignificance in comparison with a figure who was to become legendary: the Great Cacique, Don Carlos Tamoabioy, whose authority covered both the tribes we are concerned with here.

To the 'civilized', whether lay or religious, now living in the valley of the Sibundoy, Don Carlos Tamoabioy is a mere myth, the hero of a legend created by the Indians' imagination, and not a real person who ever existed. If we are to demystify a figure who, however legendary he may have become, rests on a genuine historical basis, then we have to reckon with their attitude. It is an attitude explicable only in terms of the utter contempt of the white man for all Indian traditions, and his determination to cast into oblivion all possible proof that the Indians have any right of ownership over their Sibundoy and Aponte valleys.

Don Carlos Tamoabioy most certainly existed. Though his name is only mentioned by a single chronicler, that chronicler declares him in so many words to be the founder of the political unification of the valley, having brought together all the caciques under his own supreme authority. But we find further information in the archives; he was the 'native cacique of the village of Santiago', his family's land was at Aponte, and he was a member of the *Cofradía* of Our Lady of the Rosary. In 1700 he was living peacefully with his wife, Doña Feliciana Jajamanchoy (aged 69), and his children, Doña Maria, his younger daughter, Don Marcos (aged 27) and Don Pedro (aged 31). The last-named, who married Ana Quinchoa, had delighted the last two years of the Great Cacique's life by presenting him with his first grand-daughter, Doña Sebastiana.[8]

In short, the fact of Tamoabioy's existence is well established.

In March 1700, the great man fell ill. Realizing that he was soon to die, he determined to dictate his last wishes. His relations with the white men were good, so he chose as witnesses to his will two Spanish noblemen. But the wisdom of the

Indians led him to do one strange thing: he had three copies made of his will, which he entrusted to the *cabildos** of Sibundoy Grande, Santiago and Aponte respectively.

His doing this was primarily to give the support of his authority to the sharing out of tribal territories among the different *parcialidades*,† as provided for by Luis de Quiñones. But it was also, undoubtedly, done to enable his descendants to prove their legal right to the land of the tribe's ancestors at any time, whoever might claim the right, even if only partially, to dispossess them.

It was a wise precaution: we have only been able to find the copy deposited in Aponte, which the reader will find in Appendix 2. All we know of the Santiago copy is that thirty years ago it was in the Capuchin friary of Pasto, where the historian, S. E. Ortiz, examined it. The Sibundoy Grande copy must have been in the parish archives until quite recently. Clearly, the only reason the Aponte copy is intact is that those who did everything in their power to destroy all proof of the Indians' ancient rights to the land did not know of its existence.

Don Carlos Tamoabioy began his will with a statement of his faith in Christianity, the religion of his forefathers; he also made certain stipulations for his burial: '. . . that the priest-in-charge of this village of Santiago should accompany my body with the Great Cross as usual, and that a mass be sung in the presence of my body with its bearers; for such is my will.'

A study of the document makes clear what total ascendancy the cacique held over all the natives under his rule. Listing his heirs, he leaves his goods to his sons, and to the *parcialidades* of Santiago, Aponte and Sibundoy, and he orders his fellow-citizens 'that no harm must be done to the vassals and governors of the said village of Sibundoy Grande', nor against the caciques and governors of San Andrés de Putumayo, since

*Cabildo was the name traditionally given to Indian councils, still presided over by the native governors of each village.

†This inter-tribal division into groupings, under the authority of a cacique, is comparable to the Quechua *ayllus* of northern Peru. It is evidence that some of the Incas' social structures were preserved in the Colombian southlands.

the division of the land among these different *parcialidades* was made by 'the Señor Visitor Don Luis de Quiñones, and all the Visitors who, until my own day, had the royal command and authority to fix boundaries'.

What makes this will of special interest is that in it Don Carlos Tamoabioy lists and gives the approximate position of the major holdings that made up the five square leagues – about 12,000 hectares – of the *resguardo*.

Finally, the Cacique Tamoabioy concludes with an urgent plea to his people to guard the inheritance of their forefathers most carefully:

. . . it is my will that they use [this land] and defend it if they are disturbed by any ill-intentioned person. *Item:* I declare that the said lands I here bequeath are mine, for they come from my ancestors; and that no person whatsoever has any claim to them, even Captain Don Salvador Ortiz, who has established his estates there; they are not his at all, and if he tries to invade them or use violence then appeal must be made before the Royal Court, for I declare that nothing I have is not legitimately mine in all law and justice . . .

His descendants were to take advantage of this wise advice:

After the death of the Great Cacique, his influence remained, and the respect the Sibundoy continued to feel for him was such that when the military commander Don Marcos Ambrosio de Rivera y Guzmán, Captain General of the town of Pasto and its provinces, visited the valley twenty-two years later, he noticed that the Indians had never ventured to elect another cacique: therefore he himself designated Don Pedro Tamoabioy, the Great Cacique's son, to succeed him, Don Pedro by then being already himself a grandfather.[9]

It is, incidentally, worth noting our debt of gratitude to the Marqués de Rivera, to whom we owe the second and most complete series of records for the whole of southern Colombia.* These lists of names tell us a lot more about the Sibun-

*The censuses made in the Sibundoy valley in the eighteenth century, give us the following figures:

	1711	1722	1769
Sibundoy	309	288	317
Santiago	243	317	371
Putumayo	?	46	64

doy up to the year in question, 1722. We find in them not only genealogical trees, but other most interesting details, such as:

(1) The family names (which begin with nine different characteristic sounds, and end with the suffix *oy*) demonstrate how much larger their former territory was than the area of the valley.

(2) Even at that date, every Sibundoy would have after his baptismal name that of his place of origin: Serafín Putumayo, Escolástica Quinchoa, Bautista Subundoy, Concepción Pujatamuy, etc., apart from the more acculturized families of Sibundoy Grande itself, among whom we find people called González, Jiménez, España, Criollo (Creole), Narices (nose), or with such 'Sibundized' Spanish names as Muchacha-soy, or Juan-oy.

(3) We discover to what a great old age some Indians used to live: Don Carlos Tamoabioy and Don Baltazar Juajibioy died in their seventies, the wife of Tamoabioy and the cacique Cantoca in their eighties.

(4) And wherever the *doctrineros* had not 'rectified' what seemed to them an 'error' or an 'anomaly', one can detect from the censuses indications of Sibundoy matrimonial patterns: custom in fact dictated that children should take the mother's name, not the father's.[10]

But the Marqués de San Juan de Rivera went further. During his tour of inspection he insisted that the *encomendero* of San Andrés de Putumayo 'should observe and see to it that all Indians are treated well ... that they are freed from personal service by the complete abolition of that institution ... under pain of losing their *encomiendas*';[11] incidentally, this reference to a form of exploiting the Indians which had for two centuries been forbidden by the Spanish crown shows how little respect his American vassals paid to their king's laws.

But, above all, the marqués's intervention makes it clear that he is to be ranked among those officials who, at least at the administrative level, really had the interests of the Indians at heart. So, certainly, thought the Sibundoy, who asked him for 'supporting documents, guaranteeing their ownership of the lands of Aponte which had been theirs from time immemorial'. He gave them what they asked, thus showing us yet again how stubbornly the Indians defended their lands in law against the Spanish settlers – among them the Ortiz family, who are specifically named here for the third time.

For though a long time had passed since 1680 that ambitious family had still not given up their claims. Even the intervention of de Rivera did not stop them. Therefore, in response to yet another appeal from the Sibundoy, the governor and Captain General of the province, handed over another deed in 1747, confirming the tribe in its rights. None the less, the Ortiz family remained 'in tranquil and undisturbed possession' of the estate.[12]

This fact did not discourage the Sibundoy. Thirty years later, in 1775, their cacique Leandro Agreda appeared before the provincial authorities with a full dossier of the situation, asking for the wrong to be set right, and alleging that they did not now have enough land to cultivate, and could therefore no longer pay the tribute. The inquiry that followed concluded, once again, in favour of the Indians, since those occupying their territory could adduce no proof of any right to be there. But since meanwhile the Ortizes had sold the estate in question, they were forced to justify the rights they claimed. To do so, they brought the Sibundoy to court, using the following argument:

The Indians of the village of Sibundoy carry on active trade not only with the town, but with the whole province of Pasto, and the things they trade in consist in pig's fat, domestic poultry, maize, eggs, planks of cedar wood, wooden dishes and trays, varnishes, palm wax and powdered gold; these they sell in huge quantities in exchange for hard cash, in quite large enough amounts to pay their tribute.

With such a counter-attack utterly denying their rights, rights recognized by law four times in the past ninety-nine years, the Indians put into effect the final piece of advice from Carlos Tamoabioy: they appealed to the Royal Court in Quito, where they recounted the whole history of the dispute.

Captain Diego Ortiz had links of both friendship and *compadrazgo** with the cacique Luis Narices, and had got the latter to lend him the estates under dispute. When the cacique had asked for them to be returned, the Spaniard refused. Furthermore, declarations from dozens of different clans were all in agreement as to one recent event: Don Melchor Ortiz, 'on pretence of being a surveyor, had taken their title deeds away from them'.

At this, the Court in Quito ordered an inspection of the land in question, which took place in the absence both of the inhabitants of Santiago and of the cacique of Sibundoy Grande who 'was too old to walk so far'. But this inquiry was directed not so much to proving the rights of the Indians from the Aponte *resguardo*, as to demonstrating that it was perfectly possible for those from Sibundoy Grande to pay their tribute. That is why the Clerk of the Court set about describing the wealth of this 'capital village':

Though situated in the mountains, its land is pleasant, and there the Sibundoy can, without excessive labour or fatigue, cultivate soil that produces all things in abundance. I have been informed that these same Indians once possessed prairies and pasturelands for cattle and pigs, and that at present they have over two hundred head of cattle and many hundreds of pigs.

And he laid great stress on the amount of land available all around the place, declaring that 'the circumference of the valley [would seem] to include over three leagues of usable land, and as for its swamplands, they are so enormous that one

---

*The term *compadrazgo* describes in South America the relationship existing between the father and godfather of the same child. It frequently involves a special friendship whereby, in case of need, the godfather would take on himself responsibility for the child. Such bonds are often formed under a cloak of paternalism which conceals intentions of political, social or economic domination; so it was in this particular case. It is a phenomenon still to be found, and many local notables owe their prestige and power to the dozens or even hundreds of *compadrazgos* they have formed among their peasants.

cannot see to the end of them . . .' This authoritative statement – deliberately favourable to the Ortizes and most carefully exaggerated – was signed by the leading dignitaries of Pasto, and hastened the conclusion of this lengthy legal battle. The losers were the Indians.

It had taken only a few months of legal action at the highest level for the Creole grandees to destroy the fruits of a whole century of government protection.

But the Sibundoy, like so many other tribes, also had to support the power of the great families through the system of the *encomiendas*. The entire system had been under attack as long ago as 1701, when the king of Spain, once again anxious for his coloured subjects, had declared that:

All the *encomiendas* or authorizations to receive tribute which have been conferred for two lifetimes or longer upon vassals living in the kingdoms of Spain shall cease and be annulled at the death of their present beneficiaries.[13]

And yet, many years later, the rich, whether Creole or Spanish, were still receiving these privileges. The example of the Sibundoy *encomienda* is extremely significant: its rightful owner was not officially dispossessed until 1711, and then not because of the king's command, but because of the need to raise taxes.[14] The affair might thus seem to be over once and for all: but no, because 'notwithstanding the fact of its having been restored to the Crown', it was awarded to Don Cristobal de Salazar y Santacruz 'for a first lifetime', and then in 1721 to his son Tomás for 'a second lifetime'. The latter kept it for fifty years, and only at his death, in 1769, did the colonial system finally come to an end in the country of the Sibundoy.[15]

All the documentation to which I have referred has the further advantage of describing the way the Sibundoy lived in the second half of the eighteenth century. Thus we find that even then, the valley was partly flooded, so as to push the Indians up to the hills, where there are still the remains of old Inca-style terraces to be seen. The economic potential of the natives too was, though perhaps not vast, quite enough to arouse the rapacity of the white man. These repeated efforts by the Sibundoy, together with their respect for the State and their belief in justice, provide clear evidence that they were by now anything but 'savages'.

It is noteworthy that this development was favoured by the activity of certain Dominican and Franciscan *doctrineros*, who may also have been responsible for building the lime kilns and other structures of the colonial era whose ruins were discovered early this century in the valley. Some scholars even suggest that it may have been they who introduced the Inga* dialect to the Putumayo, in order to create a linguistic unity among the tribes which would make it easier to evangelize them.

However, on a closer study, the hypothesis seems unlikely, if only because of certain morphological characteristics which distinguish the Inga and Sibundoy. It would, in fact, seem more probable that the Inga are the genuine descendants of the subjects of the Incas, who came to settle in southern Colombia, and there introduced the use of Quechua. There are two positive facts which might explain their migration:

(1) The existence of an Inca administrative class, sent by the central authority in Cuzco to live among the subject peoples; in this case, the arrival of the Inga must date back to the pre-Columbian times when they first subjected the Sibundoy.

(2) The Inca migrations towards Amazonia resulting from the Spanish invasion of Peru which, with the passage of time, might well have led the Inga as far as the upper Putumayo.

The immense intellectual ability of the Inga, their taste for business and long journeys, would seem to support the first of these hypotheses; whereas the second would explain the recent date at which the present inhabitants of San Andrés

*The Inga dialect, spoken in Santiago, San Andrés and various other villages of the Upper Putumayo, is the dialect furthest removed from the ancient Quechua language still spoken fluently in our own day by the scattered aboriginal communities of the Andean countries, from northern Argentina to southern Colombia. Indeed so great is the difference that it is very hard for the Inga groups to understand what is said by the heirs of the old Peruvian empire.

settled there, having lived further down the Putumayo up to the nineteenth century.

Be this as it may, the Sibundoy have preserved their difficult and exotic language to this day, without its doing anything to prevent peace and harmony from reigning between them and the Inga who share the valley with them, together with the same traditional dress and a reverence for the same hero, Don Carlos Tamoabioy.

The legends that have come to us indicate age-old confrontations between the Sibundoy and Inga of Aponte, the latter being eventually conquered by Carlos Tamoabioy.* But, since the family lands of the Great Cacique lay in the same area, we must conclude that there has been a certain confusion as to the events and those involved in them. The battles described would then have been fought against other tribes driven from their homelands by the conquistadors. There were, for instance, the Mocoa, who also speak a Quechua dialect, whose migration to Amazonia and incursions into the Sibundoy valley I have mentioned.

At the time of the disappearance of the *encomiendas*, Sibundoy history becomes lost under the avalanche of events which marked the end of the Spanish colonial era in Colombia; the valley, having no value either politically or militarily, returned to oblivion. Even official documents no longer mention it, which would lead one to suppose that the history of areas like this was only recorded when related to the needs of the system of exploiting the Indians used in those early days: once the Indians no longer paid tribute, the State lost interest in them, and this, in conjunction with the disappearance of the Spanish *doctrineros*, left the valley out on a limb, so to say, as far as history was concerned until the nineteenth century.

It was as though from then on only nature was alive and active in this land of the Inga and Sibundoy – and that action was in fact disastrous. Volcanic activity increased enormously in the Andes, and was accompanied by tremendous earthquakes. In 1834, an earthquake destroyed the 'Vicious City of

*See p. 269.

Concepción de Pasto' and shook the mountainous barricades which surrounded the Sibundoy valley, thus adding to the flooding. The memory of that particular quake lives still: in the evenings around the fire, old men will tell how the village of Santiago – built on a peak – had to be evacuated before vanishing beneath the floods.[16] Then the facts become interspersed with legend, thus producing the 'spoken history' that goes like this:

I, Mateo Chasoy, heard from the mouth of the caciques Francisco and Gervasio Tisoy this story, when I was still only a child:

They remembered among other things the time of their youth, when one had to go all the way to the town of Popayán to ask the bishop kindly to send us a priest to come and celebrate all the feasts at once.

Then the priest, finding that people paid too little for his celebrations, became angry, and getting into the pulpit, he began to lecture the people, and the whole village; and, at that very moment the earth began moving, and people pushed each other to get out, leaving the preacher alone. Then the older people came back into the church to take out the statues, and carrying them like so many bundles of wood, they took them to the hill of Arcanchí where even to this day a stone still marks the spot.

As they carried them, they were staggering like drunkards because of the heaving of the ground.

The hill of Tanjuanoy called out to the hill of Arcanchí to defend the statues which must not be lost, and Arcanchí told it to come closer and let the torrent pass.

The old men and the priest spent a week there, suffering greatly from hunger. After that they returned to the village by laying down planks to walk upon, and they found three candles which had been burning on the altar for but a short time, though no one had lit them.

They called the priest, who said mass, and the Indians led him back to Pasto, finding new trails.[17]

These earthquakes had tremendous repercussions: the flooding of the valley became more widespread, the Inga of La Ensillada emigrated to San Andrés, and there was great loss of human life as well as of goods of all kinds. The years that followed were uneventful apart from the visits of passing merchants from Pasto, who sailed along the Putumayo and the Amazon as far as Brazil 'bartering for shoes, cigarettes, resins, and objects manufactured in Colombia, salt, ironware, liqueurs and other Brazilian and European products'.[18]

These travellers used the Inga and Sibundoy as porters, renowned as they traditionally were all over southern Colombia for their physical endurance and knowledge of the terrain. But to the tribes they visited, this contact with the white man brought with it hitherto unknown illnesses which reached epidemic proportions and proved fatal to many.

These successive misfortunes led to a demographic and economic deterioration in the Sibundoy valley. Though the loss of human life was balanced by Inga immigration from the south (the 1851 census shows 660 people in Santiago, 837 in Sibundoy and 300 in San Andrés del Putumayo), resources remained desperately low, and the Indians only had 'some very few sheep and cattle'.[19]

Church and government were scarcely represented there. The only official personage in the whole territory was a 'prefect', living in far-off and dreary Mocoa.* The single priest who also lived there, doubling as schoolmaster, went up to the valley once or twice a year, and would travel round the district, being paid for his services in gold dust gathered from the streams. The valley did however enjoy one privilege; one of the four schools which had to cope with the whole of that vast

---

*There the remnants of Spanish imperialism were still very much in evidence. The local people, the Mocoas, were the descendants of the brave warriors who had mercilessly harassed the early conquistadors. Don Felipe Pérez describes them thus: 'These Indians, who are called Inga sometimes instead of Inca, because they still speak the ancient language of the Peruvians, are different from those in the lowlands of the Caquetá in that they have learnt to go to church when the bell summons them, and will kneel during mass; but this has nothing to do with Christianity, for they also greet travellers by kneeling before them and joining their hands together while muttering the garbled words "Most holy sacrament of the altar" as do the other Indians all over the country – a humiliating custom which reveals how arrogant was the religion of the conquistadors.'

Amazonian area was established there. It had six 'rational'*
pupils and eight Indians.

It is from about the middle of the nineteenth century that we
begin to find the rare accounts that give us some idea of what
daily life was like for the Sibundoy and the Inga. First, a quotation from the historian and geographer, Felipe Pérez:

> The Indians living in the said villages of Sibundoy, Santiago and
> Putumayo ... speak Spanish, whereas in Mocoa you can barely find
> one or two who know even a few words of it, and certainly none
> capable of reciting a prayer or speaking at any length.[20]

Don Felipe also notes that the harmony between the two
tribes was so great that they would celebrate both religious
and secular festivals together. The produce of the valley consisted of maize, potatoes, canoes, oars, nets, wooden trays,
pottery, necklaces, reed combs, baskets, chests and boxes of
wood, small round stools, hand presses (for the extraction of
sugar from cane), wool and cotton cloaks; and as for manufactured objects, harps, mandolins and violins were the speciali-
ties of the people of San Andrés who, as they themselves said,
had 'received from God a talent for the violin'.

Another traveller, the military engineer Agustín Codazzi,
also travelled the entire area. Here is his description of the
people he saw there:

> I never met with any Indian possessing any kind of deformity; nor
> did I see any with the kind of wounds or ulcers which so badly afflict
> those of mixed race – still less with goitre, that prime symbol of
> human degradation. I was amazed by the old people, far less
> wrinkled than Creoles of the same age, still fully in possession of
> their sight and hearing; and, finally, their whole physical preser-
> vation is so notable that between twenty and fifty years one can
> barely detect any difference, either because of wrinkled skin, colour
> of hair, or bodily weakness ...[21]

Codazzi praises the courage of the Indians, and their tender
care for their wives and children, though he does say this:

*There was a persistent custom in Colombia of using the term
'rational' only for whites or the 'civilized' Indians, while the non-
acculturized Indians were thought of as beings not endowed with reason
and therefore called 'irrational'.

It is the man who cuts down trees and prepares the land for sowing, but the actual sowing is left entirely to the women to do, for they believe that those who can give birth to children must also know best how to sow the ground to enable it to give birth to the grains or roots which have been placed in its womb. . . . While the women go to field or garden to weed and gather the crops – bananas, maize, sugar cane, etc. – the men go out to hunt, or look for vegetable products to sell, also devoting part of the night-time to fishing, to secure the subsistence of their beloved families, whom they love with a demonstrative affection I have myself witnessed.[22]

This evidence of Indian culture from the nineteenth-century visitor is all the more remarkable in that the religious crusaders of our own century have written entire books to show how 'savage' were the natives and how ridiculous their customs. Yet numerous instances from Sibundoy folklore – in which crows, foxes, rabbits and tigers figure largely – make clear the kind of moral qualities that have been handed down from one generation to another. Here is one of many tales, in which the owl, as the main character, symbolizes wisdom, modesty and dignity:

'I am ashamed of nothing but my nose,' an owl used to say. . . . An owl was visiting his future wife, and he was saying, 'I am ashamed of nothing but my nose.' Thereupon his future brothers-in-law took him by the hand and examined him closely, while the owl continued to say over and over, 'I am ashamed of nothing but my nose.' And they noticed that he had only just a single little hole by way of a nose, large enough for nothing bigger than a needle to pass through. So they began to abuse him – for not having a nose, for not working, for sleeping all day, and a number of other things too. They abused him so much that the owl grew angry.

He went out, and from outside he said to them: 'You say I don't know how to work! That I spend the whole day sleeping! Well, now we shall see whether you will find another young bird who can do as well as I can!'

And the owl gave a cry and flew high into the air.

After that, the bird who was to become his wife went out to sow maize, and she found the whole of the land prepared for sowing, as far as the eye could see.

Upon which the future wife was very sad.

It is amazing to see how alike these stories are both in style and in finality to the better-known fables of what is termed 'western' civilization.* Fray Jacinto de Quito describes other ways in which children are taught:

Our natives so love hunting and fishing that they can think of no better return to offer for a favour, or even for winning a wife without difficulty. The interest displayed by parents in teaching their sons how to use bows, arrows, blow-pipes, fishing tackle, etc. is amazing. They take them to the river bank and into the forest, and show them by practical example how to carry the quiver, how much poison to put on the arrows (depending on the size of the quarry in view) the amount of cotton to attach to the darts for the blow-pipe to make them fit neither too tightly nor too loosely, etc. They take the same trouble to teach them the art of fishing; showing them the times and places where the fish congregate, how to throw their hooks, etc.

When they are proficient enough in all these skills, they start a further apprenticeship, learning to give perfect imitations of bird calls, of the cries, whistlings and other sounds made by the various animals, which they learn to copy to such perfection as to be almost indistinguishable from the originals. Then comes the final stage of their education: they have to develop powerful lungs, so that they can send darts great distances from their blow-pipes, and a steady hand so that each dart reaches its objective . . .

The grandmother lets the adolescent know just when he may start going out hunting, and gives him a dog, so that he can prove his skill . . .

And while he is out in the forest, she invites friends and neighbours to come to a banquet and dance to celebrate the first bird or animal that the novice huntsman brings home.[23]

Though there is no need to form too idyllic a picture, we may conclude from all this that the life of the Indians in the Sibundoy valley was one without too many pressures, being

*It is a symptom of our alienation that we still use the phrase to mean European civilization, which is actually eastern from a South American standpoint. Another such symptom is our use of the term 'Latin American' to designate a group of Indo-American cultures which have only very slight and very ancient links with the Latin world.

divided among farm work, pig-raising (with twenty or thirty pigs per family), hunting, fishing, the weaving of traditional clothes, keeping the fire continuously alive in the family hearth, gathering the bark of a certain tree to make torches, the upbringing of the children, and the joyous celebration of all the big religious festivals at once whenever a priest came to visit them. In addition there were pilgrimages to Pasto to pray to the so-called Christ of Sibundoy, occasional trips towards the lower Putumayo by merchants in search of new contacts and adventures, elections and then sessions of the governing Chapters of all the tribes.

Each Chapter contained a governor, a mayor, and a number of *alguaciles*.* It was elected by the people at the end of December, as it is to this day. On 1 January, they celebrated the handing-over of the mace of government, and the *cepo* decorated with wild flowers was passed on to the new governor.† Afterwards the latter would provide 'those who were present with a meal and plenty to drink . . . and the party would end, as was virtually obligatory, with everyone drunk'.[24]

In those days – just as today – there was also a parallel Chapter for the children, whose function was to educate and watch over them, and even to decide what punishments they deserved,

---

*Councillors.

†The *cepo* in question was a hangover from the Spanish *encomenderos*. It was made out of two horizontal bits of wood one laid upon the other, ten to twelve metres long. The instrument was used both to imprison the rare criminals, and to beat those who infringed the traditional Indian order. The former were imprisoned by the neck, while the latter were beaten on the arms and legs. The instrument was kept in the charge of the Indian governor of each village as a mark of his dignity, and the flowers and the crucifix used to ornament it were an indication of the people's support of his authority.

The *cepo* was not, however, a purely Indian invention. In Larousse the French word *cep* is defined thus: 'Term used in the past to describe both a prison and a device for holding people down by their feet. Some *ceps* were real pillories, holding the sufferer's feet, hands and head. From the beginning of the eighteenth century, such painful instruments fell out of use.' The use of the *cepo* was also taken to Santo Domingo by the French slave-traders.

so that the children would learn from the earliest age to respect the laws and customs of their ancestors.

We may note that the major administrative duties of the caciques and governors was to look after the archives of the Chapter, which contained such important documents as copies of judgments given over land ownership, and the will of Carlos Tamoabioy. The figure of the Great Cacique had gone on growing ever larger, reaching positively legendary dimensions:

Saint Carlos Tamoabioy came into the world one morning, not like a tiny baby, but already big and well-developed. He caused seven foster-mothers to die from taking too much of their milk. . . . By midday he was an adult. That afternoon he brought together all the Sibundoy Indians, made out deeds for all his lands to them and their descendants, dividing them up and giving them well-defined boundaries, and then died at sunset the same day.*[25]

The end of the nineteenth century thus drew near in the ancient valley. Only two things remain to be mentioned: first, the economic recovery which led to a considerable increase in population, and, second, the ever-increasing visits from travellers of various kinds.

But it was not until the dawn of our own century that Inga and Sibundoy could fully grasp the effect of what amounted to a veritable white colony's becoming established in their valley, with the coming of the Capuchin† missionaries, whose arrival

*The important part played by the solar day in this story shows how a pre-Colombian base of Inga and Sibundoy tradition remained in existence until quite recent times. Another instance of this is the belief in the 'Stone of the Sun' which even at the beginning of this century survived despite the anger of the missionaries. This stone, situated in the high mountains between Pasto and the valley, served to hold back the movement of the sun so that travellers crossing those icy solitudes might reach home before night fell. According to the Indians, the sun was stopped by means of a liana which was stretched between the stone and a tree somewhat to the south. The Stone of the Sun is still there.

†Translator's note: The Capuchins are one of the three orders of Friars Minor or Franciscans (their full title is *Ordo Fratrum Minorum Capuccinorum*; hence the 'O.F.M.Cap.' after their names). They were formally recognized as a separate order in 1619, and missionary work is their main activity. Like some other orders, they do not have parishes, but in mission countries they have to do the work of parish clergy in

was to make radical changes in the homogeneous, peaceful and rapidly developing society which they were at that time.

----

practice. The areas they care for are known as 'quasi-parishes' but to avoid clumsiness I have referred to them simply as parishes in this translation. I have preserved the Spanish 'Fray' in referring to the friars to distinguish them from other clergy.

CHAPTER 3

The Indians
Protected by Church
and State

Let us give the land to those who till it and make it productive ...

(TOMAS DE MOSQUERA, President of the Republic; decree of the nationalization of ecclesiastical goods, 1861)

When the revolution and liberal teachings misled the good sense of the people, impious governments seized the Church's patrimony ... And when society regained its good sense, then the next generation brought back their filial gifts ...

(FRAY FIDEL DE MONTCLAR, Prefect Apostolic, 1927)

In the nineteenth century, while the tribes of the upper Putumayo were living in relative peace, the interior of Colombia was the scene of political and social events that were to shake the entire country, and change the whole established order: the war of independence against Spain (1810–19), the liberation of the bordering countries (1819–24), the establishment in power of Creole élites, civil wars, population increases, a great colonizing thrust, and efforts to secularize the State: all these phenomena had repercussions on both the political life of the original inhabitants of the State and the behaviour of the missionaries: repercussions which were largely to determine the future of the 'national territories' of which the Putumayo was part. We must therefore give a brief summary of the major changes which were coming into effect.

I mentioned above the principal regulations set out by the Spanish crown in the sixteenth and seventeenth centuries to modify the cruelty of the treatment imposed on the Indians. To understand the importance of such humanitarian measures more fully, let us look at the day-to-day life of the Indians on the Andean plateau by the end of the eighteenth century.

Our most reliable scientific evidence comes from Generals Jorge Juan and Antonio de Ulloa, 'Lieutenants General of the *Real Armada*, members of the English Royal Society, and of the Academies of Berlin, Paris and Stockholm'. Officially, these soldier-scholars were part of an international commission which came in 1776 to work out the precise position of the equator; but while doing so they also made certain inquiries as secret agents of the Spanish king, 'faithfully following the instructions of His Excellency the Marqués de la Ensenada, first Secretary of State, who handed on their long, confidential report to King Ferdinand VI himself'.

In it we find a description of the treatment meted out to the so-called 'free' Indians of the Andes who, the agents declared, lived 'in the most miserable and wretched state imaginable'. Of the Indians subjected to the *quinto* system,* they added:

In the *haciendas* of the first category, an Indian earns between fourteen and eighteen pesos a year, depending on the area, in ad‹ dition to which the *hacienda* allows him the personal use of a piece of land of twenty or thirty square *varas* [a measure of just under a yard]; in return the Indian is forced to work 300 days a year, and to perform a fixed task on each of those days. This leaves them with sixty-five days to cover Sundays and religious feasts, and any sicknesses or accidents which may involve interruption in their work.[1]

Furthermore, the inquiry adds, the Indians are obliged, out of this wretched wage, to find eight pesos to pay their tax, and more than two pesos for the three square *varas* of rough cloth they get to cover their nakedness; and since the produce from the tiny scrap of land allotted to them is not enough to support their families, they find themselves further obliged to buy rice from the landlord — and from him alone — at over twice the current price, thus being 'in debt by at least one peso and six reales, to pay which they have to work the following year'.

*See p. 22.

To this sketch of the classic system of slavery enforced by the settlers must be added the heavy contributions demanded by the Church, and the further obligation to pay their masters for any animals that died, 'even if they were good for nothing but to be given to the dogs anyway'.

The confidential report of Generals Juan and Ulloa includes chapters dealing 'specially with the Franciscans and the Dominicans'. After reporting on the painful treatment to which the Indians were subjected, they single out specific cases which demonstrate the collusion between the civil and the religious exploiters:

If, to fill his cup of misery to the brim, the wife or a child of the unfortunate man should die, his agony of soul is unspeakable, because he must pay the priest for the necessary right of burial. He is forced yet again to become deeper in debt to the owner of the *hacienda* ...

As to the money earned by those who celebrate religious rites, the report has this to say:

To understand more exactly to what excesses this custom leads, and the ever-increasing profits which the priests reap from these feasts, it seems to us relevant to mention here what a priest from the province of Quito told us, during his visitation of his parish, in which – between feasts and memorial services for the dead – he received each year over 200 sheep, 6,000 poultry, 4,000 Indian pigs, and 50,000 eggs. Nor is his parish one of the more lucrative ones ...

In other words, despite all the laws relating to the Indians and demanding the suppression of the *encomiendas*, their situation was just as precarious as it had been a century earlier, when the royal observer, Matías de Peralta, was so outraged by it. And it is hardly surprising that towards the end of the eighteenth century the protective powers of the Crown became even weaker, and increasing inroads were made into the *resguardos* lying near the towns and major communication links. The various extortions became so normal that in the end they no longer needed any pretence at juridical justification – as in the case of the Sibundoy lands of Aponte – and ultimately became in effect a system of government by the leading families. The colonial authorities then took to granting the settlers without more ado the ownership of those parts of the *resguardos* which they described as 'surplus' – a totally false description since they were areas which, according to normal Indian custom, were not abandoned, but kept as reserves for forest growth or game, or in readiness for the future possible needs of an increased population.

However unjust, this Spanish practice which inevitably tended towards dispossessing the native inhabitants totally – though at that time they constituted two thirds of the Colombian population – was to continue into the nineteenth century, at the instigation not of Spain, but of the leading Creole families which had seized power on the establishment of the republican régime.[2]

A true evaluation of the activity of the missionaries in Indian areas during that same period is very hard to make. The chroniclers of the various communities are only concerned to vie with each other in their efforts to claim the greatest merit in the indoctrination of the 'savages'. The internecine disputes between Jesuits and Franciscans along the Putumayo provide a very good example of this.

The Jesuits were extremely proud of the evangelization effected by Father Ferrer, and declared that their confrère Samuel Fritz had succeeded in founding *thirty-eight* villages in Colombian Amazonia, among which they included Santiago and Sibundoy Grande![3] The disciples of St Francis pointed out this error in history, and laid great stress on their own successes in Upper Amazonia. These were so great that in 1738 they had reached a total of *forty-eight* nations 'brought to submission' – a figure which their brothers, the Capuchins, rounded up to *ninety*.[4] But the Jesuits, even after their 'legal death' in 1767, were not thereby discouraged, and declared that 'they alone knew the secret of establishing missions without receiving any aid from the State', and that they alone had won large-scale submissions among the Indians.[5] A 'dishonest and unfounded allegation', was the retort of a Franciscan, who described the Jesuit author as a 'rationalist' and 'anti-clerical'.[6]

Though it may seem to be pouring fuel on the flames to say so, it must be admitted that there was good on both sides. No one will ever forget the immense work done by the Jesuits in both northern and southern Amazonia, not only in evangelizing, but also as regards economic development; it cannot however be denied that in 1797 (thirty years after the Jesuits had gone) there were still some Franciscans running missions at the foot of the Andes, as is clear from certain unpublished documents[7] which give high praise to the self-denying spirit of these men, far removed from the incomparably more luxurious life led by the churchmen on the high plateaux.[*]

As for the city clergy, their excesses are described too:

> The freedom with which the clergy live in these places is such that in itself it opens the way to disorders of every kind. In the large towns most of them live outside their monasteries in private houses – the monasteries being used only by those who are not rich enough to keep up a private home, as well as by choristers, novices and others, who live there voluntarily. The same is true in the smaller towns and villages: there is no enclosure in the religious houses, and the clergy live there with concubines in their cells, just as if they were married men.[8]

They go on to consider the kind of excuses given by these monks – 'apart from the Jesuits' – for having abandoned their monasteries and settled in the towns with their wives and children.

This not very ascetic life was rendered even less so by the

[*]A collective letter, from those in the depths of the forest to the superior of their friary by a group of Franciscans on a tour of evangelization, tells us something of the pitiable state to which their isolation had reduced them. They complain in particular of such natural obstacles as the flooding of rivers, of areas 'populated by uncivilized peoples, Caribs and well-known bandits for the most part' which make communications highly dangerous, and of the innocence of their parishioners: if they have to go through the nearest white village, they say, 'they come back changed ... for that village has not been subjected to any form of restraint, and has become a real home of vice, a bandits' lair, a miniature hell filled with wicked and perverted people'.

material advantages enjoyed by clergy and religious. They would receive legacies from the *encomenderos*, settlers and faithful, all anxious thereby to secure forgiveness for their sins. Such legacies were so considerable and frequent that the President of the Court in the Colombian capital, Santa Fe de Bogotá, wrote to the King of Spain in 1729:

> It is thus, My Lord, that the piety of the faithful in these places is excessive: it has enriched the church and the monasteries with alms of all kinds, and pious works whereby they endow churches, chaplaincies, and other benefices to be enjoyed by the clergy . . . and between this and their own industry the latter have become rich enough to buy large *haciendas*. Gradually all the really rich properties have become church-owned — so much so that one can hardly find a house or *hacienda* that is not, those that are not monasteries being the homes of secular priests who act as chaplains to their districts.[9]

To all these forms of income was added what the Orders continued to draw from the *encomiendas*, even when the latter were no longer permitted by law. For instance, the Sisters of the Immaculate Conception in Pasto by the end of the eighteenth century still 'owned' two tribes as *encomendados*.

We have little evidence about the lives of the various secular priests, Brothers of Mercy and Augustinians who came and went sporadically in the Sibundoy valley. All we know is that those who lived at the foot of the Andes had to put up with the most appalling isolation until the liquidation of the missions was decreed by the crown at the end of the century.

By way of parenthesis, we may tell the reader something of the members of another order, the Spanish Capuchins, whom we find at the beginning of our own century returning to try once again to evangelize Colombian Amazonia.

It was at the other side of the country, on the Caribbean coast, that the first Capuchins landed in Colombia in July 1647, in response to the wish expressed by the secretary of the Congregation for the Propagation of the Faith (*Propaganda Fide*)* in these words:

*This is the Vatican Department responsible for missionary activities.

It seems desirable for Capuchin fathers to take charge of the Darien mission, because it is a land of gold and great wealth, and common sense would suggest that disinterested religious like these should go there.[10]

These religious, who came from Valencia and were imbued with the crusading spirit inherited from their ancestors, were to have tremendous influence in northern Colombia. Setting out to win souls, they founded several missions on the Caribbean coast, and according to their successors, they achieved a great many conversions and founded numerous villages. But in 1800 the King handed their mission over to seculars, and told them to move to Santa Fe de Bogotá to found a friary and a college. The Capuchin historian Fray Antonio de Alcácer gives what is undoubtedly an accurate assessment of the King's reasons:

(1) The ups and downs suffered by missionary establishments in the eighteenth century; in particular the enmity shown them by the tribes they had catechized, who more than once revolted against them, and were in consequence savagely repressed by a governor who supported the friars, who themselves could be described as 'somewhat merciless'.

(2) The scandalous ecclesiastical disputes following the stand taken by the Bishop of Santa Marta about the civilization of the Guajiros. For years the bishop and the Capuchins made mutual accusations before the Spanish Court, with the bishop excommunicating the friars, and they rebelling against him. This scandal, for which there is a lot of documentary evidence, went on for years.

(3) The gradual loss of interest in that mission which, in 1793, was served by no more than six missionaries, one of whom was shut up in a hospice for 'demonic sickness', another retired 'because he had lost heart' after an attack of obvious insanity; a situation which deteriorated still further in the last year of the century with the death of two of the remaining four, and the lapse into total senility of a third.[11]

However, Fray Antonio de Alcácer records the view of one superior of the Order that the cause for the failure to evangelize the Guajiro Indians lay in the 'arrogant pride of these people, wholly opposed to the Christian religion'; it was a pride so great that the Spanish never succeeded in civilizing even those whom they brought up from early childhood, nor in getting them to give up their ancestral customs. This cultural resistance enraged the superior, who, being at a loss to explain the total lack of response from his flock, exploded:

All their laws are wicked and perverted: there is one that makes inheritance go not from father to son, but from the maternal aunt to her nephews, because in that case, they say, there can be no doubt of a genuine blood relationship; their law of vengeance, which is the chief advice given by men on their death beds, and their ingratitude to those who have shown them kindness . . .[12]

Returning to the king's decision, Fray de Alcácer concludes his book on this first Capuchin crusade in Colombia with these words:

Our Mission is officially ended, but for ourselves, in the name of history, we can only use terms of the most intense praise and admiration for these sons of St Francis, so self-sacrificing, who suffered that worst of all hardships, apparent failure.[13]

This declaration is somewhat in contrast with the assertions of most Capuchin historians, who believe the failure of the Mission to have been caused by the law expelling them made by the Colombian authorities after independence. Their community had undoubtedly been smitten to the heart of its Spanish pride, when the new government of the young republic withdrew from them their large house in Bogotá. But in their irritation over this, they were forgetting that this was in fact the application of a decree made by the King of Spain himself that any monastery that was abandoned, or had fewer than eight religious in it, should be turned into an educational establishment.[14]

This is perhaps the moment for a brief sketch of the ups and downs in the relationship between Church and State in Colombia during the nineteenth century – a sketch which, despite certain traces of local folklore, is simply a reflection of the huge scale of European and Roman imperialism all over the world.

As we have already seen, the very meagre evangelizing work of the Catholic Church during the seventeenth century had diminished still further after the war of emancipation. But since the Colombians – whether white, mestizo or Indian – continued to be Catholics, the first full republican assembly in 1821 demanded that the government establish diplomatic relations with Rome 'in order to provide these abandoned flocks with spiritual guides'. However, efforts to do so met with great opposition from Spain, and the Pope, unwilling to annoy His Most Catholic Majesty, put off nominating new bishops until 1827, and did not officially recognize the independence of the new republic until 1835. In the long run, this delay proved harmful to Rome's interests: weary of waiting, the national Congress decided in 1824 to prorogue the protection enjoyed by the Church under the prevailing system known as *patronato*.* Now, since this related to a system of

*The Colombian law of ecclesiastical *patronato* gave the legislative power the rights of

(1) granting and defining the jurisdiction of ecclesiastics, as also of the money allotted for the building of metropolitan and episcopal churches;

(2) permitting and even proposing the holding of national or provincial church councils;

(3) permitting or forbidding the establishment of new monasteries and hospitals, or the closure of those in existence;

(4) determining the payments for parish services and those of the episcopal courts;

(5) authorizing the investments and administration of the tithe, and all other offerings made for worship or for the support of the officiating clergy;

(6) sanctioning religious Bulls, or preventing their enforcement if they were thought harmful to the nation's sovereignty;

(7) determining the punishments for contraventions of such Bulls, once approved;

(8) 'electing and nominating those whose names were to go to His Holiness as possible bishops and archbishops' and 'nominating parish priests . . . and introducing them to their bishops'.

In addition to the National Assembly and the Senate, the President of privilege originally granted to the most Catholic Crown of Spain, the papacy found it somewhat against the grain to accept these distant inheritors now coming into being.[15] For the time being at least, however, the situation had to be tolerated.

Despite this position of subordination, there was peace between the two powers for some fifteen years. In fact, in 1844 the Jesuits returned with honour to the young republic. But towards the middle of the century, with the formation of two parties, liberal and conservative, in Colombia, this atmosphere so 'propitious to evangelization' deteriorated. The trouble began when the first liberal government, following the lead of its radical wing, expelled the Jesuits once again in 1850, and taking advantage of the prerogatives of the *patronato* system tried to move the Colombian Church in a democratic and liberal direction. But that Church, not recognizing the claims of the government, began condemning such 'dangerous innovations' as universal suffrage, freedom of speech, of the press, of conscience, and so on. In this, it was respecting both the spirit and the letter of Catholicism as preached by the never-to-be-forgotten Pius IX.* Sermons from pulpits became so impassioned that the conservatives set themselves up as the preservers of Catholicism, and a few months later launched a series of armed rebellions against 'corrupting principles'. None

---

the Republic, the governors and provincial superintendents could also make use of these rights.

*Pope Pius IX left a long memory, not merely because of the length of his pontificate – 1846–78 – but also for his proclamation of the Dogma of the Immaculate Conception in 1854, and his *Syllabus of Errors* in 1864. In this list of eighty propositions anathematized under pain of excommunication we find the freedoms mentioned above, and other 'errors' such as these: 'Let him who says "A man is free to embrace and profess the religion he believes to be true by the light of reason" be anathema; Let him who says "The Church must be separate from the State and the State from the Church" be anathema'; and lastly: 'Let him who says "The Sovereign Pontiff can and should be reconciled and come to terms with progress, liberalism and modern civilization" be anathema.'
Pius IX finally proclaimed the dogma of Papal Infallibility in 1870.

the less, the result of this first 'religious war' was the increasing radicalization of the government, which decreed the expulsion of three ecclesiastical dignitaries, including the Primate of Colombia, Archbishop de Mosquera. This situation combined with current liberal ideals led the government in 1853 to decree the separation of Church and State.

This unsteady balance made it possible for the Jesuits to return once again, and it soon became clear that the independence granted to the Church would merely reinforce its immense economic power. For in fact the vast concentration of landed property in clerical hands, though denounced a century earlier, still continued, and the poor use made of such large tracts of land greatly hampered the economic and social development of the country. This, combined with the greed for land of the rich Creole families, inevitably worsened the situation of the growing and impoverished mass of Indians and mestizos, thus bringing into being a new rural sub-proletariat.

With this in mind the President General Tomás Cipriano de Mosquera, brother of the archbishop, and a supporter of the liberal party, decreed in 1861 the nationalization of all goods held in mortmain.* With this measure, the Colombians heard their president condemn such a concentration of property as 'not befitting a free people, a people which, if it is to make use of its rights, cannot let itself be held in such shackles'. But, more astonishing still, he expressed the dream always so cherished in this part of the world 'of giving the land to those who work it and make it fertile'.[16] A measure so revolutionary for its period could not fail to aggravate the rage of the Church, despite its being allowed the generous compensation of six per cent a year on capital still held.

But the General, convinced that he had acted in accord with perfect justice and reason, found himself in opposition to his minister Rafael Núñez. He wanted to go so far as to force the Roman Church to recognize a constitutional ban on the im-

---

*i.e. held in perpetuity by the Church as a body, so that ownership would not cease with the death of any individual.

position of such private contributions as the tithe,* which was ruining small peasant landowners by forcing them to pay an exorbitant tax of ten per cent on everything they earned from their land and livestock. The democratic measures of President de Mosquera followed an up-and-down course somewhat as follows:

(1) When the Church, not satisfied with the financial aid allowed it, demanded tithes, he enforced an inspection of all religious ceremonies. And the Jesuits were once again made to leave the country.

(2) The clergy responded with a campaign against the régime. The President was by no means discouraged, and solemnly sent the apostolic nuncio back to Rome, together with the new primate of Colombia and other highly-placed churchmen.

(3) The epilogue of the revolutionary atmosphere thus created was not long in coming: a few months later he was overthrown in a coup d'état by the enraged liberal oligarchy, tried by the Senate, and condemned to a fine of twelve pesos, and two years' exile.

The Church was the first to profit from the new situation. It got back all its property, and also recovered the right to receive tithes and first-fruits. This restoration also made it possible for the religious authorities to codify and supervise such payments in such an efficient way that it is quite legitimate to describe it as the first system of income tax the Colombians had ever known.[17]

As might be expected, the rich families, having annulled the agrarian reform of ex-President de Mosquera, also made the most of the new situation: they bought for derisory sums almost all of the lands in mortmain which had not been restored, and sold them to the highest bidder. Then the winners, seeing in the growing power of the State a threat to their profitable laissez-faire, set about dismantling it. Having struck

*The ecclesiastical tithe was a feudal institution still imposed by Rome upon all Spanish-speaking Catholics as one of the 'commandments of the Church'. This rule is still in force in Colombia to this day.

at its foundations by a process of Balkanization, they even tried to auction off the cannon of the fortress of Cartagena and to sell the Palace of Congress still under construction! The latter did not find a purchaser.

From then on, the situation continued to develop in favour of the Church's plans, with General de Mosquera portrayed for posterity as the 'persecutor of religion', with all he had done utterly execrated in all his country's history books.

But the advantages thus gained were still not enough to satisfy the ambitions of the clergy. Profiting from the fact that successive governments dared not tread in the footsteps of President de Mosquera, a lot of bishops and priests carried on their powerful campaign against the secular state. The atmosphere of unrest which they kept in being resulted in civil wars which turned the country into a blood-bath for twenty years, and their political activity often led them into exile; but in the end they got what they were fighting for. Their first major success was the permanent return of the Jesuits. Their final great victory was in 1885. The Colombians, worn out by fratricidal struggles, at last accepted a conservative government, and a new constitution. That constitution, still in force, has several unusual characteristics, among them its opening line: 'In the name of God, supreme source of all authority . . .'

The way thus open, the Church's total control over the State became simply a matter of form. The government decreed two laws, both still in force today. The first declared that Canon Law 'was to be solemnly respected by the authorities of the Republic';[18] and according to the second, Colombians were to remain subject to the Concordat.[19]

This juridical instrument, signed in 1887, enabled the Church to be free of all civil constraint, to get whatever privileges it might wish and to have all its lost material goods back, to say nothing of the satisfaction of seeing the State admitting its guilt, making honourable amends for its past errors, and guaranteeing that 'such deviations should never recur in the future'.*

*The principal articles in the Colombian Concordat declared: The

This already heavily weighted statute was brought to a further pitch of privilege by the signing of the first 'Convention of the Missions' between the Minister of Foreign Affairs and the Holy See.[20] By this the monopoly of Catholic missions in Colombia was confirmed, and assured of financial support from the State.

Colombians recognized clearly from the first that the change of Constitution, and the whole Church–State relationship, owed nothing to any force of arms. The manoeuvring of Rafael

government's obligation to protect the Church and ensure that it be respected (art. 1); recognition of its full civil liberty (arts. 2–5); tax exemption for church buildings (6); exemption of clerics from military service (7); the establishment of privileged criminal proceedings against religious (8); the right to receive emoluments, gifts and honoraria (9); full liberty to all Catholic communities to settle in Colombia with the help of the State (10–11); the organization and surveillance of public teaching according to the Catholic religion with a ban on all ideas contrary to its teachings being propounded in the universities (12–14); the establishment of ecclesiastical boundaries and appointment of prelates to be the exclusive prerogative of the Holy See (15–16); church law made official for the marriages of all baptized persons (and divorce forbidden) (17–19). In exceptional cases, the agreements made between the Holy See and the Colombian government over the development of Catholic missions need not have the approval of Congress (31). All priests were obliged to end every mass with the Latin prayer (never audible): 'Domine, salvam fac Rempublicam; Domine, salvum fac Praesidencium et supremas eius auctoritates' (Lord, save the Republic; Lord, save its President and supreme authorities) (21).

Compensation was also to be made for the loss of interest on profits that would have been earned by the goods nationalized by General de Mosquera (22–5); and the government was obliged to devote an annual sum to the upkeep of dioceses, seminaries, missions, parishes, and the expenses needed for religious ceremonies, and to secure a regular income for communities no longer active (26–7).

This Concordat was completed by the Convention of 1892 which entrusted the church with the administration of cemeteries and made parish registers more authoritative than civil ones.

To sum up: articles 2, 7, 8, 11 and 30 of the Concordat established certain privileges for the Roman Church; articles 12–14 and 17–19 undermined the national sovereignty; articles 22–5 and 31 violated the Constitution which the conservatives themselves had produced only a year beforehand; and the first article of all contradicts the declaration on religious liberty since approved by the Second Vatican Council.

Núñez – once a minister under de Mosquera – to save the
country from chaos by securing his own position as president
with the support of his erstwhile opponents was well known.
But not for fifty years did people learn of the part played by
personal feelings in the intensely profound conversion of this
radical. What had in fact happened was that he paid with his
negotiation of the Concordat for getting his second wife accepted by the Church and high society during the lifetime of
his previous one.[21] The thing had been done by the time Pope
Leo XIII offered him a papal honour together with a warm
letter of thanks for services rendered to the Church, and an
apostolic pardon for his past errors.*

The conservative régime was beginning to make very clear
its concern to respect scrupulously all compensations and payments promised to the clergy in the Concordat and the Convention of the Missions. The government's intransigence on the
point was to be so great that it was prepared to cut back the
budget for education and even the rations of prisoners rather
than make any reduction in these burdens – so crippling for
such a poor country. For the year 1895–6, for instance, they
amounted to 466,895 gold pesos out of a total national budget
of 26,226,300.

So, the efforts of a whole generation to bring liberal reforms

*In his youth, Núñez had known a young woman, a Catholic and a
conservative, Doña Soledad. He met her again thirty years later, by then
himself divorced, and she agreed to go to Paris on the pretext of seeking
help from a heart specialist, to marry him by proxy there. But once
Núñez reached the leadership of the government, his situation became
difficult, and he asked the apostolic nuncio for 'a proof of social consideration and respect' – which he was refused. He thereupon suspended
the negotiations over the Concordat . . . and the Papal decoration
swiftly followed.

The affair ended with a splendid ball in the Presidential Palace.
According to Núñez's biographer, when the doors of the reception
rooms opened, the President 'offered the Archbishop the arm of Doña
Soledad, so that he led her to the table and sat beside her. Thus, the
supreme authority of the Colombian Church (the primate, and a Jesuit)
gave evidence of the Church's respect for the union of Doña Soledad
and the President.'

The day after the ball negotiations were resumed.

into Colombia were completely undone. And the bishops could not resist the temptation of boasting for years to come of their triumph, as we see in this statement from the Prefect Apostolic of Putumayo:

When the revolution and liberal teachings misled the good sense of the people, impious governments seized the Church's patrimony, and took from her the goods her children had given her. And when society regained its good sense, then the next generation brought back their filial gifts, and in varying ways, the Church began once again to possess land and property in town and country.[22]

The dispute, wars and other 'democratic games' which had taken place had done nothing to mitigate the greed of the ruling classes for the territory of the Indians; so much so that even during the war of independence they still found time to seize the richest lands from the tribes, always on the grounds that the latter were not making the fullest use of the 'surplus' land of their *resguardos*. When the war against Spain ended a more 'democratic' tendency had appeared: there was actually a decree to proclaim the equality between the aboriginals and the 'civilized'![23] Fortified by this measure which did away with the government protection hitherto accorded the weaker citizens, the new republicans behaved so abominably that in 1828 the President, Simón Bolívar, had to re-establish the legal protection of the Indians, with their self-governing system and other features of the past.[24]

That system, which was never very rigidly adhered to, was not in any case to last long: in 1850 the land-grabbers took a decisive step by legalizing the splitting-up of the *resguardos*. What followed from this was sheer pillage, which resulted in the proliferation of minute scraps of land granted to the Indians, and the transformation of millions of peasants of mixed blood[25] – who now form half of the Colombian people* – into a rural sub-proletariat.

*This vast group, in Colombia as in many other Latin American countries, lives for all practical purposes on the fringe of the nation – for instance, it constitutes normally no more than thirty per cent of all registered voters. This is one of the major elements in the tragedy now tearing apart the sub-continent.

Years went by, and in 1874 the radical government was moved by the plight of the Indians to promulgate a law in their favour. It condemned all use of violence against the natives, forbade their being sold alcohol or being cheated in business dealings, and above all attempted to put a stop to the continuing rape of their land.[26] The actual carrying-out of this law was entrusted to 'General Councils' whose activity could only be minimal in that period of disturbance and financial crisis.

But 'when society regained its good sense', there was a general review of the ideal for the natives in the spirit of the agreements made between Church and State. This took solid form in 1890 with the so-called 'Natives Law', Law 89, which we shall have occasion to mention frequently. From thenceforth, the natives were divided into two classes:

(1) The tribes 'already domesticated to civil life', living in villages or *resguardos*, with reasonably westernized customs. Law 89 guaranteed these Indians the preservation of their traditional forms of government, and their *resguardos*, while making the State responsible for administering all business dealings relating to their lands. Juridically, the Inga and Sibundoy were in this class.

(2) The nomadic natives, or those living in the virgin forests, 'savages being gradually brought to civilization by the Missions', who were placed wholly under the missionaries' guardianship.

To achieve this, a further law, voted three years later, authorized the government to 'delegate to the missionaries extraordinary powers to exercise civil, penal and judicial authority over their catechumens, to whom the laws for the rest of the country did not apply . . .'[27] Taking this statute as his basis, the governor of the southern part of the country gave the Fathers Superior of all missions the title and authority of Chief Superintendents of Police,[28] with full power to define crimes, select police officers and determine what penalties should be applied to such 'savages' as infringed the law by refusing to accept the western customs they were trying to enforce upon them.

Finally came the law of 1898, which completed the job by placing Colombia under the 'social sovereignty of Jesus Christ'.*

At the turn of the century, when all preparations had been made for undertaking the conversion of the 200,000 'infidel savages' of the Amazon basin, the liberals in the country attempted one final armed offensive to overthrow this régime which they hated so much. Its total defeat reinforced the conservative government, and the Church found itself endowed with privileges of which it had scarcely dared to dream.

When the Convention of the Missions was renewed in 1902 the government bound itself (once again without any authority from the legislature) to 'grant national land to the missionaries', to 'provide regularly and without interruption' for the needs of all missioners sent from Rome, to leave the academic and financial administration and direction of public education in the 'mission lands' in the hands of the mission superiors, with the title of Superintendents of Education. But the finest jewel in the whole crown was the government's commitment to 'appoint civil authorities desirable from all points of view, and known to be approved by the missions and missionary religious, after previous consultation with the Apostolic Delegate . . . Any objection from the Mission Superior based on proved facts would constitute sufficient grounds for the removal of a government employee.'

In return, the Church promised to bring the Indians towards Christian civilization, and to work 'for the development and prosperity of the Territory'. The government fully realized that

*During the next twenty years the National Congress was to approve a number of laws of a similar kind. In 1913, to 'pay homage of admiration to Jesus the King in the august mystery of the Eucharist'; to proclaim the Virgin Mary 'Queen of Colombia'; in 1929, to institute 'the national feast of Christ the King' in whose honour a vast church was built in the capital, and so on.

This feast has done an enormous amount to enrich Colombian politico-religious folklore; the President of the Republic and all senior dignitaries, whether freemasons, atheists, or Marxists, are obliged to take part in the celebrations, with suitable fervour.

as a result of this abrogation of its power three quarters of the country would become 'mission territory'.*

The ground was well and truly laid. The new crusade of the missionaries in Colombian Amazonia could begin.

*Today, though the first flush of evangelization is over, in a country with 21½ million people the 'mission territory' – i.e. areas populated by 'savages' – still covers 72 per cent of the whole, though containing no more than 50,000 Indians who live either as nomads, or deep in the forest. The administration of the missions is divided into eleven vicariates and three Apostolic Prefectures, with all the privileges guaranteed by the Convention of the Missions.

PART TWO

The New Crusade
(1906–30)

CHAPTER 4

The Start of
the White Invasion

The Whites treated the Indians as slaves, and at times even as animals.

(FRAY BENIGNO DE CANET DE MAR, 1924)

With the twentieth century we no longer face the major obstacle we have had to overcome in reconstituting the earlier
history of the Upper Putumayo: the absence of documentation.
The friars have been very ready to write the history of their
congregation, and though their accounts are somewhat smug,
tending to self-congratulation, like so much ecclesiastical writing,* their chronicles have one most outstanding merit: they
record almost every event that occurred, convinced as their
authors are of the excellence of all missionary work, and of
their consequent obligation to defend and indeed boast of its
every detail on every occasion. Basically this is no more than a
logical development of the West's cultural ethno-centrism. The
sincerity of the missionary chroniclers may give the reader

*It must not be forgotten that in the eyes of religious, apologia –
'defence of one's faith, justification for one's behaviour', as the dictionary
defines it – grows out of apologetics – 'the science of teaching how to
demonstrate the truth of the Christian religion and defend it against its
enemies'. That science was perhaps most flourishing in the second century, with the theologians; but it later spread among the clergy and
gradually developed into a defence of the Church, its ministers and its
actions. It is mostly in this latter sense that it was cultivated in the
Spanish world, not merely as a virtue, but as a duty incumbent on all
Catholics. And thus it is still understood by the missionaries of the Putumayo, who present all the tales they tell with a certain aura of heroism.

some surprises, but it will enable him to see for himself the significance and scope of the work carried out in the Upper Putumayo by these twentieth-century crusaders.

When in 1893 the Bishop of the former 'Vicious City of Concepción de Pasto' began to receive the subsidies promised by the government, his desire to organize the first evangelizing tours was thwarted by a dearth of recruits to propagate the faith. To resolve this problem, he decided to call for help on the Capuchin fathers, who, since their expulsion from the republic of Salvador in 1873, had taken refuge under the Ecuadorian dictator, García Moreno. The Capuchins seized on this chance to become re-established in Colombia, and three of them – an Englishman, an Ecuadorian and a Spaniard – at once answered the bishop's call by setting out for Sibundoy.

Fray Angel de Villava thus became the order's first chronicler in the district. His account gives us some idea of the major difficulties encountered by the missionaries: the absence of roads, and the harsh and unhealthy climate. By the second day of their journey, on the *páramo* of the Bordoncillo, the English missionary 'became extremely pale and could not stand up'. 'I was much alarmed,' notes Fray de Villava. 'The Englishman was so heavy that no one could carry him, and unable as he was to put one foot in front of the other, all he wanted was to lie down on the cold, damp ground.'[1]

The travellers finally reached the edge of the Sibundoy valley, where they managed to get their exhausted companion carried down on the back of an Indian. There, while they regained their strength in an atmosphere of the most welcoming friendliness, they noted that the population of Santiago had grown to 1,500, and that of Sibundoy Grande to 2,000, seventy of whom were white.

Ten days later, the two who were strong enough continued as far as Mocoa. Their journey became still more difficult, and indeed the description they give of their sufferings – the most minute accounts enabling us to recognize their great heroism – makes it possible for one of their successors to show how what is quite normal for an Indian is a real trial to a white man:

They went down the río Titango, and crossed it by a tree-trunk used for a bridge, which is undoubtedly quite comfortable for the Indians, but was far from being so for them. . . . They then had to go upwards again, up a very steep slope . . . to a hut known as Papagayo, where they camped that night. But their porters had not come so far, so the two explorers had to do without food, and sleep without coverings, thus suffering considerably from the cold at this high altitude . . .

On the tenth they continued their journey, clambering up and down mountains, or following river banks, leaping from stone to stone.[2]

Father Angel's account gives other details about their sufferings on low ground:[3]

We had all we could do to fight off the mosquitoes which were determined to suck our blood, following one another in droves. We also suffered from being eaten alive by jiggers. One skilful Indian woman removed eight from me, and nine from Father Collins. We really suffered dreadfully that day.*

*It may be noted in passing that jiggers – little dipterans, the females of which penetrate the skin, especially on one's feet, to lay their eggs – played a most important part in the history of Capuchin missions. Back in 1646, Fray Andrés de Concentaina wrote that one of the reasons given by his Castilian brethren for refusing to go to America was the existence of 'tiny creatures like fleas which get into one's flesh, and cause large tumours which may lead to death if they are not lanced with a knife. . . .' An assertion which one may feel to be at least somewhat exaggerated when one compares it with one Colombian journalist's description in 1968 of sybaritic Americans who 'are delighted beyond words by the pricking, titillation or super-tickling sensation they get from the tiny invader during her delicious puerperal activity'!

This sybaritic masochism, now out of fashion, necessitated a series of operations to prevent too great a reproduction of the tiny visitors. The erogenous zones most enjoyed by the sybarites were the big toe and the end of the heel. When the jigger was carefully placed in one of those spots, adepts would then scratch voluptuously with rough rope sandals specially designed for the purpose or, failing that, against the edge of the pavement.

Thus, at the risk of demythologizing in European eyes this 'great danger' of South America, we may add that in towns with a strong colonial tradition like Popayán there is a whole literature, a whole poetry, devoted to the praise of this aphrodisiac irritant.

Despite their sufferings, the two friars visited ten villages before returning to Pasto. The bishop was delighted to discover the promising future for evangelization, though there was no 'savage' tribe in the surrounding district. However, it was to be three years before in 1896 the 'Fathers of Doctrine' set up an 'experimental' establishment in the Putumayo area, while waiting for a 'contract to be drawn up with the most Illustrious Prelate of the Diocese'.[4] The Provincial of the order sent two missionary priests and one lay brother to Mocoa. Once settled there, they began by denouncing to the local authorities the 'twenty-six couples living publicly in concubinage', and 'doing so without any intention of amendment'. This problem was to be the central object of apostolic activity throughout the twelve journeys they made around the area in three years.

Encouraged by these first results, the missionaries decided to bring the Sibundoy and Inga the benefits of their apostolate; thus the first Capuchins settled in Sibundoy Grande in 1899, and in Santiago in 1900.

In the seven years since the first Capuchin excursion, the seraphic workers had not achieved the necessary acclimatization. For that reason, whether they had forgotten or had never known the humanitarian laws dictated three centuries earlier by the Emperor Charles V, they found it quite natural to ride on the backs of Indians. This system of transport which they used from Pasto to Sibundoy for ten years – and to more inaccessible places for an even longer time – is described in great detail by Fray Jacinto de Quito:

It was indispensable to have recourse to the ancient custom of the place, to ride on the backs of Indians as though they were horses, since on such paths no animals could be used. . . . There were places where it was dangerous to do anything but go on all fours, digging one's nails into cracks in the rock, and adopting various contorted postures. But with their elastic feet and legs of iron the Indians can manage to achieve the journey. . . . This posture was quite comfortable at first, though it caused unconcealed amusement; but as one gradually overcame one's first reactions . . . one's elbows would grow numb against the clammy and smelly back of the Indian; one's knees would be bruised by banging continually against the trees . . . while the Indian could go forward peacefully and comfortably, thinking only of the money he was to get and quite ready to begin over and over again.[5]

Without pausing to consider the Capuchin interpretation of how one might feel at riding on another human being, we may note that in Sibundoy and Santiago they found Indians 'who were quite Christian and peaceful in their ways, not always speaking Castilian, at least in ordinary conversation, but understanding it'. This observation, set beside the comment of Fray Jacinto about the utter spiritual neglect in which these people had lived for so long, shows how total was the cultural syncretism by now achieved by the tribes.

The missionaries also found whites* there, who had settled for very different reasons. The first to come were refugees from the frightful eruptions of the volcano Doña Juana which in 1899 had burnt to death over fifty people, 'while blackening the whole sky with ash for a radius of over 100 kilometres'. The Sibundoy had welcomed them generously, lending them huts to live in and pieces of land to grow food on. The second group were also refugees, this time from the horrors of the last civil war. And the remainder consisted of adventurers who, having failed to do well out of trading in quinine or rubber in what had looked to them like a new El Dorado, were now attempting something less risky.

And since in those days there were no houses other than those of the Indians [the Capuchins tell us] the whites took them over one by one, at derisory rents – like a stone of salt, a few metres of cloth, or something equally valueless. . . . As time went on, the whites filled the land with livestock, cows, pigs, etc., which were continually damaging the crops of the Indians, unprotected by any fencing. . . . After the harvest, and sometimes even before, the animals were left to wander freely.

*From now on the word 'white' must no longer be understood in a racial sense, because of the immense miscegenation in Colombia. 'White' by now simply means 'civilized', or assimilated to the customs of Spanish Christianity. Thus a Creole, even though his origins may be eighty per cent Indian or Negro, is held to be a 'white', and I shall from now on follow the Capuchin chroniclers in using the term thus.

Thus the Indians 'found themselves losing their lands, crops and homes, and they began to move away from the village (Sibundoy) and to take revenge on their oppressors on every possible occasion'.[6]

A few years earlier, the local authorities had quite illegally granted the settlers seventy hectares from the native *resguardo*, where they established the new village of Molina. This was the original basis for the dispute between the Indians and settlers, and since then it had continued to grow worse. Following the advice of their ancestor, the Great Cacique, the Sibundoy responded to the aggression they were subjected to in legal fashion, by laying one complaint after another before the local authorities, in an effort to get their legitimate rights respected and recognized.[7]

The seraphic workers, on discovering the situation, did not hesitate to support the Indians as against the settlers, since these were Indians who did not belong to the liberal party, or have any of the 'reprehensible habits' of the other tribes.

The atmosphere became more tense. Attacks increased on both sides, but the missionaries continued to support the Indians while defending themselves against the accusations laid against them by the settlers.

The newspapers reflect something of these battles. Thus the Capuchins, accused by the columnist Fray Candil – the pseudonym of a settler – of election-rigging, violating human rights, and confiscating the goods of settlers and businessmen,[8] counter-attacked fiercely with a volley of tracts. Some of their viewpoints, like the following as recorded by the order's historian, may be a little surprising to present-day Christians:[9]

We are profoundly convinced that the actions upon which Fray Candil bases his statement [that the sermons of the missionaries are an attack upon or denial of individual liberties] are no more than the result of their faithful fulfilment of their obligations. They can hardly be blamed for having denounced to the civil authorities people who are scandalizing everyone by the example of their evil living. Nor because certain individuals, recently arrived, have been forced by the authorities to leave women they have brought with them who are not their legal wives – behaviour which the civil law itself condemns . . .*

Thus the prime objective of the Capuchins, that of defending the interests of the Indians, faded into the background. While the whites, ignoring all government orders, continued to occupy the Indians' lands, the seraphic workers declared war on prostitutes and unmarried couples – thereby attracting numerous adversaries on whom, according to their own accounts, the vengeance of heaven was not slow to fall.

At the dawn of the twentieth century, the ancient Indian capital of Sibundoy Grande was thus the scene of a conflict described at length by Fray Benigno de Canet de Mar:

. . . It was appalling to see how whites and Indians treated each other; these two opposing races would persecute each other to the death. The whites treated the Indians as slaves and at times even as animals, using them in whatever way their fancy suggested, for purposes of all kinds. They would steal what little those unfortunates possessed, force them to work their land without payment of any kind; if a white man should decide he wished to take away from an Indian the land on which he had been working – be it a large or small area – he did not scruple to do so. The Indians, for their part, observing the tyrannical behaviour of the whites, gave as good as they got, and more, with all the energy of their savage nature. Hence a continual and fierce struggle, with the tiniest spark serving to light terrifying fires that could be extinguished only by the blood of one side or the other.[10]

It was at this point that a newcomer, Fray Lorenzo de Pupiales, finding that racial antagonism was rife even among children, determined to remove the invaders with all their insults and illegalities from among the Sibundoy. With this object, he set about convincing the Indians that they should offer the settlers a piece of land at the easternmost end of the valley, on which to build a totally white village: in 1902, the Chapter of the tribe agreed to offer them 'a broad and fine area', and ordered the four Indian families (i.e. clans) living there to

*It must be remembered that until 1938 concubinage, 'corrupt and reprehensible cohabitation', was a crime subject to a court of law in Colombia.

'leave everything'.[11] The cacique Mariano Juajibioy communicated this decision to the Bishop of Pasto in a note which gave no suggestion of the 'voice of thunder' attributed to him by legend, but only of the most sensitive feelings in regard to those whose coming had so shattered the life of his community:

> We have been asked for a piece of ground for the poor whites, and we are giving the ground known as Guairasacha or San Francisco; this we give voluntarily so that the poor whites may settle there.[12]

Fray de Pupiales needed no urging, and three days later he founded the village of San Francisco. But, contrary to what might have been hoped, the Indians' generosity was ill received by a lot of settlers who wanted to stay on the land they had already seized. Faced with their obstinacy, the cacique Juajibioy decided to go and beg protection for his people from the provincial authorities. The whites took the opportunity to attack him on the journey, 'but he defended himself bravely, and emerged unscathed'. This incident made the missionary fear that all his efforts had been in vain; but there he was wrong, because despite the attack the fine cacique kept his word, and still gave the whites the land promised them.

Now that the Capuchins' wish was satisfied, the Sibundoy demanded the return of the buildings and plantations bordering on the upper part of their main village, but to this the only response of the whites was to threaten them with death. Then, records Fray de Quito, 'the Indians reached the end of their patience, and resolved to get rid of the usurpers, if need be by force'. In the final days of 1902, 'they destroyed their homes, so as to force them out, and though there were large numbers of whites, there was no bloodshed'.[13]

This version of the story is rather different from that current in the rest of the world, which held that the priests had incited the Sibundoy to set fire to the 'village of Molina'. There is corroborative evidence, however: the future Prefect Apostolic in fact said that 'it was the Indians who set fire to a few houses which belonged to them, in order that the whites should not be tempted to come back and live in them again'.[14] His fellow-Capuchin, and the historian of the order, Fray Pacífico de Vilanova, records that 'two whites suddenly started the fire, and the Indians had to put out the blaze on their property'.[15] These varying versions do not alter the basic reality: whether or not it was the Indians who burnt their houses, it was still as far as they were concerned a measure to defend their own inheritance. And the undeniable fact that Fray Lorenzo 'incited' the Indians to take action – which is confirmed by contemporary witnesses – can only be called praiseworthy. However, the Capuchins were to have to spend the next fifty years defending themselves to the 'civilized' world for this step.

The most obstinate of the settlers were still not discouraged, and tried yet again to appeal to the authorities. Unfortunately for them, the authorities once more recognized the full right of the Indians to the valley 'as is clear from all the many public documents'.[16] Immediately afterwards, the attorney general of the Pasto area went in person to Sibundoy to see the natives re-established in their ownership. Better still: the gift of land by the Sibundoy to the 'civilized' was recognized honourably by being enshrined in a law of the national government.

Thus it remains proved that until 19 November 1904 both State and Church, in the persons of officials and missionaries, recognized and defended as legitimate the ownership by the Sibundoy of the lands left to them by Carlos Tamoabioy.*

*One thing is important to note: the way in which the Capuchins themselves recognized the validity of the natives' territorial rights. The two most important pieces of evidence are:

That of Fray de Quito: 'There is proof in the written testament of Don Carlos Tamoabioy, which the natives have in their possession, having gone themselves to get it from the archives of Quito in 1868';

That of Fray Bartolomé de Igualada, when he stated to Father Lino Rampón that 'there was in existence a title given by a viceroy (in fact the Visitor, Luis de Quiñones) after visiting the valley of Sibundoy, recognizing it as belonging to the Sibundoy people. There were witnesses to this act, though it itself has been destroyed by those whose interests were involved.'

Meanwhile, in Pasto, to make the position of the ecclesiastical authorities abundantly clear, the bishop condemned to
his flock the excesses that had been committed at Sibundoy:
'These crimes were truly horrible, for their consequences will
be eternal; they are as ugly as the devil who inspired them, and
black as the hell where they were created.'[17]

Thus calm was restored. None the less, the consequences of
the confrontation were yet to become clear: apparently the
Sibundoy had won their case, but there were now settlers established at the end of the valley, and missionaries in their own
village. Furthermore, the Capuchins were beginning to consider
how best to get hold of various material commodities. One of
them, 'with the support of His Lordship the Bishop of Pasto,
went to buy several head of cattle and sheep, and brought them
back to the village of Sibundoy by the appalling Aponte trail'.
Another 'had several hectares of land reclaimed behind the
friary of San Francisco, known as the *Cofradia* of the Divine
Shepherdess',* which was to form the basis of the *hacienda* of
San Félix.

Once established in the Sibundoy valley, the missionaries
saw that their protégés were gradually moving away from
them, often seeking refuge in the mountains – which seemed to
them either the height of ingratitude or, more probably, a
proof of their 'savagery'.

Thus Fray Jacinto recorded how, when the heralds of the
Gospel asked the Indians to help them build a house for their
own use, they met with a unanimous refusal:

It is not the custom for the priests to have a house in our village
but only to live among the whites, as they do in Pasto.

Consequently, it was 'only after a considerable battle, and
paying more than usual for the work, that we could at last get

---

On the other hand, the reader should not forget that the historian
Sergio Elías Ortiz was quite recently able to see one of the 'destroyed'
acts in the Capuchin monastery in Pasto.

*The Virgin Mary, as the 'Divine Shepherdess', is patroness of Cap-
uchin missions.

the shell of our house built, and have it covered with straw. But they absolutely refused to plaster the walls with earth . . .'

The opening of the first school in old Sibundoy Grande provided another example of their passive resistance. 'Despite innumerable announcements and notifications to those with children, the school opened with only a single pupil. It was a month before a second could be found. A third was snatched from a maize field . . .' Fray Buenaventura de Pupiales faced the same problem in Santiago, where he only managed to collect two scholars 'because the parents would hide their sons in their huge pots, or up in the trees, or under feeding troughs, or disguise them as girls', and 'when the little boys found themselves caught they would burst into tears, and have to be given a piece of bread to stop them crying'.

These envoys of the Lord simply could not realize that to the Indians they represented just one more aspect of the terrifying white invasion which had come to endanger their possessions, their traditions, and even their chances of survival.

Such was the atmosphere during the five 'experimental' years of the Capuchin mission. This period came to an end on 20 December 1904, when the Vatican decreed the establishment of the Apostolic Prefecture of the Caquetá and Putumayo.

CHAPTER 5

Powers, Programme and Methods of a Catalan Crusader

I was then in the desperate position of the man who, finding every door shut and every way out blocked, can only attempt the impossible.

(FRAY FIDEL DE MONTCLAR, 1934)

On 31 January 1905, the Holy See appointed as the first Prefect Apostolic of the Caquetá and Putumayo, Fray Fidel de Montclar, who was at the time on leave in Spain. Formerly superior of the community in Pasto, and the founder of a mission in Central America, the new prelate, short, thickset, and thirty-eight years old, combined a tremendously energetic personality with a long experience of leadership. In addition, he was a typical representative of his native Catalonia: enterprising, persistent, and preferring action to the discussion of doctrinal minutiae. Like him in this was Fray Estanislao de las Corts, the athletic fellow-countryman he chose as his assistant; his confrères described him as 'a strong and energetic character, with a will that could conquer rocks and mountains'. The character of the two crusaders was matched by their brusque military manner of speech, as we shall have ample occasion to see.

The very way in which the Prefect Apostolic set about his task was characteristic. As soon as he got to Bogotá, he demanded two absolutely imperative conditions of the government:

First, that the credits granted by the State for the individual board and lodging of missionaries be doubled;

Second, that he at once be granted the right to be 'Inspector General of Public Education', with the power to open schools and appoint teachers, according to the 1902 Convention of the Missions.*

Having settled that, he went on to Pasto to take up his office, which gave him the occasion for making this profession of faith:

O Lord, with the same ease with which you filled these vast spaces with trees and rivers, you could raise up out of these forests filled with savages and these desert lands filled with wild and man-eating beasts, civilized villages and rich towns, where you would be adored and your name blessed for years to come . . .

This missionary leader gives no details about the 'man-eating beasts', but pays honour in passing to the Indo-American Capuchins who have gone before him, recognizing 'how much work has been done in the Caquetá'. This did not, however, prevent his over-riding immediately on arriving, before the full assembly of twelve missionary priests and the Creole lay brothers, the order's motto: 'Go ye into the whole world and preach the gospel to every creature.'[1] For, to him, as the Caquetá and Putumayo were to be Christianized, every pro-Indian ideal must be abandoned in favour of an attitude of greater energy and a closer conformity with 'civilization'. Starting from this basic principle, he worked out a first project intended to 'introduce Christianity into the virgin forest'. To him that 'introduction of Christianity' had the very modern meaning of opening up the ground for economic development by a series of clearly defined operations: cutting a road through, establishing townships, getting agricultural and business enterprises on foot, and so on.

*The credits were fixed at 6,000 gold pesos. To see this in the context of the financial atmosphere of the period, it may be noted that the salary of a Minister of State was 150 gold pesos, and that of a clerk, 30. It must also be stressed that, despite the nation's state of impoverishment, commitments to the Church were always honoured: it received fantastic sums from the State in relation to those allotted to education. For instance: in the year of Fray Fidel's arrival, the State paid 183,045 gold pesos to the Church, and only spent 27,000 on public education – and remember that the sums granted to the mission schools also had to come out of that 27,000.

Though to the western mind such plans could only appear as important, progressive and modern, to the Indians they meant something very different indeed, for the measures that would open up the 'virgin forest' would also open up their society, hitherto safeguarded by the great wall of the Andes.

In the second phase, that of consolidating his Apostolic Prefecture, Fray Fidel made his intentions more concrete still: he got his Creole confrères in Pasto to sign a 'family agreement' whereby the whole of the Church's possessions in the Putumayo were placed under his jurisdiction.[2]

The transportable goods thus 'recovered' included objects in daily use, bought out of the income from tithes, offerings for masses and so on, and other ecclesiastical revenue, combined with the gifts offered for hundreds of years past by the Inga and Sibundoy in honour of their patron saints: among them were to be found, higgledy-piggledy, imperial crowns, emerald earrings and necklaces of uncut stones, as well as *capisayos*, the long red and white or blue and black striped ponchos characteristic of the area.[3]

The non-transportable goods included the ground set aside for the Church and monastery in each village, as well as sixteen chapels and eight schools, all buildings of wood or earth, covered with thatch. But Fray Fidel had also listed among these possessions the lands known as the *Cofradías* of the Virgin, whose names should be noted here.

San Félix: an allotment of five hectares of cultivated land dedicated to the Divine Shepherdess, part of the land granted by the Sibundoy to the poor whites of San Francisco;

La Granja: a small estate on the edge of Sibundoy Grande which the missionaries had taken for themselves from among the ruins of Molina, the village the Indians had destroyed at the missionaries' instigation to get rid of the first settlers;

San Pedro: a piece of land in the centre of the valley which would seem to have been granted (as a holding in usufruct*) by

---

*Note, in other words, that it was granted only for their *use*, for it was established both by colonial and republican law that the Indian lands belonged communally and inalienably to the tribes living there.

the Sibundoy several centuries earlier to those who were virtually their parish clergy;[4]

And, last, and most important of the four, the *Cofradía* of Carmen, which according to Fray Bartolomé de Igualada, covered some 'hundred hectares of swamp land'. He tells us that the land had been given (also in usufruct) to the Parish of Santiago by the Inga, in an Act kept by the Chapter of the village; but the Indian governor, Mateo Buesaquillo, is said to have destroyed the document after his tribe settled in the spot.[5]

To sum up: the Church of the Putumayo did not strictly speaking *own* anything more than a few jewels, some old buildings, and some few head of cattle, and, in usufruct, some Indian land – but this, after the publication of the Prefect Apostolic's Decree Number Two, became in fact the property of the Capuchin Mission. Actually, though, when Fray Fidel 'whom the Indians themselves carried on their backs' went to visit the *Cofradía* of Carmen, its area was not just over fifty hectares as had been thought, but 'was enclosed in a perimeter of something like a two-hour journey' – in other words, over a thousand hectares, as can be seen from the map of Capuchin possessions in 1906.

The rectification of boundaries which then took place was to incorporate into the missionaries' property the lands of the Buesaquillo, Tisoy and other families (clans) – interpreted by the Capuchins' 'inventory' as follows:

It must be made clear that the larger part of this ground is swampland. A few individuals are living on the dry part, with houses, plantations, and livestock, on the basis of non-existent claims to ownership. That is why we have allowed them the use of this land for raising crops and animals.

The results of this manoeuvre were to become clear only much later on. Meanwhile, we may take careful note of the generosity of this 'loan of land' of which the Capuchin administrator of the mission's property makes such a point:

In order not to burden these Indians with any further taxes, the beneficiaries of our loan were exempted from paying first-fruits,* and the rent for farming the land was fixed at only 80 *paires* (200 kilos) of maize per year.†

We may feel that there was something a trifle 'jesuitical' in all this loan-farming-rent business, for while the Indians believed they were paying their first-fruits, the Capuchins recorded it as rent, thus justifying their own claims to ownership of the land. This technique of expropriation developed into a regular system.

Once these administrative details were settled, Fray Fidel and his friars set about making the land pay. General Rufino Gutiérez, a friend and admirer of Fidel de Montclar – whom we shall have occasion to quote again – describes the method used:

> The Indians were obliged to spend Mondays working to build churches, schools, or houses for the priests, brothers and nuns, as well as to cultivate ground which had in fact been recognized from time immemorial as belonging to the Church and the *cofradias*; but of course it was entirely for their own good and that of their descendants.[6]

Slavery – to the glory of God and the Divine Shepherdess – was making its appearance in what had always been the ancient and safe home of the Inga and Sibundoy.

For a better understanding of the change so soon to take place, let us look more closely at the situation in the valley.

According to the North American engineer W. E. Hardenburg:

> Santiago numbered some fifty or so houses and a church built of earth with a roof of leaves. . . . The population was entirely Indian, apart from the five or six priests who looked after the village, and

*It was the custom for Catholics in the Spanish-speaking world to present their first-fruits to the Church at the same time as paying their tithes. On the demand of the Spanish Crown, these contributions were included in the 'Five Commandments of the Church' and were obligatory.

†The *paire* of maize was an Indian measure, still used in what used to be the Inca territories. It is the equivalent of about 5 lb.

one old woman of over eighty, who had been the mistress of a former president. Those Indians were strong, with bronzed and delightful faces. For the most part they had lively minds, cheerful and extremely intelligent, though when they came into contact with whites they would pretend to total stupidity. . . . San Francisco is a small depressing village with about two hundred white inhabitants, distinguishable from the Indians only by the trousers they wear.

As for the people of Sibundoy Grande, the engineer merely reports the conviction of his guide, Fray Estanislao de las Corts: 'They are lazy, dishonest, more stupid than the Inga . . .'[7]

This underlines the gulf separating the Catalans from their Indo-American confrères when it came to appreciating the Indians. The Creole Capuchins, whether from intuition, lack of imagination, or a sense of solidarity with their compatriots, based their action on the 'loving care of the Good Shepherd',[8] which resulted most noticeably in their taking up the defence of the Sibundoy against the first invasion of settlers. This evangelizing paternalism – 'Our brothers from the east, these poor little savages of the Caquetá', as the Bishop of Pasto called them – hardly tallied with the designs of the new Spanish crusaders, who were consequently to come up against certain quite unexpected obstacles:

First, spiritually, the existence in the tribes of the Upper Amazon, of a religious syncretism in which there was a quite heterodox amalgamation of Indian beliefs with those of the 'pale-faces'; and second, socially, the persistence of native customs some of which recalled the early days of Christianity: detachment from material goods, the habit of living from day to day, and the custom of working the land and enjoying its fruits in common.

There could be no hesitation: these traits from the past must be wiped out and yield to 'true culture' – in other words, orthodox Catholicism and private property, and with them economic development. But however good and desirable such plans may have been, they could hardly be expected to receive an instantaneous welcome from the natives.

Their incomprehension soon enraged the Catalans. They

became determined to 'conquer these savages' who thereupon only increased their resistance. A desperate war of liberation was obviously on its way.

The action began when Fray de Montclar, on his arrival, appointed Fray Estanislao de las Corts as acting parish priest of Sibundoy Grande. This was a step to have serious consequences for the Sibundoy, with their peaceful and conservative temperaments, still suffering as they were from the bruises of their recent confrontation with the settlers. They had in fact abandoned their village and withdrawn into the neighbouring mountains, apart from a few among them who came down temporarily to the village during the rainy season, driven by hunger and sickness, intending to leave again when the rain was over. So the valley was starting to revert to forest, and the first care of Estanislao, the 'evangelic worker', was to build a new village to his own specifications:

Today, 19 October 1906 [he wrote in a letter to Fidel de Montclar], we laid the first pillars of the first house of the new order. . . . You will see, with God's help, how we shall transform this village, or, more precisely, how we shall transform this desert into a village. I say 'this desert', because only last week there were still no more than twenty families here . . . and they, with only a few exceptions, are likely to go back into hiding in the forest at the end of the year.[9]

But Fray Estanislao was determined at all costs to prevent the village becoming totally deserted, and even hoped to get the Indians back from the mountains. The results of his first hand-outs of bread, salt and sweets to the children seemed promising: in the first week, 'eight families left their hiding places, and the following week, twenty-five more'. But Fray Estanislao, carried away by his own enthusiasm, tried to hurry the process on too fast without sufficient consideration of the means to be used: 'bounties, punishments . . . we did everything to *force* them back. This was the only possible way to civilize them.'

The result was predictable: two months later he reached the

sad realization that: 'There are now only nine families, and
even they spend all their time out of doors. Yesterday not a
single Indian came to us. . . . Today we sounded the horn at
daybreak; it is now ten in the morning, and I can still see no
one, apart from a very few schoolboys and girls to whom
we have just handed out six reales' worth of salt and sweets, to
stop them from running away'.[10]

But for all his gifts, Fray Estanislao could not stop these
'mountain-deer of Indians spending all their time hidden in the
forest'. He was forced to admit in a letter to Fray Fidel, his
superior:

> You may remember that I wrote to you in mid November that I
> had brought back *fifty-three* families to the village, whereas the list
> I made on the first Sunday of October only contained *thirteen*. Alas, I
> have made a complete tour several times this week, and to my great
> regret, I am bound to recognize that there are now no more than
> *four* families here.[11]

Despite these results, self explanatory though they seem to
us, the energetic Spaniards did nothing to modify their policy
towards the Indians – a policy unchanged since the sixteenth
century. Thus they carried on what the chronicler de Vilanova
described as a 'painful struggle'. For years and years they tried
to force the Sibundoy to live in a village built in straight lines,
which went against every Indian tradition, and constrained
them to perform obligatory toil for nothing for the advantage
of the Church.*

Some Capuchin chroniclers considered that the resistance
was due entirely to contacts between Indians and settlers. One

*(a) The Indian villages were built in scattered form for social, econ-
omic and health reasons (to keep refuse apart from the houses, and
permit of the isolation of those with contagious sicknesses). This safety
measure was impossible in the cross-shaped villages forced on the South
Americans by the Spaniards.

(b) Unpaid collective labours were authorized by Colombian law for
purposes of the common interest, like the Indian custom known as *minga*
which continues in our own day. The Capuchins took advantage of this to
include in that category (of common interest) the building of monasteries, and work in the mission farms and workshops.

attributes it to 'their pigheaded and violent opposition to the slightest progressive change in their customs, and their immorality and alcoholism'.[12] But certainly the Capuchin policy of conquest had a great deal to do with this flight to the forests. Furthermore, it is from their own records that we find the consequences of this virtual exodus:

(1) The excess of deaths over births, due largely to the inhospitable conditions of the forests, cold, steep and rainy.

(2) The appearance of degenerative sicknesses, resulting from the malnutrition which now existed not only in the forest, but also in that valley once famous for 'its rich soil and fine food'. The lack of food reached its high point in December, known as the 'month of hunger'.

Among the symptoms of degenerescence, we may note the arrival of goitre, hitherto unknown here because of the salt the Sibundoys had always got in the past from their trading with Pasto. According to the missionaries' own notes thirty-five to fifty per cent of their school children were soon suffering from this illness.

(3) An epidemic of suicides on such a scale that, around 1908, over four hundred persons killed themselves together. The missionaries and their white friends could only see this as an example of the undoubted 'barbarism' of the Sibundoy which they were so often to deplore.[13] We shall return to this phenomenon for a closer look in Chapter 9.

Finally, as one contemporary Capuchin says:

The Sibundoy found themselves in an unbelievable but evident state of defeat. They who from ancient times had been distinguished among all the rest, whose village was the metropolis of the whole of this Indian area, became aware of their appalling misfortune. That certitude led them and their neighbours to invent malicious legends explaining the reasons for it.[14]

Among those 'malicious legends' figures the brief biography of Saint Carlos Tamoabioy, and also a new version of the story of the Christ of Sibundoy. Both indicate clearly how the self-defensive reflex of the Sibundoy led them to make the supreme ideal of life and freedom part of their tradition.

But, with the gradual thrust of the Creole invasion, and the hardening of the Capuchins' methods, the traditional pacifism of the Sibundoy gave way to the acts of violence designed to discourage the whites and make them leave the valley. Nor was it terrorism: with their respect for human life, they never attacked the priests' persons, but only their most valued material goods, their cattle. Fray Estanislao reported in a letter to his superior that 'thirty-eight cows from the mission alone have vanished within a year and a half. All died from arrows, lances, machetes, or from some poison or herb which gave them diarrhoea of which they died within three months.'[15]

But the Sibundoy were not the only ones to rebel. The Inga too opposed the missionaries, even making use of arguments of piety to indicate what their own concept of religion was.

Fray Jacinto de Quito records one revealing incident which took place when he was parish priest of San Andrés. The statue of the patron saint was found to have become discoloured and worn away over the years, and the Capuchins decided to replace it. The faithful rejected the idea, but the parish priest acted over their heads, and then invited the people to come and pay honour to the new statue. The Indians responded to his appeal, but to his great surprise, laid their offerings before the old statue. Fray Jacinto then tried to take it away, but the Inga argued with him:

How, little Father, can you want to take away our San Andrés when he knows our language and our ways, whereas this *muchacho* [young fellow] has only just come and knows nothing? When we are on a journey and fall ill, we light a little candle to San Andrés, and he hears our requests; but this young man wouldn't even know why we were lighting the candle.

The priest, in this dilemma, sought the advice of the Prefect Apostolic, who replied: 'Now more than ever, I am convinced that these Indians are truly idolators. . . . You must get rid of the old statue by whatever means you can.' Yet that was easier said than done: for when Fray Jacinto put a rope round the hands of the old statue to drag it out there was a real rebellion, and he was forced to put off doing anything by popular pressure. Only under cover of darkness, and with the help of some Marist brothers, could he finally get rid of the statue by burning it.

But the story did not end there. When the Indian Chapter met in plenary session, they decided to give way to the extent of allowing offerings to be placed in front of both statues. Fray Jacinto told them that San Andrés 'was already in heaven, and could not come down again'. The enraged villagers went everywhere looking for the patron saint who they were sure could not have abandoned them; and failing to find him, they laid a complaint against *los señores misioneros* before the governor of Pasto, then before the President of the Republic, and finally before the Apostolic Nuncio.[16] When they at last had to accept that they would never see their old patron saint again, they made up another legend: San Andrés was in exile, wandering like a ghost on the waves of the Amazon and its tributaries.

This total lack of understanding on the part of the missionaries led to other manifestations of discontent; for instance, on the arrival of the Franciscan nuns in Santiago the 'Indians impudently presented themselves to the Sister Superior and told her that *tradition* forbade her coming to live in their village. "We are not whites; you go back to Pasto." '

Fray de Quito himself experienced a similar show of annoyance when they burnt a new carpentry workshop he had built to make furniture for the Mission buildings. And even the Great Crusader, Fidel de Montclar himself, was not spared. Fray Jacinto records: 'He bought a horse. The Indians knew this and . . . to prevent their doors being opened to civilization and progress, they put poison on their arrows, and in the middle of the night, they shot the inoffensive animal. True, it did not die, but it never recovered its strength and remained unusable.'[17]

However, this kind of resistance could not go on for ever. It diminished bit by bit as the most refractory of the Indians took to living permanently in the hills; the weaker ones, thus left alone, and seeing no way to escape the new system, would simply hang themselves. So there only remained to be 'civilized' by the Capuchins the sick, the infirm and the ever increasing number suffering from goitre. When the Marist brothers arrived there were forty-six goitre-sufferers among the very few Sibundoy still living in and around the capital.

However, Fray Fidel found a means of increasing the population, which was to reach huge proportions in the coming decades: he brought in religious. The first contingent of Franciscan nuns arrived from Germany, and began to give their support to the more moderate action of the Marists; but even with less violent methods, they were still not invariably successful. Brother Duque, the sole survivor of that era, has told us how the order that men must wear pants underneath their traditional garments, and the girls dresses, met with violent resistance, despite its being enforced with a whip.* But the same Marist admits that boys were more ready to have their hair cut short when given the subtle explanation that 'it was a new fashion'.[18]

There is a mass of evidence to indicate how such practices struck at the very heart of the Indians' most cherished traditions. What is surprising is the way in which the evangelizers interpreted their 'cultural guerrilla warfare'. That the children, having been forced to wear pants at school, would rush to take them off in the first field they came to in order to avoid enraging their parents, appeared to the religious to mean that the Indians were an indecent lot. This same explanation soon came to be given to all forms of resistance: thus, the records tell us, the Marists had to teach the children 'how to play ... because due to their savage state, they did not know any games'. And Fray Jacinto managed to explain the removal of a whole plantation of potatoes one night by saying that the Indians 'had not the custom' of growing them – though they were in fact one of the most typical crops in the Andes! Such examples make clear how, consciously or otherwise, the new *doctrineros* simply refused to imagine that such actions could really be intended as

*It may be recalled that the use of the whip had been explicitly forbidden two centuries earlier by the Archbishop of Villagomez.

sabotage, or, in the last instance, to recognize the chronic hunger from which the valley now suffered.[19]

Two years passed in this kind of atmosphere, while the mission went on pursuing its basic objectives: to provide itself with building materials, organize speedier forms of transport and, in short, to achieve a rational economic exploitation of the area, which was the essential condition for its future prosperity. The Capuchins themselves record their first achievements: the restoration to use of a lime-kiln dating back to the first Spaniards, and a mechanical saw imported from Barcelona; the introduction of horses, an increase in the number of cattle leased out, the setting up of several weaving machines imported from Germany. As for education, they were teaching the girls 'to embroider white linen', and 'we distributed [to the Indians] twenty-four packets of seeds of various vegetables imported from Spain'.[20]

In these two busy years, the two great Catalan crusaders tried at once to inculcate the principles of their 'native policy' among their Creole colleagues, to get rid of all latent subversiveness, and to found for the future a legal framework in which the natives' aggressiveness towards the missionaries might be pacified. All these considerations combined to produce, in October 1908, the *Regulation for the Government of the Natives*,[21] in which Fidel de Montclar codified the art of civilizing savages into forty-seven articles.*

One can, in analysing them, divide these articles into four groups:

(1) Measures of a political nature leading to the establishment of a real theocratic dictatorship in the Prefecture. In particular, they do away with the popular election of the governors

*In doing this, the Prefect Apostolic disregarded the Decree by which such rules were to be decided *by* the government *in agreement with* the ecclesiastical authorities. For in this case, it was he who composed the document and presented it *a posteriori* for the approval of his good friend Bucheli, elected first governor of the new province of Nariño, of which Pasto was the capital. The name of this family will recur several times in my book, illustrating the continuity of the power exercised by the pseudo-aristocracy of South America.

and other members of the Indians' Chapters. In the future these were to be chosen from among candidates put forward by the Chief Missioner, and could only act under the enforced chairmanship of the parish priests, whose authority was to be reinforced by the presence of a body of police, chosen and led by a Supreme Chief — none other than Fidel de Montclar himself.

(2) The internal rules of the police dictatorship: the natives were to be obliged to reside in the village for a fixed number of days each week, leaving their plantations untended. Private meetings were to be supervised, and must end at nine p.m. 'as signalled by the bell'. There was to be a daily inspection of people's private life, day and night, with houses and lands inspected to safeguard 'the morality of the village'. The establishment of this network was intended to catch potential victims for the whip of the *cepo*: minor delinquents, and Indians of either sex guilty of serious or light infringements of chastity.

(3) Rules for the purpose of keeping the natives in a state of servitude. These gave careful details of the punishments, fines, or labours to be enforced on all delinquents. Among the faults to be punished were not coming back to the village on the days designated, not taking part in public works, not working a week for nothing in the police service according to the rota system in operation, not fulfilling one's obligatory share in the free work to be done on land where food was grown for the police, the missionaries, the workers, etc.

All these measures were to stifle the Indians' economy by diminishing their capacity for production, thus accelerating the very exodus the missionaries were trying to prevent.

(4) Powers given to the missionary leader to 'redistribute' Indian lands, without regard to the Indians' rights or to their tradition whereby the valley belonged communally and inalienably to its tribe.

This final measure gives an indication of one ambition that was deep-rooted in the heart of the Catalonian missionaries: the final eradication of the community spirit of the Indians (which had for centuries enabled them to defend their lands), which was to be replaced by the western cult of private property. The Capuchins boasted openly of this several times in such terms as the following:

> The missionaries preach this attachment [to riches] to civilize the Indians ... to bring them into a civilized way of living, that they may learn to enjoy working, and no longer let themselves be exploited by the whites ...[22]

It is hard to see how the Indians could be the gainers when only Capuchins and settlers were masters in this property system. But what is quite clear is how the Regulation affected matters in practice: the disputants began to lose ground, and their 'delinquency', so fiercely attacked by the *doctrineros*, gradually diminished. With the help of some free labour, the religious could now ensure a regular supply of food – which had up to then been uncertain – and they gradually acquired more comfortable houses, while the *Cofradías* of the Virgin were developed into 'fine pasturelands'.[23]

With this new 'spirit of collaboration' on the part of the Inga and Sibundoy, the Prefect Apostolic was able to set about building roads suitable for wheeled vehicles, an operation which, according to one chronicler of the order, began very successfully:

> Two new roads were opened, one from Sibundoy to San Francisco, the other from Sibundoy to Santiago, the first 6·4 kilometres long, the second 7·2; they crossed twenty-three bridges and were perfectly adequate for horses. From Santiago a road was begun to Pasto, and work went so fast that in five weeks' time it was already 14 kilometres long.[24]

But with this we enter a whole new phase in the life of the Great Crusader.

General Rafael Reyes, who had just become president of the republic, was an enthusiastic admirer of the Prefect Apostolic. Therefore he gave his immediate approval to Fidel de Montclar's great project of linking together the various parts of his territory.

Thus there seemed no need to wait before beginning the

work, but scarcely had the engineers mapped out the route and begun operations, when the money ran out. Fidel de Montclar sent demand after demand to the government, but in vain, for its intense poverty made further grants impossible. So the Great Crusader decided to act for himself, and he ordered his assistant Fray de las Corts to get the Sibundoy–Pasto part of the road begun by whatever means he could.

All went well, and only three months later Fray Fidel was able to write to his friend the President: 'Without help from anyone, we have already opened over eight leagues of road passable by horse traffic.' This would certainly be true if one did not count the free labour provided by the natives as 'help'. For the hardest work fell on the 'volunteers' dragooned by the agents of Fray de las Corts, as he himself admitted in the circumstantial reports passed on to his Superior:

The work teams will be organized this week, and I myself shall go next Monday to the work-site to get the *peones* to work. God grant that my agents manage to get hold of the Indians; if they are successful, then I think you will soon be able to come on horseback.[25]

. . . We have almost completed 35 kilometres! There is a lot of mud on the part we are now working on. . . . A good road is better than any number of good sermons when it comes to civilizing these Indians.[26]

A year later the reports become less optimistic in tone:

Last Friday I had to stop the work for lack of labour. . . . If new people cannot be found for me soon, my presence here will become pointless. But if they can be found, then I promise, with God's help, that you will have this road.[27]

There is one piece of photographic evidence of this heroic period that is of great interest: in it we see, on the work-site, two whites and a group of Indians being directed by Fray de las Corts. Among the labourers is a quite elderly woman, carrying two huge stones for the road – which suggests that the Capuchins were not terribly strict in their own application of the principle of respect for and advancement of native women which figures so markedly in their declarations.

On the other hand, the problems of recruitment did not arise only from people's refusal to do forced labour, but from the fact that the Indians *did not want the road*. This may seem odd; if we are to believe Fray Estanislao de las Corts, it was because 'the horses which would use the road would help them enormously in transporting the merchandise the whites have brought to the area, thus taking away from them their sole means of earning the reales they needed to buy their salt'.[28] But the still fierce resistance among the Sibundoy and the Inga suggests that they were even more concerned over the danger it represented to their own culture and the preservation of their racial identity, by opening the way to the white man's civilization.

As a man of action, Fray Fidel could not brook such setbacks and delays. To get things moving faster, he opened a public fund in November 1908. It only brought him in 400 gold pesos, accompanied by a timid warning from the Ministry of Public Works: 'The government ... cannot allow the road from Mocoa to Pasto to be paid for by public alms collected for the purpose.' The Prefect Apostolic then determined to address himself directly to Bogotá, where he 'warned' the ministers of the Interior and of War 'against the abandoned state in which these areas are, and the imminent risk Colombia is running of losing the whole of the Putumayo district to the Peruvians and Brazilians'.

It was a compelling argument. To a hastily convened Council of Ministers, he made it clear 'that it was pointless to send the detachment of armed troops they were planning to safeguard their frontiers, for as long as the road was not usable, nothing positive could be achieved'. The next step was even easier. The government placed itself entirely at the Prefect's disposal, immediately voting him a further credit (40,000 gold pesos), and appointing him 'Inspector General of Public Works'. All this fitted in very well with his plans, even the fact that the direct administration of construction work was entrusted to the governor of Nariño, for the latter, our old friend Bucheli, immediately delegated his powers to Fray Estanislao de las Corts, with the right of recruiting workers at will, deciding what they should be paid, and — perhaps even more important — appointing supervisors and foremen 'to keep order, plan workers' mobility, etc.'. A month later, Fray Estanislao reopened operations.

Thus, by the end of his fourth year in office, the prelate of the Caquetá and Putumayo had fully put into effect his plan of action for conquering the territory:

The *final* objectives were the teaching of the Catholic religion, and the development of the economy.

The *immediate* objectives were establishing missionary estates, and concentrating the Indians into new villages, built according to the Spanish pattern in a criss-cross of straight lines.

The *means* were economic aid from the state, and unpaid forced labour from the natives.

And with Indian subversion gradually subsiding, as the police system worked out by Fray Fidel became consolidated, he himself was able to leave for a brief holiday in Europe, and deal with the other problems which concerned him.

During this time the Sibundoy population was decreasing almost visibly. However, the 'malicious legends', used by them to teach their children the values of their own race, continued to proliferate in the valley. Here, for instance, is the representation of the historic figure of Our Lord of Sibundoy:

A hunter had been living for a long time at a place known as 'The Cedar' near the San Pedro river. One morning, he put poison on his arrows, and having put them in his quiver, took his bow and set off hunting in the direction of Sibundoy. He had been walking for some minutes, when he saw a huge bird, rather like a condor, flying very fast. He watched to see where it would land, and it alighted on a myrtle. Since the undergrowth around the tree was very thick, the hunter had to bend low, and force a way through with his hands, thus approaching his prey rather as a wolf would. But when he stood up in front of the myrtle ... he remained motionless, paralysed by what he saw: at the foot of the tree, in a hole shaped like a niche, Our Lord of Sibundoy was sitting barefoot, his hair long, clothed in *cusma* and *capisayo*.

When the Indian Chapter were told of this, they came to the spot, and the Lord spoke, ordering them to build their church there, where it has been ever since.

The end of the century-old legend was modernized thus:

The sacristan, noticing that the Lord's clothes were wet through every morning, suspected him of going out at night, and decided to find out. Under the pretext of renewing the candles, he went to the church late at night . . .

The Lord had vanished. He told the governor, who, in agreement with the other leading men, ordered that the culprit be beaten with twelve strokes of the whip. After this punishment had been carried out, the Indians expected that the Lord would ask forgiveness and promise not to do it again; but instead he stood up, turned his back upon them, and went off on the road to Pasto. . . . They tried to catch him but he became invisible, and all they could do was go back to the village sadly, and repent of having beaten him. Their remorse became even more acute when they discovered that the reason why the Lord had gone out each night was to take their place working on the road from Pasto to Mocoa.[29]

This they discovered from the 'wax tears' they found lying alongside the road. And their grief was indeed great, for they wondered whether their own special patron had been working in support of the white men's plan.

CHAPTER 6

An Open Road
and White Barbarism

When we were informed of such abominations, we doubted that they could be true, so unbelievable did they seem.

(PIUS X, the encyclical *Lacrimabili Statu*, 1912)

The chief business which brought Fray Fidel back to the home of his forefathers was the matter of the ecclesiastical status of his Prefecture. In point of fact, when he was appointed, the vast mission of the Caquetá and Putumayo was part of the Ecuador and Colombia *custodia*, a dependency of the Capuchin province of Catalonia. Thus, with its civil, economic and police privileges, it was independent of the Colombian hierarchy, while still being very far from Rome.

But in January 1907 the superiors of the order decided to separate the Ecuador–Colombia *custodia* from the Mother House, thus placing Fidel de Montclar under the authority of a Colombian Provincial. The chroniclers of the order make no secret of the fact that this decision 'was not well received by the Father Prefect'. And though he appealed to the Vatican, the change-over took effect without any conflict, and the Prefecture continued to draw its missionaries from Pasto.[1]

Faced with this *fait accompli* – but far from resigned to it – Fidel de Montclar began a campaign of letter-writing to the highest Capuchin authorities to win back the Mission's former status; at last, realizing that he was achieving nothing, the great Crusader decided to go himself to Barcelona and to Rome, resolved 'to move heaven and earth to achieve his object'.[2] And so successful was he that in March 1910 a new decree came from the Congregation for the Propagation of the Faith which he found wholly satisfactory.*

After a few weeks' rest, Fidel de Montclar, with eight missionaries from his native province, returned in triumph to Colombia. But the addition of the new men brought no outstanding development to the activities of the Prefecture, for it was counter-balanced by the dismissal on their arrival of four out of the five Colombian Capuchins who had been seconded to the Father Prefect.†

Another event which had taken place during the prelate's absence was once again to put to the test his skill at out-facing his enemies: the fall, in March 1910, of his friend the dictator Rafael Reyes, whose government was followed by one concerned to adopt a critical attitude towards anything touching on national policy. This change resulted in immediate and serious consequences for the Catalan mission:

(1) The suspension of the credits allotted for building the road to the east, following on information received which cast doubt on the way the missionaries were handling the work; this resulted in an immediate slowing-down of the labours of Fray Estanislao.‡

---

*The chief argument adduced by Fidel de Montclar was the inability of the Creoles to carry out his large-scale plans. The Colombian Provincial, on the other hand, held that in view of the sparse population of the area, it was quite adequately served by the evangelizing tours of a few missionaries recruited on the spot. This was an ill-considered argument, since both the Colombian government and *Propaganda Fide* wanted 'the missionaries to work to civilize the infidel Indians', as directed in the Convention of the Missions.

The consequence of all this was somewhat paradoxical: the Creole Church, anxious to evangelize unbelievers, was put to rout by the Catalan priest whose immediate objective was the social and economic development of lands and tribes that were already acculturized.

†These four went back to the diocese of Pasto. Fidel de Montclar's team now included only four Latin Americans, of whom only one was a Colombian.

‡In his report for 1911 Fidel de Montclar explains the matter thus: 'Certain enemies of the Mission, unable to tolerate the idea that the Church should be providing such an example of patriotism and civi-

(2) The replacement of the governor of Nariño by an official less devoted to the interests of the Capuchins, which provided the Prefect Apostolic with an opportunity to condemn in no uncertain terms the 'enemies of the missionaries'.[3] However, the new governor nevertheless declared the valley a 'civilized zone', thus temporarily removing its so-called *savage* population from the administration of the Capuchins.

(3) The setting up of a special commission to inquire into the accusations brought against the *caucheros* of the Amazonian forest. This was a somewhat awkward measure, because, though the genocides and other atrocities denounced by it had been going on for years, the Capuchins, 'the guardians of the nation's frontiers', had never breathed a word about them.

But of this there is more to be said.

The rubber trade had begun in the south-east of Colombia at the end of the nineteenth century. At first the *caucheros* were the traders who cheated the Indians. The missioner Angel de Villava gives this description after his journey in 1893:

> Few people realize the unfortunate condition of the Indians. Truly slaves of the traders, they have not even the freedom to work their own lands; they are forced by their masters to keep moving on, and if they attempt to rest, they are forced to find the rubber to pay for some garment or knick-knack they have been given by the trader. The Indian does not know what he is earning, nor what he owns, nor what he owes – as is clear from this case: a trader had given an Indian several things, for which he demanded fourteen *arrobes* of rubber [about 175 kilograms]. At the end of a certain time, the Indian came to his creditor with the rubber which, having been weighed by the creditor on his own scale, registered sixteen *arrobes*; so the trader said to the Indian: 'You owed me fourteen *arrobes*; you have given me sixteen; you therefore owe me another eighteen.'[4]

After adding that the Brazilians made frequent incursions into Colombian territory to attack the Indians, Fray de Villava concludes: 'This slavery of the Indians has been the major and

---

lization, have directed their attacks against us. The government, wrongly informed, thus became suspicious of our work.'

almost insurmountable obstacle to our administering the sacraments to the Correguaje and Tama.'

Twelve years later, information provided by other missionaries suggests that the number of *caucheros* operating in Colombia in 1905 was something like 2,000 on the plains of the Caquetá, and just over 100 on the banks of the Putumayo. These adventurers, according to these missionary sources, would normally live in the forest, and behaved in a semi-savage way 'especially in regard to the depravity of their habits, with only a few fortunate exceptions'; they made use of 4,000 to 5,000 Indians. The native population of Colombian Amazonia then amounted to a total of about 200,000.[5] This was all the information the Capuchins had on the matter because, as they so often said, 'the natives' lack of freedom in such areas made it impossible to do anything with or for them'.

But with the fall of General Reyes, the situation grew dramatically worse. The Peruvian firm Arana, having become a vast enterprise, imposed its own law, with fire and bloodshed where need be, over thousands of square kilometres. Its appalling reputation reached the Anti-slavery Society of London, which created a worldwide scandal over the extermination of the aboriginals.[6]

Faced with the resulting outcry, the Colombian and Peruvian governments set up a combined commission to make an on-the-spot inquiry. The atrocities which came to light were incredible: collective massacres of thirty and forty people, including women and children; the murder of 170 white Colombians; young Indians buried head down in the holes dug by the traders for placing stakes; and innumerable instances of euthanasia, justified by one *cauchero* in these terms:

Pablo Zumaeta, manager of the Company in Iquitos, continually sends us orders to get the Indians to work as hard as possible and without stopping, because our purpose is to send enormous amounts of rubber to Europe. . . . That is why there can be no question of giving up [corporal] punishments; if an employee hurts or wounds one or more Indians, it is hardly his fault that they don't know how to look after themselves. That is why their wounds remain unhealed, become infected and cause such suffering. . . . Surely it is heartbreaking to see a human being suffer? . . . That is why, from sheer humanity, it is better to kill them, so that they will not suffer any more.[7]

To the great astonishment of the Capuchins, it was clear that the reality was far more horrible than anything recorded in the old chronicles of their confrère de Villava. The situation was even more embarrassing for their highly placed protectors: what justification could there be for the Capuchins having failed to recognize the atrocities committed by the most powerful white men in the area? Equally galling for the Mission was the fact that it had been left to a foreign and non-Catholic body to denounce these outrages.

All this explains the coolness with which the new government received Fray de Montclar on his return from Europe, and the intense activity required on his part to overcome the mistrust of the authorities, and, still more, to undo the unfortunate impression made all over the Catholic world by this neglect of one of the most vital elements of his mission. He did his best to clear himself by uttering a fierce denunciation of the crimes, in his Report for 1911. But this belated response did not prevent the scandal from reaching the ears of Pope Pius X, who hastened to add his word of condemnation in the encyclical *Lacrimabili Statu* (June 1912) — a document of some importance, not only because it was specifically addressed to the bishops of Latin America, but also because it constituted the first official statement by the Vatican in favour of the South American Indians since Benedict XIV's letters apostolic in 1741.

The Pope did not only condemn 'the slavery to the devil and to criminals' into which 'the original inhabitants of America' had fallen. In response to the anxieties of the governments of Great Britain and the United States, he set up an English Franciscan Mission to take charge of the inhospitable central regions of the Putumayo which the Catalan missionaries did not visit.

This action by the Pope left the Catalans unmoved, and for the next twenty years they took no more interest in that area or its people. One of the official chroniclers explains this 'by the fact that at that date the boundaries between Colombia and Peru had not yet been finally settled':[8] a not very convincing argument, if one recalls that the region in question, several hundred kilometres from the border zone, was in the very centre of the Apostolic Prefecture. (This latter fact is clear from the maps of the Prefecture which the Capuchins themselves published . . . on postcards!) It seems that we must opt for a different explanation: that of the Capuchins' perfectly human preference for the Sibundoy valley and the land near the Andes, far healthier places to live in, and more suited to their policy of economic development.

However, let us return to our central theme.

The indefatigable Fidel de Montclar returned to his labours. As the initial enthusiasm of the new government became tempered with time, the determined Catalan had begun to regain his lost ground before the year 1911 was out. He had already got annulled the decree removing the Sibundoy valley from his jurisdiction; then, when he was in Bogotá to try to get back the money he needed for the road he had dreamt of for so long, fate came to his assistance. A confrontation between Colombian and Peruvian military detachments in the Amazonian forests had just led to an outburst of patriotism in the city. The wily prelate had only to remind people that he himself, two years earlier, had warned the republic of the risks existing on that frontier, in order to find himself basking in a new wave of sympathy. He made such good use of this unhoped-for situation that not merely did he get the government to restore the credits that had been suspended, but actually got them increased fivefold.[9]

Fray Estanislao's road-works started up again with renewed vitality, and under the pen of the Capuchin chroniclers, the whole episode takes on a certain epic quality:

No one could resist the determination of these religious, so self-sacrificing were they, with their vocation to bear the light of the gospel into the darkest forests of the Caquetá and the Putumayo; they realized that to fulfil their mission, and free so many thousands of savages from slavery, there was nothing for it but to break a way through the Andes . . . and the Andes crumbled under the attacks of these heroes of civilization . . .[10]

And missionaries transformed themselves into pioneers, priests into engineers, as the peaks of the mountains were shattered to fragments, and whole lines of hills flattened before the advance of their road. And with the road, a whole new life penetrated into what had only yesterday been a land of mystery.[11]

From the report of an inspector of finance, impressed by the Capuchins' ability, we get more details about how the enterprise was carried out:

The construction works are organized in a simple and economical way: the father-director negotiates with a *caporal* or middle-man for the building of a certain length of road for a fixed sum; the contractor gets together the twenty or thirty *peones* he needs and pays them an agreed sum per day, setting up his *rancho* and ensuring food supplies from among the goods provided by the mission or whatever he can himself procure.[12]

With this system work advanced rapidly. However, we have to look at other Capuchin documents to discover the secret of this 'simple and economical way' by which the missionaries were able to get the job done for so small a price per kilometre: a large part of the food for the 1,600 workers came from the 130 hectares which were intensively cultivated by the Indian pupils of the Marists in Santiago and Sibundoy.

Taking advantage of this excellent situation, the missionary leader decided to get his plans moving faster than ever. A new village was founded at the foot of the Andes, at the point where the river Putumayo became navigable; it was called Puerto Asís. Thus, once the road reached the spot, there would be easy access to one part of Amazonia, and to that 'king of rivers' which was the most direct route to the civilized world. The plan was duly supported by the government, and its carrying out entrusted to Fray de las Corts; but in fact it was to meet with a number of obstacles.

The fathers describe how the inadequacy of local food production, and the lack of any spirit of collaboration on the part of the Indians in the area, forced them to import their supplies from North America and Europe, in particular, wine, oil, clothes and holy pictures.[13] But the impatient and brusque character of Fray Estanislao de las Corts also created certain additional difficulties. According to the Ecuadorian Fray Ildefonso de Tulcán, all went well for the first fortnight:

> The interest evinced by the Indians living round the port caused in us a mixture of admiration and astonishment. Even the *caucheros* were not slow to admit that they had never seen them so cheerful and willing. The Indians of San José worked for two whole weeeks on the road, men, women and children all joining in.[14]

However, to the energetic Fray de las Corts this did not seem rapid enough, and two months later, he complained to his superior: 'Accustomed as I was to having hundreds of *peones* at my disposal, and now having no more than eighteen, I am deeply distressed, in fact quite in despair.'[15]

But it was not in his nature to give way to despondency, and his tone soon changed: 'Finding myself without *peones*', he wrote, 'I forced the villages of Guamués, San Diego and Ocano to plant five hectares each; this work has been going on now for four days.'[16]

As usual, he provides no details on the methods with which he 'forced' the Indians to work, but it was not long before their results became apparent:

> As though the difficulties of nature were not enough, an appalling campaign has grown up among the *peones* the missionaries have employed for the road-works. We have had to promise them fantastic wages, pay their travelling expenses, and offer numerous other promises.[17]

These concessions granted against his will were to make it possible for Fray Estanislao to complete the founding of Puerto Asís, which was to be the most important single achievement of the Capuchins along the Putumayo.[18] The great day, 10 March 1912, came at last. The two crusaders, hardened horsemen that they were, spent three days leading the triumphal journey inaugurating the road from Pasto to Mocoa – to the 'frightened astonishment of the natives', as the general who went with them noted.[19] In consideration of their immense efficiency, the minister of public works decided on the continuation of the road to Puerto Asís.

Never had the Mission received so much cooperation from the State – but then a chance incident occurred which brought the whole operation once again into doubt: with the coming of the first rains, the completed part of the road became impassable. At that point the government decided to take over its upkeep, while leaving it to the missionaries to get the stretch from Mocoa to Puerto Asís finished. But Fidel de Montclar saw this as part of a campaign against the Church, and demanded the formation of a control commission 'so that the enemies of religion can at no point find there any excuse to calumniate the mission'.[20] That commission, consisting of three influential figures from Pasto, produced a report that was highly favourable to the missionaries' engineer, but suggested reservations about the proposed route.

Meanwhile the expert engineer sent by the government had just sent in his own, infinitely more critical, report. Then, as Fray Jacinto de Quito would say, 'there was a fine to-do'. The Great Crusader responded with his usual energy, and published a leaflet denying that the report of the qualified engineer was of any value at all, while also pointing out that 'he is an infidel and impious man, who profaned certain sacred vessels in Ecuador'.[21] His detractors took the opportunity to publish evidence showing how the pay of the workers had been reduced and the money given to the Mission. So there opened a fresh controversy, and for several years laymen and religious were to be engaged in battle.[22]

But the first results of the incident were most displeasing to de Montclar: the government, though a Catholic and conservative one, finally relieved him temporarily of his responsibility to get the road built.

This blow was only short-lived. A few years later a new

government came in, which restored to the missionaries both the duty of maintaining the road already built, and that of carrying it on as far as Puerto Asís, which the missionaries took to be a fair reparation.[23]

While, despite all these ups and downs, the Catalans felt satisfied that they had successfully completed one of the major projects, the Indians on the other hand were far from being similarly satisfied. One Capuchin historian reports:

It was at that time that a number of whites invaded the aforesaid Sibundoy valley; the fantastic ambition that possessed them led them to commit the most appalling atrocities against the natives; so much so that one of them, passionately greedy for land, began to pillage the Indians whose plantations bordered on the small area he had cultivated; in some cases he broke down the fences protecting their ground, and let his animals through to ruin their crops, thus condemning them to total poverty. In others, he would visit their homes, and with threats and even violence, would force them to give their land to him at derisory prices. If any of his victims attempted to stand up to him and refuse to be dispossessed, he would throw three or four pesos on the ground to force him to give up his property.

There was another white man who, to avoid later complications, bought twenty hectares of ground from an Indian for 150 gold pesos. A deed was drawn up before a notary, and the Indian received the agreed sum with all due legal formalities. But when he got home, suspecting nothing, the purchaser leapt out at him, took back his money by force, leaving him with only two pesos and . . . the new settler then went calmly off with both the land and the money.[24]

In short, then, all the fears of the Inga and Sibundoy had proved fully justified: the opening of the road brought with it a daily increase in the white invasion of their lands.

CHAPTER 7

Fray Fidel Makes His Own Laws and Steals a Valley

It was at our instigation that Laws 51 of 1911, 106 of 1913, and 69 of 1914 . . . were put forward and adopted.

(FRAY FIDEL DE MONTCLAR, 1916)

Did the Indians have any exclusive right to live on those lands? What is quite clear is that they were unable to prove the existence of any such right.

(FRAY PACIFICO DE VILANOVA, 1945)

The opening of the Putumayo road, however, was only the first in the triptych of successes achieved by Fidel de Montclar in 1911. Aware that he must make the most of this moment of opportunity, he set on foot his two other major projects: to secure for himself more help from the government, and to extend and consolidate the mission lands.

He began by publishing the profit and loss account of his Prefecture for that year to show how poor its position was. But this document brings in certain new elements. Here are its main points:

Receipts

Received by the terms of the Convention of the Missions	3,000	gold pesos
Annual aid to the Caquetá mission	2,880	,,
Salary of the two fathers teaching in the school	720	,,
Salary of the Prefect Apostolic as Inspector General of Public Education	360	,,
Total	6,960	gold pesos

Expenses

Food for the missionaries and their employees	3,500	gold pesos
Travelling expenses for nine religious, two carpenters and a blacksmith recruited in Europe	2,400	,,
Salary for carpenters	1,600	,,
Help to schools	1,230	,,
Purchase of holy pictures, altar wine and books	620	,,
Missionaries' travelling expenses	340	,,
Missionaries' clothing	320	,,
Bonuses and clothes for the Indians	220	,,
Expenses for travelling to Bogotá on mission business for the Prefect and his secretary	200	,,
Maintenance for the police	160	,,
Total	10,590	gold pesos

The deficia, 3,630 gold pesos was covered by alms and mass offerings from outside the mission.[1]

This straightforward account, and the final codicil, leads us to form the following conclusions:

(1) All the credits listed come from State payments.

(2) The receipts published do not include the board and lodging or payment of teachers other than Capuchins – mainly Marist brothers and Franciscans; if one adds these resources to the published figures, then the amounts available to the Mission seem to be several times larger than those allotted to the extremely poor regional government.

(3) The statement of a 'deficit covered by alms and mass offerings' makes it clear that the whole of their mission work was seen by these new crusaders as a State service rather than a work of the Apostolate.

(4) Immigrants from Europe were receiving privileged treatment in the Prefecture's budget: 22.6 per cent of expenses went to cover the travelling expenses of twelve missionaries and workers from Catalonia, and 15 per cent to the wages of Spanish carpenters imported by the mission for its own use. In other words, having consolidated his theocratic régime, Fidel

de Montclar was beginning to give the most important positions in his territory to Spaniards.

Some of these points were made by various deputies speaking against the plan of granting the Mission Council the extraordinary credit of 20,000 gold pesos. But the Church in Colombia was too strong for them, and with the active support of Fray de Montclar,[2] the law was passed. Better still, it laid the ground for the law of 1912 which increased the allotted sum to 100,000 gold pesos – a figure that was to remain constant for a great many years.[3]

The wave of optimism which swept the Capuchin mission of the Putumayo was thus fully justified; the Great Crusader was also winning on this second front.

His third success related to the colonizing of the Putumayo. In this plan too there were two other interests involved: the government, anxious to reaffirm national sovereignty in the south-east, and the governing class of the neighbouring province of Nariño, who continually proclaimed the need to 'uncork Sibundoy' so as to have a means of access to the Lower Putumayo, the new businessman's El Dorado. This was a convincing argument for, as long as the high Andean plateau suffered from over-production and a lack of outlets for selling what was produced, the rubber companies of Amazonia – whose exports were approaching the fabulous sum of 40 million dollars – would continue to suffer from a permanent lack of consumer goods.[4]

Consequently, once the road to the east was begun there remained only one obstacle to the coalition of these three forces: the animosity of the Inga and Sibundoy, which was so intense that they refused to have inns or staging posts for whites on their land. It thus became necessary at all costs to get more white people into the area, so as to unleash a 'rush to the East'. Yet we are left with one question-mark: how could Fray Fidel reconcile the work of evangelization to which he was dedicated with the arrival of settlers which must inevitably accentuate the disbanding and persecution of the tribes in his care?

The answer can only be found in the missionaries' view of the 'inferior nature' of their aboriginal flock, a deeply-rooted view which we find expressed in a number of documents, among them the official organ of the Mission, which declares that the 'Indian is thieving and lazy by nature and by education'.[5] Such an estimate, given their belief in equality and other human rights, may perhaps perturb other Christians, but was open to no doubt as far as the *doctrineros* were concerned.* The Great Crusader himself was so convinced of the superiority of the white race from every point of view, that he declared bluntly in his Report for 1916:

> To become civilized the Indians need contact with white men; by being with them they receive practical lessons in their ways and customs which, however bad they may be, are the customs of civilized men, and consequently, less repugnant. [He is hence forced to conclude]. . . . It is clear that the whites often scandalize them by the spectacle of their misbehaviour, and cause them to suffer by their ill-treatment; but such disadvantages are considerably reduced if the whites can be settled at some distance from the Indians' villages.[6]

After having thus reconciled the white invasion with the interests of the Indians, there only remained for de Montclar one major problem to solve: the Inga's and Sibundoy's right of ownership of their ancestral lands. It looked like an insur-

---

*These were conclusions reached by the Putumayo missionaries after being there for seventy years. From the opposite end of Colombia we have evidence of another Capuchin, after years of evangelizing the Arhuaco Indians of the Sierra Nevada of Santa Marta, Fray José de Vilanesa. Here is how this 'specialist scholar' speaks in the official review of the National Ethnological Institute of Colombia in 1952: 'The Arhuaco Indian has the same defects common to almost all Indians: they are generally selfish, mistrustful, lacking in aspiration, inclined to idleness, and with a tendency to drink. . . . Further, like all Andean Indians, they have no love of cleanliness.' One may perhaps form one's own judgement as to the anthropological insight of this priest from noting comments like this: 'The continual effort they make to breathe [because of the altitude] makes the upper part of their noses sunken in and their eyes and foreheads remain small because for the same reason they cannot develop normally' (*sic*).

mountable obstacle: on the one hand, because it was a right that had been recognized on various occasions by both the Spanish and the Republican governments; and on the other, because in the eyes of the Colombian government it was an inalienable right. All the Prefect Apostolic could do was simply deny the facts, and turn justice upside down by making new laws, annihilating the *resguardo*, and getting this once 'heavily-populated valley' declared a *baldío** – in other words, unused land. This was a fantastic piece of sleight of hand which, by what looked like chance, would enable the Capuchin mission to round off the *Cofradías* of the Virgin and establish such rights of ownership as made it possible to turn them into genuine *haciendas*.

The enterprising prelate did not hesitate: he explained his intentions to the authorities in Pasto, who received them enthusiastically, and agreed to help to get the stratagem through the National Congress[7] where the law must be ratified, using such considerations as this:

> The valley will soon be a place of great importance to the nation, and though up to now it has remained outside the movement of world trade, the time has come to bring it into contact with civilization and incorporate it into its life.[8]

Thus, after only a brief debate, Law 51 of 1911 was passed. It sanctioned the founding of a white village in the Sibundoy valley, and the re-allocation of the whole district among the Capuchin mission, the settlers, the province of Nariño – and the Indians, whose 'ultimate rights' were to be defended by a lawyer paid by the province of Nariño. This small concession was due to the fact that during the debate, one deputy, a stranger to Pasto, dared to point out the existence of the Carlos Tamoabioy tradition.[9]

It was a tiny concession indeed if one bears in mind that the same law was proposing:

*In Colombia the term *baldíos* is used of vacant lands which the State reserves the right to grant legally to the first settler who can prove that he has made good use of them, at a time, or in conditions, specified by the law.

For the Church, as represented by the Capuchin mission in each of the villages of San Andrés, Santiago and Sibundoy: 100 hectares for the provisional parish, 100 for the Committee for Good Works, 50 for the model farm of the Marist brothers, 100 for establishments of education, and 1,000 for a future seminary;

For the settlers: up to 59 hectares apiece;

For the Indians: 300 hectares to a village, which meant that each individual could have . . . two.

Whatever remained after all this was to go to the province of Nariño.

It is evident that on that 15 November the legislative body as a whole was guilty of appalling partiality towards the whites. Every right, every law, every Indian custom which had always been respected up to then was suddenly rendered non-existent. Though the legislators sanctioned the setting up of a 'possession judgement' to pronounce on the 'ultimate' rights of the Indians to the land in the valley, the payment of their defence lawyer was entrusted to the province of Nariño, one of the interested parties in the matter. The allowance of two hectares to each Indian made it quite clear that in the eyes of the law they were inferior to the settlers. The Inga and Sibundoy found themselves suddenly made part of 'civilization' – but as inferior beings, owning only tiny patches of land, and with all possibility of economic advancement withdrawn from them. Furthermore, the fact that the Capuchin mission and the province of Nariño were to be allowed thousands of hectares, whereas each native village was to have no more than 300, established yet one more unjust and wildly disproportionate discrimination. Even the apparently benevolent measure of allowing tiny pieces of land to the Indians – pieces soon to be given the significant title of 'missionary *resguardos*' – was a two-edged weapon. On those tiny patches, the Indians would be 'concentrated', in order, said the Capuchins, to 'prevent their being dispersed', and thus to become civilized; what was forgotten or not mentioned was the fact that this concentration of natives placed a painfully cheap labour force at the disposal of the whites – a labour force which became not merely cheap but free for the missionaries because of the old 'Regulation'. In other words, this law, passed well into the twentieth century, perfected the former system of colonial serf-dom, but this time under the aegis not of the government, but of Capuchin friars.

Reactions of various kinds were not slow to appear. The settlers already established in the valley were infuriated by the prospect of other invaders coming, and were unexpectedly reprimanded by Fray Fidel: 'If the Sibundoy were the rightful owners of this valley, why should this half-dozen protesting settlers have set about cultivating land that was not lying unused?'[10]

Then too, there were Indians who were well aware of the trap being laid for them in the 'possession judgement', and who decided to appeal to the highest authorities, including the president of the republic, with messages such as this:

> The village of Santiago was founded five hundred years ago with boundaries fixed as follows [description inserted]. . . . We are the owners of five leagues bought by our ancestors Carlos Tamoabioy and Leandro Agreda from the king of Spain for 400 *patacones* (ounces of silver), as stated in the deed of ownership which was given to them.[11]

No answer was ever given to this appeal which was, in fact, the last written statement by the Indians that they possessed the title-deeds to the land in question. For, as Fray Bartolomé de Igualada, administrator of the Mission Funds, was to say, 'because of the interests involved, the title has disap-peared'.*

All of 1912 and part of 1913 passed in an atmosphere of excited anticipation. The Great Crusader, despairing over the inactivity of the government, once again began litigation,

*Declaration made in 1962 to Father Lino Rampón. We may also recall that the historian S. E. Ortiz reported that he was able to consult the copy of the document belonging to the Indians of Santiago in 1935 or thereabouts, which was then 'in the hands of the Capuchin com-munity in Pasto'.

always through other agents. The new laws he managed to get passed – Laws 52 and 106 of 1913 – confirmed the dividing-up of the valley, while granting him still further benefits:

(1) Presidency of an Immigration Council, allotted a large budget, and provided with all needful powers;

(2) Presidency of a Vacant Lands Council, whose job it was to effect the division of the valley;

(3) A limited period of eight months, in which the 'arbitration tribunal' could receive complaints both from individual Indians and from groups receiving grants.

Obviously these measures could only reinforce the discretionary powers of the man who inspired them, while the elimination of the 'possession judgement' of the valley lands – now irrelevant owing to the curious disappearance of the deeds of the *resguardo* – removed any possibility of the Inga and Sibundoy getting their rights recognized. On the other hand, the perfectly 'legal' robbery to which they had just been subjected marked the final failure of the law-abiding policy they had inherited from their ancestors. They had learnt to their cost that the law is always made by the strong, and often goes against the interests of the weak.

To leave no room for doubt about the Prefect Apostolic's behaviour, it may be noted that on this occasion in particular, he made no secret of his responsibility, so certain was he of the excellence of his intentions. However, in his report to the government in 1916 he does give a rather deceptive account of his legislative activity: 'It was at our instigation that laws 51 of 1911, 106 of 1913, and 69 of 1914, giving the department of Nariño *the unused lands, belonging to the Nation*, were introduced and passed . . .'[12] [italics mine].

In effect, this half-truth was intended to make sure that his friends in Nariño fully appreciated what he had done for them. For it must be made quite clear that the Capuchins were well aware of the facts of history and of the rights they were violating in order to achieve their objectives. There are several indications in this chapter which prove this, chief among them the Great Crusader's apostrophizing of the settlers who had grabbed land which he knew belonged to the Indians. And one is left speechless by the arguments put forward by the Catalan historian of the Mission to justify the side-stepping of the law by his Superior:

Law 51 of 1911 could not have been made with a greater concern for safeguarding justice and harming no one. True, it broke a historic tradition by introducing a white population into the centre of Indian villages. But one has to ask the question: did the Indians have any exclusive right to live there? What is quite clear is that they were unable to prove the existence of any such right.[13]

Before concluding this sad episode, there is one further characteristic of Fidel de Montclar's colonizing plans worth mentioning. In his Report for 1913, he wrote: 'I have asked Don Julian Bucheli to put before Congress the outline of a law intended to assist the immigration of *Spanish families* into this area.' The italics are mine, but it was the missionary leader who was so convinced that these would be the best settlers to take over the richest of the Indian lands. And should there remain the smallest doubt as to the brilliant future he dreamt of for Amazonia, he made the attacks against him the occasion for publicly admitting his total agreement with an article entitled, 'Missionaries are the Same, Always and Everywhere', an article by a Colombian writer of the period:

We ourselves have had the chance to read about and study the redemptive, effective work, unsurpassed in its heroism, done by Belgian missionaries in the Congo: [that Congo] once totally savage is today covered with a network of railways linking such important towns as Léopoldville, Elisabethville, Albertville and many others, where there are thousands of Belgians working in huge industrial operations – men who, following the wise advice of the great Léopold II, have had no hesitation in investing millions of francs in the area which are now yielding an enormous return. . . . And what was so recently a colony is now an integral part of the kingdom of Belgium, as well as a vast and remunerative field of action for Belgian labour and capital. . . . To whom is all this progress due if not to the valiant missionaries?[14]

In other words — as Fray Fidel de Montclar must have been fully aware — missionary establishments 'all over the world' constituted the advance posts of European economic colonization. But it must be allowed that in his mind the colonialist ideal was not unmixed with other sentiments.

It is a point of honour and a cause of legitimate pride for the civilized nations bordering on areas still under the yoke of barbarism to see those borders pushed back further all the time, as people become won over to the ways of civilized society; but this does not make it right to use means which the most basic humanitarian feelings reject, such as the criminal killing-off of those unfortunates.

This humanitarian consideration also had the advantage of preventing the disappearance of a valuable labour-force, which the Spanish settlers were proposing to use in creating another Congo.

CHAPTER 8

The Great Crusader
Sends a General Packing

The aforesaid Mission has carved out for itself a landed estate of over two thousand hectares in the valley of Sibundoy, according to the official study.

(GENERAL JOAQUIN ESCANDON, special commissioner, Resolution No. 7, 15 November 1913)

Special article: it is forbidden, under pain of mortal sin, to read the paper signed by Joaquín Escandón, and addressed to the Reverend Father Prefect Apostolic . . .

(MGR LEONIDAS MEDINA, Bishop of Pasto; Episcopal decree No. 16, 3 February 1914)

From 1912 to 1914, the hectic activity of Fray Fidel de Montclar was not restricted to the legislative sphere. He devoted himself eagerly to the material development of his Mission, taking a leading part in the war of abuses and open letters whereby his political adversaries began to make clear their views.

The disputes between settlers and priests indirectly originated in the protests of the Inga and Sibundoy against the invasion of their land, protests which had been growing continually since 1910 until by 1912 they had become such a storm that the government sent a senior official to make an inquiry on the spot. The result was a contradictory report, recognizing for the most part the justice of the Indians' complaints, but at the same time completely exculpating the Mission, and giving lengthy praise to its civilizing work.

Things would have remained where they were, but for the fact that relations between missionaries and settlers had also deteriorated, since the mission's territorial expansion was proving an obstacle to the settlers' ambitions in the same direction. For their own purposes, therefore, the settlers quite unexpectedly became the natives' champions, recalling their right to vote freely and the defence of their individual dignity. The liberal press took up the matter, and a war of mutual abuse began.

Let us, however, look closely at just what put the spark to the gunpowder: on Christmas Day 1910 the people of Santiago were to choose as their new governor one of two candidates presented to them by the Father Prefect. According to the Pasto press, the 'election' seems to have turned into a riot, with a number of people badly hurt. Fidel de Montclar's response was to issue a tract explaining how, when everything was ready for the voting to begin, two white men had come 'to protest against the arrangements made by the Prefect Apostolic, in his capacity as Police Superintendent of the native villages which he was working to civilize, for the election of an Indian governor . . .' He added:

But my two opponents were not in a state of mind that made it possible for them to understand so lofty an ideal, and so decided to remain silent. Obviously this was an agreed signal, for an Indian named Francisco Quinchoa immediately appeared on the scene and began shouting. Having repeatedly ordered him to be quiet, without success, I ordered him to be taken to prison. At once a group of natives began punching the three policemen who were trying to remove the objector. In the tumult that ensued, I asked several white men present to help the police in taking the rioters to prison. When this had been done as I ordered calm was restored, and the election of the governor took place peacefully. Juan Tisoy, a most intelligent native who reads and writes very well, was elected by the majority of the voters.[1]

There is little need to tell the reader that the new governor, thus elected after the opponents had been put in prison, was a great friend of the Capuchins, as he was to prove three years later, in getting a petition signed against one of his successors in the office who opposed the payment of tithes and first-fruits as demanded by the Mission. But not long after this a second scandal took place. The authorities in Pasto had just started a lawsuit against Francisco, a member of the influential Tisoy family, who was accused of having beaten one of his sons brutally with a whip. The missionaries' opponents started a rumour that it was they who were in fact responsible for the beating, and the prelate stood up publicly to defend the accused, declaring that he was being persecuted simply 'because he was a friend of the Capuchins'. Written statements then flew back and forth, making it clear that the Prefect Apostolic and the Judge dealing with the case were openly at war.[2]

All of this made the government determine in 1913, after the border fighting between Colombia and Peru, to separate the territory of the Caquetá from that of the Putumayo, and establish the latter as a special commissionership. One of the most respected men in the country, the pious Catholic and conservative General Joaquín Escandón, was put in charge of it.

Fully convinced that the circumstances well justified this innovation, the Special Commissioner was no sooner established than he decided to reorganize the administration of his territory, returning it to the direct authority of the State. Although he was anxious not to hurt anybody's feelings, his doing this could not fail to put the civil authority in a position of opposition to the theocratic government operating at the time.

The first brushes arose out of some carefully formulated observations in General Escandón's first report on his activities. The first was the way in which the Indian Chapters, presided over by the missionaries, were punishing certain crimes which should have gone before the civil courts. Another suggested that the administration of the larger villages in the area 'should perhaps remain under the jurisdiction of the Commissioner'. Though the questions concerned were settled fairly soon, it was by no means so simple to resolve the dispute between the

Catalan missionaries on the one hand, and Francisco Tisoy and his son Diego on the other. The whole affair gravitated around the *Cofradia* of Carmen in Santiago. The missionaries, wanting to 'round off' this estate of the Divine Shepherdess, decided to cancel the 'loans' granted seven years earlier to a number of Indian families when they made that sudden immense enlargement of the Mission's estates. But the Tisoy and Buesaquillo families stood out firmly against this, and were absolutely determined to defend the heritage of their ancestors. The lawsuit that ensued resulted in General Escandón's delivering a judgement in favour of the Indians, and further declaring that 'the aforesaid Mission has carved out for itself a landed estate of over two thousand hectares in the valley of Sibundoy, according to the official study already referred to, and that in spite of the fact that law No. 51 of 1911 has not even been put into effect'.[3]

In his wish to preserve good relations with the government, Fray Fidel would probably not have taken up this reference to the property which the missionaries had carved out for themselves out of the former Indian *resguardo* well before the laws they got through had actually come into effect, had not an unexpected event occurred to complicate the situation still further. For the Tisoys, not satisfied with their recent triumph, published the text of the Commissioner's statement as a leaflet with the somewhat provocative title 'And Now?':

The law should not be a spider's web which the powerful can destroy with impunity, as long as the authorities, knowing the law, and knowing therefore what is right, have the courage to reject the claims of those in high places.

By their solidarity, twelve Galileans won the hearts and minds of men. No one will take from us that which is our rightful heritage, nor restrain our freedom by forcing us to work like serfs in a feudal system of old, under pretence of converting our souls for a paradise to be gained only on condition of passing through hells of ignorance, poverty, and merciless slavery.[4]

The indignation of the Father Prefect was such that his violent counter-attack was directed as much against the General as the Tisoys. Two tracts and an inflammatory article – with a very telling title – followed in rapid succession: *The Eighth [Commandment]*, *Woe to that man through whom scandal cometh*, and *To love is not to argue over details, but to act.*[5]

Francisco and Diego Tisoy, he declared,

led on by their unlimited greed, have tried to seize not only the goods of the Church, but those of other natives too. We missionaries, who have in the past done so much for Francisco and his son, find ourselves today forced to call them to order, and correct their evil ways; we must state that they are rebels and enemies of the very missionaries who have done so much to protect them.[6]

After uttering this public condemnation, Fidel de Montclar sent a telegram to the national government demanding that they put into effect the clause in the Convention of the Missions whereby 'a well-founded objection from the head of the Mission constitutes sufficient grounds for the dismissal of a government employee . . .'

A few days later, he got a telegram back:

Prefect Apostolic. San Francisco. Situation will be remedied rapidly. Will change commissioner. Reference your telegram. Under-Secretary of State.[7]

But the final episode in the war between the Great Crusader and the General-Commissioner was to arise out of the matter of an illicit still! For in fact two weeks later tax inspectors discovered barrels of home-made spirit belonging to the Capuchins, about which Fray Fidel had this to say:

On 10 January 1914 Fray Lorenzo de Pupiales received Luis F. Medina, the head of the gang, with great honour and solemnity. But the gentleman had just seized a quantity of spirit which he had been informed had been smuggled into the mission. 'Here we know nothing of such things,' said the friar; 'they only concern common people. The spirit we have comes to us from a Swiss Marist, Brother Manuel, and is used as fuel for the lamp we use to project slides every Sunday to help us explain doctrine to the Indians.'[8]

Other versions of the incident, from secular sources, add

only a few additional details, particularly in regard to the man described by the Prefect Apostolic as the 'head of the gang'. The affair was recounted to the National Congress as follows:

It is possible that the reverend fathers are no longer dealing in contraband; ... on 19 January of this year, in the Sibundoy monastery at nine a.m., and at five p.m. in the Santiago monastery, bottles, demijohns, and eleven casks of excellent aniseed liqueur were seized. This seizure was the work of Señor Luis Felipe Medina, Tax-collector, accompanied by Señor Graciliano García, the authority's representative, and of Señores Julio M. Moncayo and Julio Moreno. On the 12 of the same month, the tax collector for Mocoa, Lauro F. Arturo, confiscated one more barrel from them. All of this was definitely contraband.[9]

In short, the proof against the missionaries was overwhelming, but, whatever the purposes – pious or commercial – for which the 'excellent aniseed liqueur' was intended by the reverend fathers, the Great Crusader was determined to have his revenge: he obtained the instant dismissal of General Escandón from the government, and he persuaded his ecclesiastical superiors to excommunicate the General for sacrilege.[10]

The day after this spectacular victory the Prefect Apostolic, in order to clarify the point of the 'reputed' wealth of the Mission, published a list of the ninety-five permanent workers employed on its four farms and thirteen other establishments.*

*According to that list, the three missionaries in the valley had the following staff:

Forty-one *peones* employed in the pasturelands, five day-labourers in the fields, three day-labourers chopping the wood needed for the buildings, four sawyers, nineteen carpenters, four cowmen, four joiners, four men to carry salt, three weavers, four ox-drivers.

The whole of the Mission included the following buildings some still in process of construction:

In Santiago: the house of the Marist brothers, a convent of Franciscan sisters, the church and Mission House and the Mission carpentry shop.

This list[11] unfortunately does not provide us with any kind of statistics on the unpaid labour force of Inga and Sibundoy, or on the actual area occupied by the Mission's *haciendas* and farms. We only know from the Treasury official Rufino Gutiérrez that his great friends the Capuchins had, they said, something approaching three hundred head of cattle. The writings of Rufino Gutiérrez also give some idea of the scale of the agricultural undertakings carried out by the Mission: 'They have the most varied and extended crops I have seen in Colombia, making it possible for the children who have worked there, and for the Brothers and Sisters, to be supplied with books, furniture, etc.' As we have seen earlier, these crops also, and indeed primarily, provided food for the missionaries and their workers.

Limited though they are, these data bear witness to the economic strides made by the Mission. Compared with this obvious advance, the people of the valley themselves had virtually nothing to show. And though there were a few exceptions, the reason for this was that the most important of the Inga families were still trying to defend their right to the land.

But the struggle had taken on a new aspect: it was no longer a matter of the economic terrorism which the Indians had tried at first to use against the ambitions of Fray Fidel; the Inga, from now on, returning to a far older tradition, had once again begun trying the kind of legal action against the missionaries recommended two centuries earlier by their ancestor Carlos Tamoabioy, but with new, more subtle and more flexible tactics.

One example of their flexibility is most striking: the immensely diplomatic attitude adopted by Francisco Tisoy, his son Diego, and other Inga leaders when the General-Com-

---

In Sibundoy: a new church; a convent of Franciscan sisters, the Mission House and the house and school of the Marists.

In San Andrés: the Mission House with space for a school and a church.

In San Francisco: church; mission house; carpentry shop.

missioner was sent away, and Fray Fidel finally recognized as the undisputed authority over the district. The Inga in fact rushed to seize the first chance to make their peace with him. This arose when certain 'calumnies' were spread about the Capuchins about the payment of tithes. They wrote to Fray Fidel:

You must know that we are not complaining of the fact that the missionaries demand that we pay tithes and first-fruits; for we are well aware that such a payment constitutes an obligation for all good Christians, and such was indeed the teaching of our ancestors.

But they continue with a carefully worded protest over the theft of their land:

It is true that we are grieved to learn that there are those who wish to take our land from us; and it is for this reason that the village has asked the governor Miguel Jansasoy to appeal to the higher authorities to prevent our being dislodged from our peaceful ownership. For if the whites finally divide the valley among themselves, where are we and our children to work? What will happen to so many boys and girls who can now be seen in the village, when they reach adulthood?

And the latter ends with what seems to be a request for help:

We have also learnt that the government has named your Reverence a member of the council that is to study the territory of the Sibundoy valley.
Therefore, in the name of our people, we beg your invaluable influence in preventing them from taking our land from us, in letting the whites take possession of what we have built up in the sweat of our brows.[12]

Charmed by this tone the Great Crusader at once made this letter public, without noting the final paragraphs which, in the light of the known facts, placed him in a rather different position. For in them the natives were making the Prefect Apostolic face his responsibilities, the first of which was to admit his own guilt in regard to the sufferings they had undergone, as the author and executor of what amounted to simple theft.

But the letter did restore the Tisoys to the favour of the Prefect Apostolic, thus ensuring the future fortunes of the subtle Diego.

Fidel de Montclar could certainly be satisfied with his achievements at that point, the beginning of 1914. He had removed the threat posed by General Escandón, and been granted a formidable concentration of powers: spiritual leader and police chief of the Caquetá and Putumayo, he was also in charge of public teaching, road building, the reclaiming of unused land, and of immigration; and for all this he got help from the governor amounting to several times what had been granted the Special Commissioner. The Prefect Apostolic could now really get his programme of selective colonization under way.

When it came to the point, however, the agreement of the Nariño officials could suddenly no longer be taken for granted. The reason for this was simple: during the past year the Mission leader had brought a new contingent of immigrants from Spain — ten farm labourers, two joiners, two weavers, and two shepherds.[13] And the Creoles were beginning to fear a wholly Spanish colonization. Thus, when the newcomers began to set themselves up in saw-works, carpenters' shops, factories for producing building materials and Mission *haciendas*, the local settlers or would-be settlers described the situation to the rest of the world as a modern version of the Spanish conquest of the past.[14] Fidel de Montclar tried to neutralize their campaign with such statements as this:

The undersigned has worked unremittingly to get the rights of the Indians respected, and after that to get all land lying unused in the Sibundoy valley distributed among the poor families from Pasto . . .

But this wary attitude was undermined by a most intemperate statement from his good friend the Bishop of Pasto:

In my view, to get the best results, this immigration must come primarily from Spain; for apart from being similar in race, language and religion, the Spanish are also a people of energy and initiative, as is clear from all our experience, as well as from the splendid qualities of the aforesaid Barcelonans who run this mission . . .

The second most desirable immigrants are Germans . . .[15]

It is not possible to estimate just how much influence this stance on his part had on the later development of the situation. But we do know the first result with absolute certainty: the Immigration Council, which had normally up to then left full power in the hands of the Prefect Apostolic, rejected the plan for Spanish immigration which he had put before them. This snub was the prelude to further vexations to come.

CHAPTER 9

Indian Culture
and Christian
Acculturization

The power to punish has had a very beneficial effect on the Indians.

(FRAY FIDEL DE MONTCLAR, 1915)

The reader must have wondered how the Inga and Sibundoy, whose economic advancement he has been following, and whose exceptional degree of culture is evident, can be those same 'barbarians whose moral and intellectual faculties are totally atrophied' described by the Great Crusader, or the practitioners of those 'iniquitous and bestial customs' which so enraged the indefatigable de las Corts.[1] Can it be that the Indians had degenerated because of the misfortunes which beset their tribes, or are we faced simply with the Capuchins' own peculiar interpretation of the situation?

Some light may be thrown on the point if we consider the faults for which the Capuchins never ceased lecturing their flock.

Chief among these 'faults' were all the practices and beliefs which are so helpful in informing us about the ancient culture of the valley, of which they were by then the only survival. Their funeral customs, which became linked with the Christian burial rites, are a good example: a meal was prepared as a farewell to the dying man, with the final good-bye occurring at the moment when he himself took off his *chaquiras* (necklaces); the custom of dropping small sticks into all the rivers and streams passed by the funeral cortège, to provide symbolic bridges for the deceased to use in crossing them in his journey after death; placing a burning candle in the tomb, to light up the darkness of the after-world; and finally the offering to the dead person of a gourd of *chicha** and the building of a thatched roof over the tomb, to prevent its occupant suffering from thirst or the rigours of the climate on his long journey.[2]

As well as the rite of the 'Stone of the Sun' described earlier, there was also that of the 'Stone of Marriage', which has been recorded for us by Fray Jacinto de Quito: the tradition was that any bachelors who passed by that stone, standing half way between the villages of Santiago and Sibundoy, should throw two sticks of wood at it, and if they fell in the form of a cross, it meant that the time had come for the young man to marry, while the way the cross pointed indicated the direction in which he would find his future bride. The same missionary adds that this superstitious practice was not taken wholly seriously, and that it was common for a young man to repeat the operation until the bits of wood fell so as to point to the house in which the girl he wished to marry lived. This, however, did not stop the Capuchins from ordering that the stone be buried – but it was in vain, for after a very short time the stone was back on the surface, once again covered with sticks![3]

Another belief which angered the reverend fathers was that children who died could only get to heaven if they had not yet reached the age of reason, and adults only if they had made what was known as the pilgrimage to Our Lord of Sibundoy.

Quite a number of details relating to worship faced the fathers with problems of this kind: for instance, the Indians' preference for their old holy pictures and statues, even when badly disfigured by time; the fact that they disliked the idea that Sunday mass attendance was obligatory; or, again, their obstinate refusal to accept a diversification of religious feasts which, according to their tradition, should all be celebrated at once, sometimes at Santiago, sometimes at Sibundoy.

It is not hard to perceive that such beliefs and practices were simply the result of a syncretism which had grown up over the

*A nourishing drink made from fermented maize, and used by Indians and peasants throughout the Andes.

centuries, with the traditions of the ancient religion disguised under a layer of Catholic ritual – a situation which had partly come about because of the total pastoral abandonment of the valley throughout the nineteenth century. But the Indians did not see themselves as 'infidels'; still less could they be said to have rejected the Catholic religion, since as a group they had accepted it for several centuries. The term 'idolatry' employed on numerous occasions by the Catalan Capuchins to describe such traditional customs as those of the Stones of the Sun and of Marriage was also quite inaccurate, for in them the Indians saw something far more like a game than a religious ritual. As for their devotion to their old statues, it seems very little different from the same kind of attachment one finds in Europe; and the belief in some form of predestination similarly seems to have a lot in common with tendencies to be found in some of the most old-established Christian communities.

It seems that we must conclude that the opposition with which the missionaries met in their will to implant more rigorous Catholic orthodoxy in the valley was merely an indication of the Indians' efforts to preserve their own original understanding of the world. There is surely nothing either shocking or surprising about that; in fact, it is upon such an understanding – which must inevitably be different as between Indian and white man – that the cohesion, liberty and security of any society depends. It was for that reason that the Inga and Sibundoy defended their 'pernicious errors' with a pigheadedness which convinced the missionaries 'that all this was so deeply implanted in them . . . that they would not make any great effort to commit to memory the things we explained to them . . .'

The only missionary to have an insight into the true nature of the Christianity of the Inga and Sibundoy, and how little danger was really presented by their 'errors, idolatries, etc.', was Fray Jacinto de Quito. He pointed out that if they wanted to celebrate all the religious feasts in one, and in a semi-secular manner, this was simply a survival from the days when 'a priest would visit them once a year to celebrate the feasts all

together'; and that they interpreted the tradition of the Last
Supper on Maundy Thursday 'somewhat in the fashion of the
agapes celebrated by the first Christians'.[4]

But the missionaries as a whole were not prepared to tolerate the slightest deviation in forms or teachings, and still less
the right to survive of any culture other than their own western
one. Furthermore, with blind fanaticism, they denied the possibility of man's living any kind of ordered life outside Christianity. When the Great Crusader came into contact with a
hitherto unknown tribe, he could actually say:

> When I see these Indians, when I consider their gentleness of
> character, the peacefulness of their customs, the order existing in
> their families, it seems to me quite clear that this is due to Chris-
> tianity. . . . I cannot believe that nature alone could have brought
> them to this praiseworthy degree of civilization.

No doubt the close contact which the *doctrineros* maintained with the Inga and Sibundoy made it impossible for them
to recognize the presence in them of similar virtues, for, according to Fidel de Montclar, it took 'the patience of a saint' to
'drive their absurd notions out of Inga and Sibundoy
heads'.[5]

However it did not take long for the patience of the seraphic
fathers — with the assistance of the Father Prefect's police
system — to prove itself quite capable of achieving the desired
modifications in the outward religious manifestations of their
parishioners.

Fray Jacinto records that in thirty-five years of evangelization only one Indian refused to make his confession on
his deathbed; and another chronicler adds that 'in 1912, when
the population of Santiago had reached 3,000, there only remained three couples in the whole village whose union was not
blessed by the Church'. The attraction of Christian marriage,
which would seem to have arisen spontaneously among the
Inga and Sibundoy, is explained by the Great Crusader thus:
'We have worked hard to get rid of disorders, especially by
making the young people get married immediately on leaving

school . . .' And to prevent any misunderstanding, he adds that these young people finished their two or three years' schooling 'at the age of sixteen or eighteen'.[6] This preventive measure (which the Capuchins were still enforcing in the 1960s) was immediately seized on by their opponents to accuse the missionaries of marrying off the Indians by force. The Order's historian gives the following rebuttal:

> Such an accusation can only be based on an ignorance of the peculiarity of the Sibundoy Indians, whose custom it is to wait for the priest to call them to get married. They simply start living together, and if the priest does not do anything, they will see that he gets an anonymous message. When the missionary then reproves them for their behaviour, they will quite naturally reply, 'But we were waiting for the father to call us!'
> Surely there is something of a gulf between this and saying that the missionaries marry off the Indians by force.[7]

None the less, the Capuchins were to continue to hand out to adolescents 'certificates of celibacy' to guarantee their 'suitability for marriage', and it would seem that their zeal did not end there, since even today one can find dozens of couples who only received the nuptial blessing after several sessions of beating and the *cepo*.[8]

Furthermore, these practices were reinforced by the preservation of the *camarico* (an ancient offering in kind, made up of animal or vegetable produce, and presented to the Church to celebrate certain feasts) as well as of the traditional church taxes, tithes and first-fruits, which the Indians paid 'according to their ability', as we saw in the previous chapter.

Thus it is clear that the evangelizing activity of the Capuchins resulted in rapid advances as regards church worship, the administration of the sacraments and the payment of ecclesiastical taxes. But at the level of doctrine, progress was far less spectacular; in fact, it only really affected the children, who were educated by the Marist Brothers and Franciscan Sisters. This was hardly surprising, considering that the Capuchins lived in their friaries and tended their estates, while the adult natives barely left their homes, except on Sundays to go to mass and on Mondays to work for nothing for the Church.

We may also pause for a moment over the innumerable references of the missionary chroniclers and their Creole friends to the 'abominable', 'indecent', and 'unhealthy' clothes worn by the Indians of the Sibundoy valley.[9]

The clothes worn by the men, first: these consisted traditionally of a black tunic (*cusma*), sleeveless and collarless, knee-length, belted with a long woven white girdle; a long poncho (*capisayo*), with vertical stripes of blue or red; masses of necklaces (*chaquiras*) of blue and white beads that could weigh anything up to nine kilos; and a narrow, woven, coloured band (the *llacto*, now no longer worn) with a bobble at each end, to tie their long hair back. The women's clothes consisted of three pieces of woollen cloth, without any seams: one, usually red, with a hole for the head, was attached to the second (black), which formed a skirt, by a long, broad woven girdle wound several times round the waist; the third, generally blue or green, was worn as a shawl.

We may perhaps leave it to those qualified to judge whether or not this traditional costume is indecent, but it is noteworthy that Fray Jacinto de Quito admiringly compared the majesty of the men's costume with the tunics and togas of the ancient Romans, and saw a likeness between the garb of the women and that worn by the Jewish women as described in the Bible.

But to those not versed in missionary morality, let me make it clear that according to the chronicles of the Capuchins the most appalling element was the totally pagan habit of their parishioners of not wearing pants. Even Fray Jacinto was troubled by this, but from one Indian to whom he tried to point out the indecency of it, he got the reply: 'But you must see that the Lord on the cross isn't wearing any pants'; and another Indian added: 'But if one should wear pants, then why do the reverend fathers conceal theirs?'[10]

It is clear that Fidel de Montclar cannot have been unaware of *why* the Indians so disliked western clothing, since he himself says that the Inga and Sibundoy would allow their sons to wear European clothes at school, but not at home. He also cites the case of a young man recently returned from the town who, despite every appeal from his family and the missionaries, was refused entry by his own fiancée 'until he takes off those white men's clothes'.[11]

To cut one's hair meant giving up the *llacto*, the headband to be seen on the mummies of the Inca emperors (then called a *llautu*). As for giving up wearing the *chaquiras*, that would mean abandoning the only external sign of wealth which made it possible for the Indians to settle their differences without recourse to weapons; they would have struggles in which the winner was the one who could get his opponent's necklaces off. Clearly, then, for the natives to give up their ancestral garb would indicate the beginning of the slippery slope to a perilous acculturization.

The list of complaints made against the Inga and Sibundoy went on to consider their 'undoubted tendency to steal', and the difficulty of getting them to grasp the principle of private property, so inseparable from Christianity. The Capuchins had perhaps forgotten that the first Christians themselves practised a similar holding of goods in common, thus securing solidarity and equality among the members of each community. Such simplicity as the Church had in its early days was surely exactly the same as that of the Inga and Sibundoy, who had put some of their lands at the disposal of the first missionaries, and the 'poor whites'.

It is hard to see how the missionaries could have seen 'theft and sin' in the taking of a few head of cattle to satisfy the hunger of people who looked on the goods of the *Cofradías* as communal; or why they should have been blamed still more for their laziness, lack of ambition and failure to value private property (though this last was only during the early years of the mission, before the whip and the *cepo* had given them a stern lesson on the values of the West).

But there are other points which the Capuchins deliberately ignored. Fidel de Montclar refused to see the arrival of the first settlers as anything but a good means of breaking down the Indians' communitarian society, apparently ignoring the atmosphere of violence it produced, for he could write:

In fact, those who used in the past to wallow in permanent idleness saw no value in property, easily yielding up their land without objections of any kind; those who showed no desire of giving up their routine way of life; these people have now decided to rise up from their torpor, since they find themselves obliged to defend themselves against the immense greed of the whites, who want to take possession of their plantations and profit from the revenue they provide.[12]

The Capuchins' own behaviour was ambiguous; though trying to inculcate into the natives the superiority of private over collectively owned property, the Capuchins were actually taking what land they owned away from them.

It was impossible for the Sibundoy to make any economic progress by the very fact of the restrictive measures imposed upon them by the Mission: the narrow limitation set on their ownership of land; the exhortations to place it 'voluntarily' under the protection of the *Cofradias* of the Virgin; the obligation to pay taxes of tithes and *camaricos,* and also to work for the Church for no wages, etc. Such treatment could only lead the majority of them to take refuge in the forest, or to 'sell' themselves – to work for a ludicrously low wage – to the missionaries and settlers.

Another argument used by the Order in its publications to indicate the 'state of savagery' in which the Inga and Sibundoy were content to live was the resistance met by the first Marist Brothers and Franciscan Sisters who attempted to teach them to read and write. It was the period when the Brothers 'would go stumbling over rocks and find ways through the forest in search of Indian children to take to school', while, according to Fray Fidel, 'the Sisters used every possible means to get the girls out of their huts and into the classroom'; in other words, 'into those veritable nurseries which the Sisters tried in a thousand skilful ways to make attractive, in order to remove from the tender hearts of these children the seeds of savagery and degradation which are there both as an inheritance from, and by the example of, their parents . . .'[13]

By the Capuchins' own admission that resistance was originally due to the Indians' 'fear that their children would become whites'. But the situation soon improved: by 1914 there were thirty-one schools in the Putumayo, among them 'some supported by missionaries' own money' with 'over 1,300 pupils enrolled in them'. What brought about this changed situation? We may look first at what the teachers wrote about their pupils:

They are taking so well to their studies that we often find a pupil coming to Sibundoy with another [young Indian], completely savage, won over from the depths of the forest.[14]

. . . In their hearts, which at first seemed closed to any sensitivity of feeling, there are already arising truly noble aspirations. By teaching them to sing we are taming their habits, and by agriculture developing their sense of ownership.

. . . The results could hardly be more gratifying. Children we received not long ago in the most lamentable state are now speaking Spanish fairly correctly, and reading and writing it quite passably; they have learnt basic arithmetic, and above all, they are beginning to have clear ideas about our holy religion.[15]

The last paragraph is singularly revealing: that the Indians finally agreed to send their children to school was undoubtedly due to the kindness of the Marists and the Franciscan nuns; but it must also have had something to do with their realization that the basic knowledge offered to their children would provide them with so many weapons of self-defence. Knowing how to read, write and reckon also meant being able to show their superiority over the great majority of the invading settlers, who were for the most part totally illiterate. This is not just guesswork: the missionaries themselves indicate several cases of children who went home and taught their parents, and refer to the alteration in the relationship between whites and Indians as a result of the intellectual advancement of the latter:

It quite often happens that when a contract has to be drawn up, or an act signed between two whites, they are forced to ask an Indian to sign it for them, for they cannot even write their own names . . . and this is a matter of considerable pride to the natives . . .[16]

The Prefect Apostolic quotes certain cases more striking still, especially this one, in which there figures a character we have met before:

Quinchoa himself has been overtaken by the present native Commissioner of Santiago, Diego Tisoy. The latter has sent me several communications which would compare favourably with those of any well-established official. Indeed, this same Indian has even sent the Señor Commissioner [of the Putumayo] such a well-written report that the Commission has kept it as an unusual curiosity . . .

The *Corregidor* of Santiago, having employed several white secretaries, has finally engaged an Indian who does the job so perfectly that he has no hesitation in declaring him better than any white man.[17]

One may then wonder how this competitive spirit – so much in conformity, we may recall, with the suggestions of the Great Cacique Tamoabioy – could be reconciled with the Capuchins' theory of the 'seeds of savagery and degradation the Indians get both as an inheritance from, and by the example of, their parents'.

The missionaries' observations in regard to the traditional festivals of the Indians, when examined closely, present two curiously contradictory points of view.

The first is that expressed by Fray Jacinto de Quito, who as a Creole is more sensitive to the customs and rites of the natives than his Catalan superiors. His observations, filled with interesting details, related to the feasts of patron saints, the Carnival, the Corpus Christi. From him, we know the complex ritual that was observed in celebrating feasts: how a *sindico* was appointed to organize the preparations; how it was the custom for the people of Sibundoy to go to Santiago one year, and those of Santiago to Sibundoy the following year, a few weeks before Corpus Christi, and how the Indians of both villages would meet halfway along the road, both accompanied by statues from their churches, 'wearing hats and *capisayos* to prevent their getting wet or sodden in pools of water'. Fray Jacinto also describes the time it took to prepare the costumes of those taking part in the various performances: those of the twelve *danzarines,* decorated with sequins, sixteen mirrors, splendid crowns and a cascade of necklaces 'weighed down with silver coins from the days of the Spanish kings'; those of the twelve *zaraguayes,* similar to the former but less magnificent; and the disguises of the *matachines* with their crowns of feathers and their masks, white, mustachioed and hideous. The latter had the job of preserving order, while the first two groups had to lead the dance, playing on guitars, tambourines and castanets.

Fray Jacinto notes that the two tribes would come together to celebrate these festivals, notwithstanding their different languages. He tells us too what the dancers did, that they followed the processions up to and even into the church, since such was the tradition. He has this to say of it:

The laws of decency were in no way infringed by these jollifications, in which the devil could have little part, for there was not an ounce of evil anywhere in them, nor was there even the suggestion of any contact between the sexes.[19]

The style of this good man becomes positively gentle when he describes the night of Maundy Thursday, when the Indian governors presided over a frugal meal with all the tribes gathered together, and reminded their subjects of Christ's death and the attitude appropriate to recalling it, ending with the words: 'This evening we are happy because we are joined together as brothers; we may not be able to be so next year.'

It is clear from both such descriptions, and the traditions still persisting, that such feasts did not exist solely for the purpose of honouring Christ. They also provided for the Inga and Sibundoy an occasion for celebrating the memory of their ancestors, and strengthening the bonds of brotherhood among tribes and individuals: as an outward sign of this they would present one another with the most valued of all gifts – salt.

The other point of view was the one endlessly put forward in the more official writings of the Capuchin community. There, the Indian feasts were described as 'pagan customs', and were only mentioned in order to be condemned out of hand. Thus, in regard to the carnival celebrations, it was said that 'especially during the three last days, it became a repellent kind of bacchanalia of indecency', because of the excessive amount of *chicha* being drunk, and further, that it led to 'numerous suicides'.

To explain this phenonomen, the seraphic brothers would often cite the following lines from the pen of their great friend Don Rufino Gutiérrez:

On the eve of Corpus Christi, the procession of dancers, with musicians at their side, go from door to door to invite their neighbours to join them, and in each house they are given a drink. They then go to the church to pray and celebrate Vespers for the feast; there they dance to the music of harps, mandolins, drums, flutes, etc., and on leaving the church, they go to the home of one of those organizing the feast where they dance, drink and eat until a good number of them fall stupefied to the ground . . .

Finally, worn out by dancing and excessive drinking, their health damaged, having lost all power to act, and now owing debts which they are quite incapable of repaying, the Indians will hang themselves from trees in their gardens. Dozens of them thus settle their accounts by paying with their lives for the excesses they have committed.[19]

And the missionaries' reports go on to boast of their successes in getting Roman orthodoxy accepted by 'these Indian children who at first seemed closed to any sensitivity'. Year after year they would publish the same statements from five or six missionaries, or officials on tours of inspection, all impressed by the beauty of the Spanish hymns used to 'tame their habits'. And they would send postcards showing Capuchins surrounded by children holding European musical instruments; or a priest teaching adults – dressed in European clothes – how to play *pelota* as in Spain.

Once the 'barbarism' of the Indians had been demonstrated

so briefly, one can see why the Catalan Capuchins – so civilized that they preferred to use 'fine aniseed liqueur' even for their magic lantern! – blamed the Indian *chicha* for the 'bacchanalia of indecency' in which the Indian festivals ended. They were certainly not wholly wrong in complaining that too much of it was drunk, though this natural and undistilled drink is infinitely less toxic than the drinks produced by the 'civilized'. But it simplified matters, to say the least, to blame that drink for the epidemics of collective suicide mentioned above, which regularly took place once the Carnival celebrations were over.

In effect, there cannot be found a single missionary who would admit even the possibility that such indications of despair – following the rare occasions on which the honour, tradition and cultural heritage of the Indians were recalled with ceremonial – might have indicated a protest, or even a despairing rejection of the white invasion which, when all was said and done, was taking from them everything that might have made life seem worth living. There are four pieces of evidence to justify such a hypothesis:

The self-inflicted hecatombs which had decimated other Indian groups during the era of the conquest;

The choice of a particular tree, which suggests that such suicides had an element of ritual about them;

The fact that this practice seems, according to all the chroniclers, not to have existed before the arrival of the Capuchins;

The studies of a great many anthropologists, not only laymen but missionaries too. For instance, the North American Father Louis J. Luzbetak notes that 'evangelization introduced an imbalance into the way of life of these natural beings', of which the major consequence was that they 'lost the desire to live'.[20]

Yet there were innumerable examples which might have led the missionaries in the Sibundoy valley to reflect more deeply on this serious problem. At other times of the year, too, their protégés would commit suicide, not by hanging, but by throwing themselves from the top of a peak which the Great Crusader called 'the cliff of hell'.

Let us for a moment forget the missionaries' point of view whereby 'Indian barbarism' was enough to explain everything, and try to see how the Indians themselves may have seen the situation.

Among the Inga and Sibundoy one can distinguish three groups, who reacted to the invaders in three distinct ways: first those who were chieftains or important personages, whom the missionaries tried to win over by treating them in a privileged way and taking special care over the teaching of their children, so that a lot of them would eventually turn into good secretaries or minor officials, especially the Inga of Santiago, whose cleverness at times rebounded against their masters, as we have seen in the case of Francisco and Diego Tisoy. In the second, smaller group, were the most rebellious, who opted for flight, or emigration to the towns, and the despairing for whom suicide was the only way out. Finally there was the mass of those in between who tried, as far as they were able, to resist the enforced change in their culture.

While a great many families realized that the best means of defence ultimately consisted in assimilating the most basic part of the culture imposed on them by the Catalan missionaries, they none the less stubbornly defended their own habits and customs, especially their traditional games, their usual way of doing agricultural work in common, and the building of new homes which had to be completed in a day. And the Sibundoy were careful to preserve among their children the traditional virtues which had made it possible for them to survive over the centuries, virtues of which no doubt the most important was the self-mastery which they inculcated in their children by stories like this:

Once, very long ago, the tiger was afraid of thorns. A family had to go away to the town, and left one of the daughters to look after the house. She was a good little girl who prayed to Our Lady; but she was wild, because she did not know the local villagers or anyone else. One would have likened her to a forest deer, perhaps.

That day, while the little girl was cooking maize and potatoes with a little meat and some eggs, the tiger, attracted by the smell, came out of the wood. Terrified, she prayed to Our Lady, and went up to the attic, while the tiger set about cooking the eggs.

Up until then the tiger was quite quiet, but when the little girl, from her perch, stuck a needle into his head, he fled, leaping and roaring, and became the raging beast he is today. He began to look for men and animals to shed their blood and kill them. And all because he could not control his anger.[21]

The sensitivity and subtlety of Inga and Sibundoy customs also emerges from their dedication to friendship, which they celebrate with an unchanging ritual: new friends consecrate their friendship before a crucifix, with each giving the other a few words of good advice, kneeling as they do so, after which they will embrace one another and swear brotherly friendship.[22]

The number of examples which give the lie to the Capuchins' assertions about the 'simplicity of their minds' and their lack of sensitivity is so vast that it is unfortunately impossible to mention them all here.

From that time forward, however, a major change began to occur in the customs of the valley. The matriarchal society of the past became weakened, and the father's name began to replace the mother's as the family surname.

Obviously Fidel de Montclar was too intelligent not to recognize this. But could he possibly see any positive value in the traditions of the Indians, or realize that he was dealing with a culture which, though different from his, was equally worthy of respect? If so, he would have had to reconsider the whole basis of the Capuchin Mission's civilizing action.

One must therefore conclude that the Prefect Apostolic only made such a point of exaggerating the 'barbarism' of the Indians in order to make the changes brought to the valley by the Capuchins appear all the more praiseworthy, and thus justify the vast government subsidies he demanded for his colonizing work. But he was also able, when the aggressiveness of the settlers endangered what he was trying to do, to extol 'the childlike soul of the Indians' and their 'repugnance for the evil habits of the white men' – thus proving that it was vital to keep them in isolation, and protected by the missionaries. Such an analysis leads one to wonder how much remained of evangelical principle in the Capuchins' behaviour.

We may begin to note that the kind of phrase most often recurring in Capuchin writing is of this type: 'Estanislao de las Corts, one of the missionaries who has done most good to the Indians due to his energy of character.'[23] And the official mission historian points out:

The Indian must be considered as we found him at the beginning of the century, like a grown-up child, without any awareness of personal responsibility, or rather, perhaps, with a completely atrophied moral conscience. Only the fear of punishment could put any brake on his ungoverned behaviour . . .

Simple demagoguery about [corporal] punishment is something everyone can understand, especially those who have no sense of responsibility. It is hardly surprising then that there are legends and certain *more or less probable-sounding accusations*. The missionaries have followed a true path, in the best interests of the Indians themselves.[24]

It is clear, then, that the Catalan priests set a high value on authoritarian methods, and the use of such means of persuasion as beating and the application of the *cepo*.

As we have seen the *cepo* had been already in use in the Putumayo a century earlier. There are also documents proving that in 1907 the civil ruler of the area banned what he called the 'barbarous torture of the whip'.[25] However both practices had returned in full force, despite everything in Christian law, the moment that particular official left – which enabled the Mission's adversaries to blame the Capuchins for their reappearance.

As might be expected, the Prefect Apostolic in his Report for 1911 rejects the accusation, declaring that, on the contrary, he had ordered the use of the whip to be abandoned 'in all the villages'; of the *cepo* he says nothing. But a year later, his admirer, Rufino Gutiérrez, writes:

If the crime is not too serious, the simplest thing is what is generally done today: the governor of the *parcialidad* puts the criminal in the *cepo* he has in his possession, for whatever length of time he thinks fit; if it is a frequent offender, then he himself gives him several strokes of the whip – a venerated object never removed from the cross on the *cepo* except in exceptional circumstances, and then with much ceremony. In addition, in consultation with the priests, the culprit will be condemned to work for a determined number of days in some form of public work. The Indians still have to be treated as badly brought-up children with certain evil tendencies.[26]

All the Prefect Apostolic had really done was to return to a medieval tradition introduced to this continent several centuries earlier by his predecessors, the *doctrineros* and *encomenderos*: he declared in 1915 that 'the power to punish has had a very beneficial effect on the Indians'. This elegant euphemism is no more than a partial admission, for he goes on to mitigate it by a statement that is quite flagrantly untrue: 'Before the missionaries arrived, beating was in use, but I had it abolished, and insisted that culprits be punished in a more humanitarian manner.'[27] With a few strokes of the pen, he thus denies the assertions of a number of official documents, as well as the evidence of thousands of those living in the valley who are still able today to declare that the missionaries presiding over the Indian chapters 'tolerated' the use of both *cepo* and whip, the former until 1940, the latter to this day.

Though at first sight the missionaries may seem wholly responsible for the preservation of these vicious practices, the reality is somewhat more complex, for the Indians themselves certainly contributed to it. It is worth looking at the reasons of both. The Indians saw this custom as a survival of a still-remembered time when it was the job of their own authorities to administer justice. The *cepo* then served the purpose of a cell, and also constituted a symbol of the authority conferred on the governor for his year of office, an authority which everyone accepted in virtue of the ancestral adage that 'no one rebels against the governor's stick'. The Catalan missionaries, for their part, could hardly have found a better means of getting their way through the intermediary of the Indians. This explains how carefully this mission has, even until our own day, sought to keep in effect the clause in the Great Crusader's *Regulation* whereby the election of Indian leaders could only be made from among candidates chosen by the missionaries, and during the course of a meeting at which one of them must preside.

This was quite good enough a reason for the Capuchins to take care not to abolish corporal punishment, though in their double capacity as police superintendents and Presidents of the native Chapters they had every authority to do so. Instead they actually extended such punishments to further types of crime, as defined in the missionary *Regulation*. As we shall see later on, sexual intercourse outside marriage blessed by the church held pride of place, but the crimes of disobedience and lack of piety could also lead to the *cepo* and the whip.*

Their use of *cepo* and whip earned the Capuchins a name for 'barbarism' among their adversaries, including the liberals of Nariño who maintained that 'those looking after the villages of Mocoa and the Sibundoy valley ought to be priests of the Pasto diocese'.[28]

Given the persistence of such suggestions, Fidel de Montclar once more took up his pilgrim's stick and went to ask his

---

*The 'power to punish' also extended to a number of other infractions which would never have occurred to the Sibundoy of old as is clear from this observation recalled by the most educated of them all, the anthropologist Alberto Juajibioy:

The St John dancers go on Saturday to greet the governor and ask his forgiveness. He asks them whether they have done their duty in cleaning the village square and *whether they have been to mass*. If they have failed in either of these duties, the *alguaciles* first whip them, and then follow that up with good advice. After which they are given a gourd of *chincha* which they swallow in a single gulp.

protector, the President of the Republic, for official approval of his policy towards the natives. And once again he got what he wanted: on 23 December 1915, 'by request of the Apostolic Prefecture', decree no. 1484 was promulgated, in which the government recognized Fidel de Montclar's position, as expressed in his *Regulation*, as arbiter of 'public morality', and Superintendent of police and of education, as well as having authority to grant land to the natives. Only one point in the *Regulation* was not accepted by the State: that of obliging the Indians to work for nothing on the *haciendas* and worksites of the missionaries. But that did not stop this devout practice on the part of the Capuchin fathers from continuing, as already described by Don Rufino Gutiérrez. Indeed, according to the evidence of the Sibundoy themselves, it was at that date that another day besides Monday was set aside for working for the Church: work was to be done on Tuesday in honour of the Blessed Virgin. More serious than the extension of the land-grabbing of the mission was the fact that this called for a corresponding increase in the labour needed to tend it.

This aspect of the Capuchins' work caused attacks to be made on them in the Nariño press, more forcefully than ever, while adventurers on the make, both settlers and traders, joined in the chorus of protest against the diminution of the Indian labour force thus available to them. In short, this became an endlessly fertile cause of local controversy.

CHAPTER 10

The Critical Year

There are some failures in logic which really deserve to be punished by whipping.

(FRAY FIDEL DE MONTCLAR, 1916)

The brake applied by the leading families in Pasto on Fray Fidel's plans for Spanish immigration, did not discourage him for long. Aware of the fact that at all costs he must keep such influential people as allies, he showed no annoyance. Indeed, he actually set off with his Immigration Council to select the most suitable areas at the foot of the Andes in which to settle the first Creole groups. Shortly afterwards, while the authorities of Nariño province, without waiting for the legal division of the Sibundoy valley, were publicly auctioning the 'unused' lands of the former *resguardo*,[1] the Prefect Apostolic launched a huge-scale campaign throughout the area in support of his new plans for settlement.[2]

This readjustment, forced on him by circumstances, certainly did not mean that Fidel de Montclar had simply abandoned the major part of his colonizing aspirations. Though he had to give up the idea of settling his own compatriots in Amazonia, it was only in order to replace them by the most similar group of people he could find locally. Forgetting all his grand statements in favour of the working people of Nariño with their desperate hunger for land, he announced that he would be recruiting new settlers from the far-off district of Antioquia,* of sober, healthy and Catholic stock'.[3]

*Antioquia, a province over a thousand kilometres away from the Si-

At first there were 535 applications, from twelve different municipalities. But various publications describing the piteous state of the area caused the first rush of enthusiasm to die away, though the Father Prefect, in consultation with the Immigration Council, promised very considerable benefits to those who would volunteer to come: transport, provision of tools, etc., lodging, six months' supply of food, medical service, medicines and even hospital care 'should the need arise'. According to the rules set up to meet the situation, would-be settlers must be 'healthy, Catholic, of good behaviour, and above all sober. To apply for concessions and privileges, they must have a medical certificate to guarantee their state of health, and a declaration signed by the priest of their parish and the local mayor to guarantee their moral standing.'[4]

Having thus carefully laid the ground, starting in August 1915, the Prefect Apostolic had his morally impeccable recruits moved not to Sibundoy but north of Mocoa, to a site he had chosen himself and named Alvernia, in honour of St Francis. Plans for this new village were made immediately, and a start was made on a road to link it with the capital of the Commissionership. This done, Fray Fidel and the governor of Pasto looked together towards the Sibundoy valley to start work on the founding of the town of Sucre which had been planned for in the Great Crusader's very first law. The newly established settlers viewed this step very coldly, and fearing that newcomers would limit their own hopes for expansion, they set about every sort of manoeuvre to prevent the project being carried out. But the Great Crusader, as usual, defended himself vigorously. As one of his admirers wrote:

He left no journey unmade, no speech unspoken, no manifesto unwritten. In this instance, he wrote a tract pointing out the absolute need to found the town of Sucre; it would be done because it had to be done; it was necessary for the poor of Nariño, it was necessary for the Indians of the Sibundoy valley, it was necessary for Pasto, and, above all, it was necessary for the nation as a whole.

---

bundoy valley, was populated by Creoles well known for their enterprising and colonizing spirit.

This really struck home as far as the settlers were concerned. There followed a strange battle of tracts in which each party tried to defeat the other by presenting itself as the protector of the Indians:

Surely [cried Fray de Montclar] it is the sheerest cruelty to prevent the poor Indians from receiving what is theirs by right? And if the Sibundoy are the owners of this valley, why should this half-dozen protesting settlers have taken it on themselves to cultivate land that was not lying unused? By what right have they assumed the title of cultivators here when by law it is one that can only be recognized to those working land belonging to the nation? There is a lack of logic here which must really be punished as such. [Extract from the tract *The Law of the Funnel.**]

And once again Fidel de Montclar won his point. Note, however, that he achieved his object without for a moment failing to observe every 'legality' of form. The lawyer appointed to defend the interests of the Indians was paid by the Nariño government, which may help to explain how, in the eight months allowed for by the law, he had still not managed to get hold of copies of the title-deeds of the Sibundoy, or even of proof that such deeds existed, though we know they were available. Thus the tribunal decreed that since the valley did not belong to them, it could be divided among the whites, according to the interpretation of the laws first suggested by the Prefect Apostolic. Indeed the only defects in the proceeding were its total disregard for the truth, and its failure to consider the spirit of all the previous legislation intended to preserve the land rights of the Indians.

Not merely did the Inga and Sibundoy thus lose their age-old patrimony, but they were actually driven out of the area selected for the establishment of Sucre. 'The interests of the Indians were certainly respected as far as was possible,' notes Fray de Vilanova on the point, 'and though some forcible expropriations were necessary, they were at least carried out in perfectly legal conditions.'[6]

*By the term 'law of the funnel', the Prefect Apostolic meant receiving a lot and giving only a little. It was his passion for everything relating to 'legality' that led him to publish a tract with such a title.[5]

So families settled in Sucre between February 1916 and August 1917. But endless disputes between the new arrivals and the established settlers led three quarters of them, sick of the battle, to leave, so that only 120 families finally remained at the end of the year. The Capuchin historian was led to comment sadly: 'Sucre is not, alas, growing as had been hoped. It is a bureaucratic town, seeking the source of its wealth and economic life outside itself, and thus remaining anaemic and paralysed.'[7]

At Alvernia, the Father Prefect's most cherished colonial experiment was hardly any better, because of the growing antagonism between the Nariño Creoles, and the settlers from Antioquia. Fidel de Montclar noted with bitterness that 'people are trying to discourage the Antioqueños by making them believe we have brought them in to fight the Peruvians'.[8] But far from letting himself be depressed, Fidel de Montclar tried to describe the situation in the most hopeful colours to his patrons in the government:

The colony [of Alvernia] is going well, and everyone is working there with the greatest enthusiasm; there is no note of discord; you won't find a single man loitering in the village on any weekday. We celebrated Corpus Christi for the first time last Sunday. . . . Almost all the settlers came to communion that day. . . . I am daily more confident that these Antioqueños are splendid people, and far the best fitted to colonize these areas. . . . There was joy on every face, a joy expressed verbally by enthusiastic cheers for the Capuchin mission, for Colombia, for Antioquia province and for Spain . . .[9]

But the members of the government had barely finished reading this heart-warming text when they received the following telegram in October 1917:

President Senate, Chamber of Representatives, Bogotá. The undersigned Antioqueño settlers, come at request Prefect Apostolic Fidel de Montclar to work the Putumayo region, beg Chamber reaffirm laws guaranteeing settlers cultivating for nation against outrage and exploitation, regard contracts with missionaries and Spanish workers who, abusing immense power with administrative authorities of region, ignore Colombian laws. Said Mission pre-

venting real material, intellectual and commercial progress, by arbi-
trary monopolization of land, livestock, goods and men subject
again to old Spanish slavery destroyed by nation's martyrs.[10]

The government was of course stupefied: what could explain
such an attitude on the part of such carefully selected settlers?
The Senate ordered the governor of Nariño to make an inquiry. He was a friend of Fray Fidel's and member of the Immigration Council for unused land, and his report came back in
short order. As might have been expected, he rejected all accusations against the missionaries. From information received
from the Father Prefect he was able to say:

I wish it to be understood that the twelve individuals who signed
the telegram to Congress are those who, by order of the competent
authorities (that is, the Prefect Apostolic, superior chief of Police),
have had to be put in prison in the town for having attacked and
looted the Mission in Alvernia, profaned the Church, and mocked
the sacraments to the great scandal of the pious and honourable
settlers of this area.[11]

What reply could the accused give? That the Capuchins,
having failed to distribute the food ration stipulated in the
contract, and supplied by the State, left them with no option
but to help themselves to prevent their families from starving,
and they had therefore entered the Capuchins' storehouse —
the door of which was not even locked — to take what was
owed them. Clearly their grievances must have been genuine,
for a fortnight later the civil court ordered them to be released
without more ado, despite the accusations of the Mission.[12]
They then sent the liberal daily paper of Pasto this open letter,
which was to lead Fray de Montclar to an outburst of rage
exceptional even for him:

The head of the Mission, despite his intelligence and his brilliant
and remarkable activities, is keeping the national government in a
state of deliberate ignorance; for he writes and publishes pamphlets
and letters which falsify factual information in innumerable ways;
he sends telegrams in praise of the Mission which he gets signed
uncomprehendingly by illiterate and simple Indians; he takes photo-

graphs in which, ten leagues away from the capital of Nariño, Franciscans are to be seen surrounded by 'cannibals' – whereas everyone here knows that these Indians, daubed in paint for the camera, have in fact been civilized since the days when Don Hernán Pérez de Quesada, brother of the founder of Bogotá, first settled in Sibundoy, two hundred years ago. It is by trickery of this kind that this prelate manages to falsify the nation's judgement and win ill-informed support.[13]

Fidel de Montclar responded with a further inflammatory pamphlet, describing these settlers as 'faithless, lawless ingrates . . . empty-handed as sinners at the moment of death'. But the worm was in the bud, and in November 1918 the Father Prefect himself was obliged to admit to his first serious setback:

After what has happened, feeling ourselves under no further obligation to dispense favours to creatures so totally degenerate, we have decided to withdraw the missionary establishment from Alvernia, and leave that colony to its fate.[14]

But the settlers were well able to defend themselves for, following certain government pressure on behalf of these 'degenerates', the Mission found itself obliged to give the poorest of the families a small allowance of food, and 'that they might clothe themselves, give up some of the supply of clothes intended for our own use [*sic* in the Mission's own report], brought from Europe before the 1914 war . . .' The account concludes sadly: 'The mission's enemies have had the last word.'[15]

Government circles, though traditionally favourable to mission rule, felt a certain uneasiness over the setbacks of their highly paid protégé. For some years now people had been daring openly, actually within the ruling conservative party, to criticize the Capuchins, and the president of the republic himself had used the term 'missionary-businessmen' before Congress, while pointing out the instability of the results achieved by the missionary Church.[16] This situation, combined with an unprecedented financial crisis – the national budget had had to be reduced from 18·3 million pesos to 13·8 — obliged the president, despite his friendship for the missionaries and the fact that his own son was a priest (he is now Cardinal Luis Concha Córdoba, the primate of Colombia), to annul the subsidy of 100,000 gold pesos allotted to the missions. Having received advance warning of this, the Colombian Church appealed to Congress; there ensued a heated debate, with the liberals proposing, as a conciliation to both parties, that the subsidy be simply cut by half, while the unquestioning supporters of the missionaries talked in terms of religious persecution, and demanded a public show of hands in order to unmask these 'traitors to Catholicism'.

It was just at this point that the troublesome business of Alvernia became public, and bitterness against the Mission really came to the surface; so much so, that the deputies, having once again affirmed the law in honour of the Virgin Mary, were hesitating over the proposal of an unimpeachably orthodox senior official that *something must be done* to stop the money of the ordinary people being 'used simply and solely for the personal enrichment of the missionaries; for it is quite clear that though they are flattening mountains, they are only doing it to settle themselves on fine estates whose revenues they alone receive'.[17]

But faced with threats of anathema, the nation's representatives ended by preserving the subsidy in its totality in 1918.

All this, and the rumours that went with it, had one unexpected result: the Council of the Missions, whose job it was to divide out the money, decided to appease public opinion by using the sum allotted to the Putumayo mission for other purposes. But the Great Crusader rapidly dealt with this new and 'incredible' plan:

It is hard to imagine the effect this news had upon us. . . . We were literally struck motionless. . . . We should have had to pay dearly for our lack of foresight. . . . For though it is true that we had received funds regularly, it is equally true that we had invested them all, without saving a penny for ourselves. . . . [But at last] the Lord, in his infinite goodness, has deigned to assist us, and ensured that justice be done, with the result that we shall continue to receive our normal monthly payments.[18]

A year later, the financial situation was even worse, and opposition to the subsidizing of the missions took on new force, nourished now by the earlier, but only recently divulged, scandal of the 'excellent aniseed liqueur' of the Putumayo Capuchins. The debate had the great advantage of making a number of things public, among them the petition addressed by Fray Andrés de Cardona to the judge of the 'white' village of San Francisco 'asking him to have most of his parishioners put in prison because they owed him for several baptisms, masses and marriages', and the order from the judge demanding that a police officer be sent to force the parishioners to pay up. The deputy who made this particular attack was filled with indignation that in this the twentieth century, and within so Catholic a country, people could still be imprisoned for debts for religious services 'against all justice and law'. But what specially struck the Catholic conscience of the nation and the government was that it should be a 'Roman and Apostolic Catholic' deputy who should be trying 'by presenting his accusations before us with an honesty and courage which do him credit' to save the honour of his religion, so compromised by the Catalan Capuchin missionaries.[19] Not a happy situation for Fray Fidel.

It is not hard to see that these stormy debates should have shaken the government's confidence; so much so that one minister proposed in Congress that colonization and the integration of the natives should become once again a State responsibility. This suggestion was not in fact taken up, and the Council for the Missions kept its allotted sum undiminished, but nevertheless times had definitely changed.

But this period in the Father Prefect's life gives us an insight into his tactics for gaining government support: on the one hand he tried pressure on public opinion, endeavouring to convince everyone that the work of the Capuchins was indispensable for civilizing the tribes placed under their jurisdiction; and on the other, he worked to secure the success of a presidential candidate so dedicated to the interests of the missionaries that there could be nothing to fear from him.

A few lines from one of his letters to the Minister of Agriculture and Commerce sum up the arguments he used in his first move:

I do not think it would occur to anyone to look upon the Indians of the Caquetá and Putumayo as civilized people, for though the Mission has achieved noteworthy results in this field there yet remains a great deal to do. ... The clothing, language, instincts, superstitions, the dislike of living together in villages and numerous other persistent traits making it clear to anyone who ventures into these places that the Indians are not always civilized.[20]

Once again, Fidel de Montclar did not scruple to contradict himself, for in his Report for 1916 he had said of the Ingá and Sibundoy:

The pomp with which they celebrate religious festivals, the ceremonial with which they surround Catholic worship, the harmonious singing in which they all take part, make it clear that we are in a society very far from meriting the description 'savage'.[21]

Thus, from tactical necessity, de Montclar was presenting 'the Indians subject to his jurisdiction' by taking his examples at one moment from the Sibundoy valley, and at another from the distant forests and lowlands, where the Capuchins were afraid to set foot. By thus merging the two areas, or bringing them out each in turn, he managed to preserve among both government and public opinion – neither of them in a position to discover the truth for themselves – a sense of confusion enormously to his advantage.

As for the second point in his campaign, his preparations for the 1918 presidential change-over, his attitude was completely clear. Of the two candidates belonging to the Conservative party, he decided to support the one whose Catholicism seemed to him firmest, Marco Fidel Suárez, in whose favour he outdid himself in praises of the warmest kind in publications with such significant titles as 'All for the Fatherland, and the Fatherland for the Faith'.

However the candidate supported by the liberal party was admonished, preached against and even condemned by the Prefect Apostolic in statements so absolute as to deserve quoting here. Here, for instance, is an extract from the 'Circular on the Elections by the Very Reverend Prefect Apostolic':

The liberals are known for their systematic hatred of Catholicism. We do not need to remind anyone of the outrages their party has committed against religion. . . . The candidature of Guillermo Valencia is supported and defended for that same reason by the freemasons whose motto is 'War on all religion, and everything relating to the supernatural order. . . .' So there we see who Guillermo Valencia's friends are: the masonic lodges of Cartagena and throughout the country. . . . Can there be Catholics so innocent as to be unaware of the objectives being pursued by these enemies of God?

By sending his portrait and the Apostolic Blessing to Marco Fidel Suárez, an eminent son of the Church, our Most Holy Father Benedict XV has given him deserved praise, and expressed a wish that this worthy champion of Christ should be imitated by many others . . .

Nor did the Father Prefect stop there. The more intense the campaign, the more direct grew his language. This is clear from everything he wrote at the time. In his tract of 27 January, entitled 'The Scrupulous Cats', he returns to his polemical style:

Ten journalists from *Gil Blas*, the *Gaceta Republicana* and *El Tiempo* went to ask the Papal Nuncio whether he would order the secular and regular clergy of the Republic to abstain from preaching about political matters because, they said, doing so is not evangelical, does great harm to religion, and finally is contrary to the wise dispositions of the encyclical *Humani Generis Redemptorem*.

Really! What an extraordinary idea!

Finally, Marco Fidel Suárez won, getting 304 votes in the Putumayo as against 131 for Guillermo Valencia. Fray de Montclar, who had just had his fiftieth birthday, could celebrate it in the happy certainty that even in the worst moments financial help from the State would not be lacking in the future. But the blows he had taken over the past few years were too much,

even for him. All the more so in that even his friendship with
pious President Suárez was not enough to enable him to get
new laws for the Putumayo through the National Congress.
This sad discovery came to him twelve years after he had
initiated his 'civilizing' policy, and at precisely the moment
when the Sibundoy were decreasing fastest. After twenty-five
years of Capuchin domination the tribe was reduced by half.*

*From a study by Haydée Seijas, based on figures quoted by the
Capuchins themselves.

CHAPTER 11

Theory and Practice of Missionary Colonialism

Society, then, has need both of poor and of rich, of small and large landowners, and it would run counter to the dispositions of divine Providence to exclude either of these two important groups.

(FRAY FIDEL DE MONTCLAR, 1916)

It is strange to note that the most violent attacks made on the Capuchins inside Congress were not in relation to their total scorn for all things Indian, nor to their curious methods of evangelization, but to the way they administered the land they had taken for themselves. It seems worth examining a few points. First, how did the missionaries justify their greed for owning land? Second, just which of their investments caused such criticism? Third, what effects did the Great Crusader's policy have on the economic development of the valley? Fourth, what means did the Mission use for achieving its territorial and economic expansion?

Before attempting to answer these questions, it is important to be clear (a) that we are here concerned *exclusively* with the goods owned by the Mission in the Sibundoy valley, and not those in other parts of the Apostolic Prefecture; (b) given the absence of official statements as to the way in which the credits allotted to the Mission were used, and the impossibility of getting any access to the Capuchins' own accounts, we have to take as our only evidence those maps and documents published or preserved by the Mission whose veracity cannot be questioned.*

*According to the actual terms of the Concordat, and of laws still in

As regards the first point: as we have seen, Fidel de Montclar blamed himself for 'lack of foresight' in failing to ensure the continuity of the credits allocated by the Council of the Missions. We may point out to start with that that confession is contradicted by its author himself:

We are not so blind as to be unable to see that it is vital for us to secure the means to enable us to be an independent Prefecture; for the possibility that there may one day be an adverse government which will withdraw all funds from Mission work always exists, and this would represent the most certain and fearful setback for the whole area; we could no longer support ourselves here.[1]

There could hardly be a clearer admission on the part of the Mission that in its anxiety to secure its future existence it was pursuing a policy of acquiring capital, in the form of continuing increase in landed property and buildings. In addition to the justifications already mentioned – which are still used today – there is the canonical argument that in any event all such goods belonged not to the Capuchins, each of whom had made a vow of poverty, but to the Church, a body less open to criticism.

As regards the second point, the first quantitative reference to the goods owned by the Mission in the countryside dates from 1916, the year when Fray de Montclar stated that 'the area of land now cultivated or developed into good pastureland exceeds a thousand hectares. It is so well tended that it can compare favourably with the finest farmland of the South. We

---

force in Colombia, the Catholic Missions are obliged to give the State an account of how they use the money placed at their disposal. This obligation has never been fulfilled. First, because during its first year of existence, the Council for the Missions alleged that there was no government ruling as to how the use of the funds was to be verified; then (since 1915) because that same Council took refuge behind the Arbitration of a Revenue Judge who felt that the absence of such a ruling dispensed him from further action. The argument continues to this day.

All efforts made later by various members of Congress to get the obligation fulfilled have been in vain – which is why the sporadic Reports from the missionaries are limited to a few descriptive details and accounts of their own virtue.

have imported forty Durham heifers to improve our cattle; we have also introduced horses, sheep and pigs.'

In 1918, he makes further mention of the Mission's investments, in a note to the Council of the Missions describing the evangelization of his area:

The Prefecture, for its part, has consistently and regularly – in so far as the resources at its disposal have permitted – carried out the drainage of a large stretch of land whose richness is well known. . . . Encouraged by this success, it has continued digging canals, and there is now a vast network of these which has made it possible to drain and transform into farmland considerable areas that were swampland.

Obviously, and we are the first to admit the fact in all honesty, this undertaking has cost a great deal . . . in spite of which we have continued the work once begun because of our awareness that it would secure the future of the Mission.

Finally, the statistics given as an appendix to the Report for 1917 provide a picture of the allocation of goods and of land cultivated by the white colonies of the Sibundoy valley:

Goods of the Mission

	Houses	Cattle	Horses	Hectares cultivated
Santiago	—	—	—	300
Sibundoy	25	400	130	1,300
Total	25	400	130	1,600

Goods of the Settlers

San Francisco	71	322	84	434
Sibundoy	6	50	—	157
Sucre	148	63	58	225
Total	225	435	142	816

Goods of the Marist Brothers

Santiago	—	18	2	15
Sibundoy	—	18	1	25
Total	—	36	3	40

To understand this table one must note two points: (1) the white population consisted on the one hand of seven Capuchins and six Marist brothers, and on the other of 928 settlers, 583 of whom were men, either bachelors or with families; (2) the list of the Mission's goods is incomplete: it omits not only the saw-mills, marble quarries, work-sites and piggeries, but also the *haciendas* in San Francisco and San Andrés.

The plans made by the Marist Brother Pedro Claver, worked out with the most praiseworthy care and precision, fortunately enable us to fill these gaps, and discover the true extent of the 'Mission lands'. The Capuchin community kept secret the existence of these plans for fifty years. We feel justified however in mentioning them now; and by projecting them on a modern map of the area made with scientific instruments, it is possible to resolve the controversies which have surrounded the estimation of the value of all these possessions for so long.

It is clear from the calculations of Pedro Claver that the land claimed by the Mission then represented 2,196 hectares, half of that being swampland and stubble-fields. When rectified against a modern scientifically made map the figure emerges more precisely at 2,561·8 hectares. From this we may draw two conclusions:

(1) That the Capuchins' *haciendas* occupied the richest lands in the valley, and completely encircled the Indian settlements of Sibundoy, Santiago and San Andrés.

(2) Further, if we accept the statements of the missionaries that they had occupied these lands for many years, it must be realized that General Escandón had told the simple truth in the report which caused him to be excommunicated and dismissed from his job as Special Commissioner for the Putumayo.

As to the third point, a summary analysis of these figures also leads us to draw certain conclusions in relation to the economic development of the valley in 1917:

With less than two hectares per family, the white settlers

were in a situation of economic underdevelopment, and thus of alarming dependence on the missionaries;

The Marists, upon whom the entire responsibility for education in the area rested, possessed hardly anything, since the 'school farms' which should have come under their administration, were included as part of the 'Mission lands';

From the missionaries' figures it would appear that the whites' possessions *per capita* can be broken up this:

	Houses	Cattle	Horses	Cultivated Hectares
per Capuchin	3.5	57	18	228
per family of settlers	0.3	0.7	0.2	1.4
per Marist brother	0	6	0.5	6.6

If there was such a disproportion in the resources of these three categories of 'the civilized', one may well wonder what was left for the Indians. There is no indication of this either in Fray de Montclar's reports, or in any government sources.

In only a few years, the Catalan missionaries had joined the small ranks of the *latifundiarios*, the descendants of the original conquistadors, making both the Indians subject to their jurisdiction and the white small farmers they had themselves invited to share in the colonizing of the Sibundoy valley, pariahs with no possible hope of any improvement in their lives in this world.

This was not, however, how the matter looked to the man mainly responsible for this 'civilizing work', Fidel de Montclar, who spoke thus in defence of his theory of agrarian development, based on the dialectical mutual interaction of two extreme situations:

Where the land is occupied by a great number of owners, it has a more charming aspect, with the multitude of small holdings and the variety of notes presented by the diversity of cultures providing it with a peculiarly attractive appearance. ... I do not by any means wish to suggest that there should not be large properties as well — far from it: without them, I am sure the small property-owners could not carry on. For they need someone to give them a helping hand, to provide them with work when their own land needs no further attention. ... Society, then, has need both of poor and of rich, of small and large landowners, and it would run counter to the dispositions of divine Providence to exclude either of these two important groups. So let rich men set off for the Sibundoy valley, and let them develop vast estates there, but never let them push out those who must form the largest proportion of any human association.[2]

So Divine Providence provided the Great Crusader's policies with all the justification needed, and the socio-economic balance which was bound to result could hardly be called evil since it formed part of God's plan. From this point of view, the results were splendid: with thousands of dispossessed natives and a few hundred settlers with tiny holdings, there were also a handful of huge landowners, chief among whom was the Mission itself.

Fray de Montclar was after all perfectly logical in following out his theological-cum-capitalist theory when he replied to his detractors:

If a secular company had done all this in the area would it not be praiseworthy, and would not the entire nation remain immensely grateful for the surge forward it had given the country as a whole? Why should we be judged by different rules, in other words the law of the funnel? ['A lot for me, a little for you.']

Has it not been continually said that we Capuchins have done nothing in our Mission, and that everything we have undertaken has failed, etc.? How then is it that things have changed so suddenly that we have now become so successful that we seem to have outshone the sun itself? Please, gentlemen, may we have a little logic and legality – but not logic lacking in common sense, not the legality of the funnel.[3]

Unhappily for the Father Prefect, in attempting to justify the Mission's success in the economic sphere, he simply provided so many arguments for those who accused him of having misused public funds intended for the development of the area. And it is quite understandable that scholarly distinctions between the

wealth of the Church and the personal poverty of the missionaries should have failed to convince the settlers: while they
were struggling in poverty, the Capuchins could declare 'for
the physical health of the missionary he must have the fewest
possible material difficulties to contend with', and that for his
psychological health he must from time to time take holidays
in Spain.[4]

Equally useless were de Montclar's other arguments: the
costliness of evangelization, of dignified ceremonies, and of the
work of colonization; for it became a matter of public notoriety that the Capuchin Mission received from the national
government sums more than five times greater than those allotted to the civil administration of the area.*

These facts are quite sufficient to explain the bitter complaints made by the settlers, and the failure to colonize Sucre
and Alvernia. They also cast some light on the material successes of the Mission in what was once the domain of the
Sibundoy.

As regards our fourth and final point, it is worth considering
the other aspects of the *modus operandi* of the Capuchin expansion which began, as we saw, with a pure and simple invasion of the Indians' lands, and continued by a denial of
their rights in law, so that the Mission's establishment as
'settler and cultivator' should not appear too illegal.

The first collateral operation of the Capuchins was directed
to preventing the dispersal of the labour force by setting
bounds to the 'Indian lands' or missionary *resguardos*. The

---

*The 1917 budget granted the following credits to the civil and ecclesi-
astical administrators of the Putumayo:

To the Commissionership of the Putumayo: 8,500 gold pesos;

To the Apostolic Prefecture: 40,050 gold pesos, divided thus:

   For the upkeep of schools: 12,600;

   For the maintenance of the Pasto–Puerto Asís road: 24,000;

   Emoluments to the Prefect Apostolic as Inspector of Public Education: 570;

   Subsidy to support the missionaries' living expenses: 2,880.

To all this must be added the huge credits allotted by the Council for
the Missions which were discussed earlier.

areas at issue were two portions of the valley, of which theo-
retically one was for the Inga and the other for the Sibundoy,
which were divided by a larger and more level piece of ground
reserved for settlers.[5] These 'Indian lands' had nothing Indian
about them except the name, for – as can be seen from the
maps – a large part of the *haciendas* of the Blessed Virgin were
in fact established there. In other words, Fray de Montclar was
violating even the minute property right he had himself allowed the natives, while preserving this valuable area for apostolic work and a compact labour force.

The next operation was the evacuation of Indians who had
lived on the 'Mission lands' for generations. As examples of
this, we may perhaps look at two cases, one concerning the
Inga, the other the Sibundoy. The first involved a piece of land
at the very edge of the *Cofradía* of Carmen, in Santiago, next
door to the ground which the Tisoy and Buesaquillo families
had defended so fiercely. This ground had belonged to the Jacanamijoy family for centuries, until one of its members sold it
to a white man under immense pressure. The Mission did not
oppose the transaction, despite the ground's being situated
within the 'Indian lands', and certainly did not think of claiming ownership itself. But once the Capuchins began to work the
land of the *Cofradía* of Carmen, they found that this piece of
land cut off their access to the río Tamauca; so the Mission
began a lawsuit against the whites who had got hold of the
land and, without waiting for judgment to be given, had the
house they had built razed to the ground.[6] The case in fact was
decided against the Capuchins, whereupon the Superior, appointed by Fray Fidel, Fray Benigno de Canet de Mar, wrote a
letter to the parish priest of Santiago, of which I give the
following extract:

Since things are going badly in the Commissionership, I shall go
this week to Pasto, and will return with the lawyer and the judge.
... Consequently I have urgent need of good witnesses for the case.
And I think it would be useful if you were to get in touch with the
five sisters of 'Rillon' Jacanamijoy, and see whether they would be
ready to state that their father really rented from the Church the

land he tilled at Pacay. You can tell them that I will pay for his funeral . . .

P.S. If they are willing to give evidence to this effect, let me know, so that I can get their statements recorded at once.*

In this kind of way the missionaries would try to persuade Indians to attest that the lands of their ancestors belonged to the Church when — as was known by everyone — the Pacay holding was part of the ancestral heritage of the Jacanamijoys (which can be proved by reference to a deed given by a tribunal in Pasto).[7] I leave it to the reader to form his own judgement as to the integrity shown by the Capuchin Superior.

On the other hand, these protectors of the Indians showed little concern to defend any Inga possessions they did not themselves want to seize. This is clear from looking at one of Brother Pedro Claver's maps, dated 1922, in which we find the *haciendas* of eight settlers established well within the so-called 'Indian lands' that the Capuchins were supposed to be protecting.[8]

The case of pieces of land reserved to Sibundoy families was similar. In his Report for 1917 the Prefect Apostolic noted the presence of 'forty-five white men, some bachelors, some with families' inside the 'Indian lands' surrounding Sibundoy Grande; this provides us with a second example of the methods used by the Capuchins in pursuance of their territorial aggrandizement.

The Sibundoy, 'apathetic and lazy' — or, rather, totally discouraged, and having lost even the slight hope that had inspired their earlier acts of sabotage — were far less effective in opposing the infiltration of the missionaries than the Inga, whose procedural skill we have seen. Weary of the battle, they ended by agreeing to place themselves under the 'mediating authority' of the missionaries, rather than suffer the extortions of the settlers. When one settler named Medina invaded some of their land, east of the San Pedro river, the Sibundoy at once

*I myself studied the original of this document in the presence of the parish priest and two witnesses in the archives of the Santiago church, on the afternoon of 2 January 1967.

hurried to beg Fray Fidel for his help. He certainly stood up against Medina . . . but only after simply annexing the land in question to his Mission. Medina appealed, and the Prefect Apostolic won his case by quoting twenty-three witnesses to the effect that: 'The lands in question were part of the *Cofradia* of the Divine Shepherdess'; 'that the Indians had owned them from time immemorial, and the missionaries now some years'; and finally: 'that their sole owner is the Capuchin Mission'.[9]

The Capuchins made this judgment an excuse to claim all the land on the left bank of the San Pedro – land they were to re-sell some dozens of years later to white families, despite protests from the Sibundoy; they are still doing this in 1970.

One final point remains to be clarified: the use of the Indians as a labour force for draining swampland, and tending the lands of the Mission. This question will be dealt with more fully later on, but the statement of one Indian brought forward as a witness in the Medina case gives us a sense of how it happened:

In the swampland of the *Cofradia* of the Blessed Virgin, I never worked for my own gain; and I was only able to cultivate a small holding there and keep a few animals because the Fathers allowed me to do so, as they usually did with all the other Indians, in return for our services to the Church.[10]

Thus the Catalan Capuchins were continuing to force the Indians to do unpaid labour for them, four centuries after this had been forbidden by Charles V, and almost a century after the government of the republic had renewed the ban. These 'voluntary' contributions, though sometimes paid for by the 'loan' of a small allotment, were not always restricted to the same area, and often caused large movements of population of which it would be interesting to discover more than we now know. Such at least is the conclusion we must draw from the case of the building of the church in Sucre, concerning which the missionaries said that they 'had engaged a Spanish foreman to see to the framework and roofing, since the less important work could be done by the voluntary labour contributed by the Indians from the village'.[11]

One wonders just what the missionaries meant by the 'Indians from the village', since their reports which I have already quoted state that the population of this settlement, created as part of the process of 'colonizing' the Sibundoy valley, were whites from either Antioquia or Nariño.

All this may enable the reader to form a clearer notion of the invasion and exploitation of the Inga and Sibundoy perpetrated by the Capuchins during the second decade of this century. This analysis will, I hope, make it clearer why certain officials and members of parliament, 'conservatives and apostolic Roman Catholics', were driven to making the timid protests I have described against the activities of the Mission.

But, outside this little valley, what did Fidel de Montclar's Mission do during all these years in the vast, almost virgin land of Amazonia that was also entrusted to its care – an area stretching from the foot of the Andes to the distant frontiers of Brazil and Peru? This is the question to which I shall next attempt an answer.

CHAPTER 12

Evangelization in Upper Amazonia

The day after the Missionaries arrived, the six savages were baptized and confirmed, after the most basic religious instruction. And the oldest of them also received communion.

(FRAY ESTANISLAO DE LAS CORTS, 1926)

Have you had indecent thoughts? Do you want to receive God in the host? Have you believed in witchcraft? Have you worked on holy days?

(Capuchin catechism for the conversion of savages, 1926)

We may recall that during the first five years of the existence of the Apostolic Prefecture of the Caquetá and Putumayo, when the Capuchin mission was largely staffed by Creole priests, it used from time to time to send out teams on evangelizing expeditions in the lowlands at the foot of the Andes, places explored centuries beforehand by the *doctrineros*, and later by traders and would-be rubber planters. In 1911, Fidel de Montclar wrote:

Some of these trips would last up to ten or twelve months, during which the missioners underwent indescribable hardships, sleeping on river banks, or beneath trees with only the sky for a roof, always at the mercy of the thousands of insects with which those places are infested, and in permanent danger from wild animals.

Despite our small numbers, and the fact that we had to care for the Indians who were already baptized, we made some twenty expeditions within quite a short period through the impenetrable Caquetá forests, seeking out infidels.

But once the Mission became annexed to the Capuchin province of Catalonia, these expeditions grew fewer, because, as Fray de Vilanova explained:

In the period from 1910 to 1917 the opening of work on the Pasto–Mocoa road, and the many different labours involved in colonization, made it necessary for the missionaries to remain at home a great deal more, and this inevitably resulted in fewer apostolic excursions.[1]

In other words, what was the policy of both the State and the Vatican — an effort to civilize the still savage tribes — was not being and would not be carried out.

The reason given hardly seems enough to explain why the missionaries preferred to devote their care to the more civilized parish-type communities. Their lack of knowledge of the terrain and of the facilities needed to cope with that vast area of 'pestilent and demonic' emptiness which comprised the larger part of the Prefecture must also have had a lot to do with it. The Prefect Apostolic himself recalls how even the journey from Mocoa to Florencia presented enormous obstacles:

Between leaving and returning one has to spend at least twenty-eight days canoeing, through regions almost totally uninhabited, with all the hardships and sufferings that involves; first of all going down the Caquetá, and then going back up the Orteguaza, in the most primitive craft without comforts of any kind.[2]

This, combined with the missionaries' lack of interest in, and indeed fearfulness of, the southern region, explains why Capuchins were so seldom to be seen there – giving their adversaries the fun of asking with a certain malice: 'How is it that the Caquetá is developing more rapidly than the Putumayo, since it gets no help from the missionaries?' To which Fidel de Montclar replied (to the Council for the Missions) that he was less concerned for this territory because it was inaccessible to the settlers in the interior, whereas the little valley of Sibundoy, the object of so much covetousness, needed the permanent presence of the Capuchins to defend the 'aboriginal race'.[3]

This is how matters stood when the scandalous incidents of 1918 and 1919 came to put a stop to the colonizing dreams of the Great Crusader. And though his spirit was sorely tried, he had at least the satisfaction of seeing his personnel reinforced by the arrival of a fresh contingent of evangelical workers from Catalonia, which enabled him to enlarge his field of evangelical action, so restricted up to then. He now proceeded to reorganize the administration of the Prefecture, appointing Fray de Pinell as Superior, and establishing the most developed townships as 'quasi-parishes'. In addition, considering that the twenty-two Capuchin fathers and twenty-one Marist brothers available to him were not adequate for putting his new missionary plans into effect, he asked Rome to make the territory of the Caquetá altogether separate from that of the Putumayo – which in fact was later done.

His next step was to re-deploy his troops: ten missionaries for the Sibundoy valley, eight for lowlands at the foot of the Andes, and four for the rest – that is for over five hundred thousand square kilometres of Amazonian forestland over which nomadic tribes of 'veritable savages' were dispersed! These figures confirm the Capuchins' preference for the highlands of the Putumayo, far easier to cultivate and more populous, where thirty-four of the Prefecture's forty-one schools were established. Thus it is hardly surprising that the starting point selected for the new evangelizing thrust should have been Puerto Asís.

In that village, which was Colombia's port of access to the Amazonian basin, the missionaries had started a unique form of pedagogy. The education of children took place in an 'orphanage' in which the children of all the near-by Indian tribes were incarcerated. The missionaries have left the following account of the difficulties they had to face in removing these children from their families:

It is impossible for anyone who has not had the opportunity of studying the character of certain of the Indians to grasp the immense labour involved in bringing the children together and keeping them under constant discipline. They are used to living in the forest, and therefore to complete independence; once they have scattered, it is hard to bring them together again. Furthermore almost all of them, or at least the great majority, belong to tribes living three, four, or even six days' journey away, which makes it intensely difficult to succeed in getting them to understand that they have to remain in the orphanage; not only do they have to abandon their *dolce far niente*, but they also have to leave their families who live so far from Puerto Asís. The opposition of the parents is a terrible problem; it can only be overcome by force of promises and flattery.

As for the future which missionary education offered to these 'orphans' against their wishes, it was to be the same as that of all uprooted people — simply to swell the masses of the local sub-proletariat. A photograph shown in Fray Fidel's Report for 1918 depicts a group of young Indian girls with the title: 'Franciscan Mothers and their servants'.

But let us glance at the further expeditions undertaken up the main affluents of the Amazon. Here are some extracts from the diary of the trip made by Fray Anselmo de Olot, who led the first one in 1917:

Aguarico. . . . A long journey on foot from San Miguel because the track was appalling. The nature of the inhabitants is friendly, but they like living according to their traditional customs. As in San Miguel, the population is small. I only stayed a few days among these Indians, to administer the sacraments, and instruct them about the mysteries of our holy religion . . .

Cuyabeno. . . . The place was enlivened by the presence of a large group of river-dwellers both white and native. I took advantage of their hospitality to make a census of the population, which always makes our sacred ministry easier. To sum up briefly, I found the same situation as in the village of Aguarico: some married, others baptized, some bachelors, others living together unmarried; but to all I gave advice. For myself, after receiving great kindness from all these excellent people, I set off again in my canoe towards Napo after four days. Apart from seeing the waters of the Lagartocacha for the first time, and noticing a few river-dwellers' huts, this next trip had nothing special about it, except for the unfortunate effect it had on the macaws, *Paujils,** etc. which came within range of our guns.

*The *Paujil* or *Pajuil* (*Penelope superciliaris*) is a kind of large wild

La Bocana. ... I must say something of what happened to the poor Inga Indians I had met in the Cuyabeno during my first visit. A group of white men, led by an Ecuadorian, a former employer of these Indians, living at La Bocana, attacked them one night in their homes as they slept. After some resistance all those lacking the strength to flee were put into chains, taken to a canoe prepared for the purpose and transported to La Bocana. ... I could hardly fail to act when I heard this. I assembled all possible evidence of what seems to me to have been nothing but an unprovoked attack, and sent them with a report to the political official in La Bocana, with an urgent demand that the Indians be freed . . .[4]

During that same year, 1917, various other trips were made round the foot of the Andes, including those parts of the provinces of Nariño and Cauca which fell under the Prefecture's jurisdiction.

But our glance at the Mission's evangelical activity would be incomplete without giving the apostolic balance-sheet for the year:

Marriages: 270	Confirmations: 745
Christian burials: 288	Sermons: 1,978
Baptisms: 636	Communions: 99,766

The apostolic fervour of the parish priest of Santiago, Querubín de la Piña, deserves special mention: he marked up 14 marriages, 84 confirmations, 111 baptisms, 194 sermons, and 15,000 communions.[5]

This fresh series of evangelizing tours had the major result of giving the missionaries a more accurate notion of the problems of navigation on the local rivers, as well as of showing them that the forest around the foot of the Andes was already covered in a network of tracks regularly used by Indians, traders and rubber men. But the greatest surprise these tours brought them came at the end of a year, when Fray Ignacio de Barcelona discovered the speed with which secular col-

---

gallinaceous bird to be found all over equatorial America. Its meat is extremely good.

onization was proceeding in the north, in the territory of the Caquetá:

> I must admit in all honesty that Florencia* has impressed me agreeably from all points of view. The prejudices I held against this part of the Prefecture – as Your Reverence well knew – vanished as though by magic. I expected a virtually empty area, without communications of any kind with the rest of the world, unhealthy – a desolation. ... Imagine my surprise then, when, two days before arriving at this village, we began finding along the banks of the Orteguaza broad areas of cleared ground being used as pasture for large numbers of cattle. .... Believe me, Reverend Father, it seemed almost like a dream ...
>
> My admiration increased still more when, on first entering Florencia, I found it not a collection of *ranchos*, but a well-planned village, made up of several streets and having two large squares. ... All the streets were already built up along both sides, as were the squares. Indeed they would have to be so in view of the size of the population which, according to the Commissioner, is over 6,000 ... [6]

It would be unfair not to mention the work done among the whites in Florencia; as one missionary reports:

> All the pious societies which have been founded there have flourished remarkably. They may be said to have fallen upon ground that yields an hundredfold.[7]

This statement is confirmed by Fray Jacinto de Quito, who mentions specially the growth of the Third Order, and the Congregations of Doctrine and of Perpetual Adoration, as well as the great advance made by the five *Cofradías* of the Scapular, and so on. But what were the Capuchins doing in response to the spiritual needs of this mass of new settlers who continued to develop not only Florencia, but even more isolated parts of the Caquetá? In 1919, Fray Ignacio de Barcelona drew the attention of the Prefect Apostolic to this problem:

> That you may know what evil there is – spiritually I mean – I

*The capital of the territory (*intendencia*) of the Caquetá. Today, linked by road and air with the centre of the country, Florencia is the largest centre in Colombian Amazonia.

will speak only of cases in which I have incontrovertible evidence; of such I have made a list of nineteen unmarried men living in sin, not including two or three doubtful cases. Among married men I have discovered at least thirteen whose lives are evil: you may guess what labour this has cost me, but with God's protection I have managed to ascertain these things. ... I have administered 104 baptisms in the past few days and 105 confirmations, and have officiated at fourteen marriages.[8]

We must bear in mind, however, that the Capuchins had two different forms of marriage, depending on the colour of the skin. For the 'civilized' they had a veritable 'card-index' of souls, of which we can get some notion from comments made in their notebooks. For instance:

R.R., married at Timaná, left his wife and went to Napo where he married an Indian woman; on returning to Florencia and finding his first wife there, he left them both, and went back to Napo.

M.M., married at Timaná, left his wife and went to the Putumayo where he is living in adultery with Bárbara.

A.G., married to Alejandre Palomares in Huila, left her husband and came to the Putumayo to live in concubinage with M.P. (she died leaving children).[9]

It is not hard to see how such a policy contributed to making the Capuchins unpopular with the settlers, who viewed it as an intolerable interference in their private lives.

But when it came to the Indians living along the rivers, the missionaries adopted a far more flexible attitude, reducing the instruction considered necessary before baptism to a minimum. The notes made by Fray Estanislao de las Corts during his 1921 trip along the tributaries of the upper Caquetá indicate this very clearly:

Among the Huitoto of Peneya. ... The leader of the tribe welcomed the missionary pleasantly. He had been baptized by Fray Gaspar de Pinell during his tour ...

Ten or so families met together at the leader's house, and the priest began his catechism class. One of the men present, who had only recently come up from the Carapaná, asked to be baptized with his family, and this was done the next day. After baptism, they received the nuptial blessing, and made their first communion.[10]

The Capuchins made thirteen trips of this nature between 1917 and 1921. One can follow them and their results in detail in the rich descriptions written by the explorers themselves. None of the expeditions had an unhappy ending – at least for the Capuchins; the only deaths to be mourned were those of two of their guides on the search for the Tetete. This southern tribe was the only one in the entire Prefecture to have withdrawn *in toto* to the forest, after having been decimated by the *caucheros* and others in search of slave labour, and was still desperately resisting the white man.[11]

These tours determined Fray Fidel in 1925 to widen the scope of his activities so as 'to exploit the vast eastern part of the Mission which, owing to its appalling climate, our lack of personnel, the vast distance and the problem of communications, is still in a state of impenetrable chaos'.

There followed a fresh series of journeys, the first of which was made by Frays de las Corts and Tortella, who went down the Caguán river and then back up to Sibundoy by the Caquetá. They were astonished in the extreme to discover that these so-called 'impenetrable regions' had been the site of Jesuit missions centuries earlier, before having more recently become the *caucheros*' empire:

The whole river [writes Fray de Montclar] is surrounded by a mass of ruins, providing telling evidence of the movement, the wealth, the life there was here in the days of the rubber boom and of how that wealth was wasted. Everywhere one sees broken machines, things left to rot, empty boxes and chests. It looks like a battlefield. . . . The whole river speaks of blood and crime. . . . Its loneliness is like that of a cemetery that some enemy has profaned . . .[12]

During their four-month tour – from January to April 1925 – the missionaries encountered three tribes, among them the Jaihon, 'the only savages the length of the Caguán'. The six people left in the tribe were, within the space of twenty-four hours, instructed, baptized and confirmed, according to Fray Estanislao; and he indicates another aspect of his civilizing effect on them — the Castilian names given to the new converts.

The two following expeditions, in 1926, were directed to converting the Jairuya and the Muimane, whose whereabouts Fray Estanislao discovered earlier. But, as the missionaries had to admit, 'our results on the spiritual level were poor, because of the difficulties of instructing them without a good interpreter'.

The final tour was, on the other hand, more fruitful. It was led by Fray Gaspar de Pinell and another missionary who was beginning to be recognized for his energy and strength of character: Fray Bartolomé de Igualada. This time they had excellent interpreters and, after visiting the same tribes, they went on to begin the religious instruction of some of the Mocaguaje and Huitoto. This time, Fray de Pinell was careful to note down the translations of prayers and spiritual readings made by the interpreters, so that he was later able to put together a little Huitoto catechism. Here are some of the questions intended for using when hearing their confessions:

Have you had indecent thoughts?
Do you wish to receive God in the Host?
Have you believed in witchcraft?
Have you done impure things? Alone? With a woman? With a man?
Have you committed adultery?
Do not be afraid; this is not to punish you, but to open the way to heaven for you.[13]

This is one of many examples from catechisms for natives which make it quite clear not only that the missionaries were making no effort to express Catholic practices in a form the Indians could understand, but that they were presenting them with ideas, and even with a vocabulary, quite meaningless to them — yet of whose strangeness the missionaries were quite unaware:

Jesus Christ had no true father . . .
Hosts are made of wheat . . .
Wine is made from grapes . . .

In these books, we also come upon all the teachings that were meant to give the Indians an understanding of the sacredness of private property, and of the respect and collaboration they owed the white man, and missionaries in particular. Here for instance is a quotation from Fray Melchor de Barcelona's Moskito catechism:

Those who steal cattle or other things ... can only save their souls if they give back what they have stolen, and admit their sin in confession ...

Catholics who refuse to sell whatever they may be asked for to Spaniards, Creoles or Americans who are passing through, or who sell it at too high a price, are committing a sin; and it is equally sinful to refuse to hire them canoes, to serve them as guides or refuse to let them sleep in the house; for God has commanded that we help one another ...

Catholics must support their priests and pay for the expenses incurred in worship. God will not bless the labours of those who evade this duty.

Fray Melchor also teaches that religious tolerance has its limits:

Catholics who go into a non-Catholic church, or attend prayers said in their homes by non-Catholics, or who invite non-Catholics to their own prayers, are committing a sin, because this shows a lack of respect for God and for the prayers of the Catholic Church.

These last interdictions were directed specially to the work of English speaking Protestant ministers who had been coming to these regions for many years, and taken advantage of the Capuchins' total lack of interest in them, so much so that the catechism quoted above condemns those who have received baptism or the sacrament of marriage from a Protestant, or been taught in his school, as 'guilty of serious sin'. Fray Melchor could hardly have been unaware of the influence of the Protestants, however, since he was forced to use the Anglo-Saxon lexicon which they, his predecessors, had introduced for the conversion of the Moskito — some of which passed into their own language: Holi Spirit, Gad, Jisesrais, Help, Greip winn-a, Virgen Meri, Catolic Chorsh, Glori, Manking, Bless, etc.

The cultural peculiarities of the tribes themselves were also listed among 'serious sins':

Q: Is it a serious sin to do the things commanded by the *Sukias* when we are sick?

A: Yes, because that means failing to trust in Divine Providence which has provided us with natural remedies to heal us.

Q: Is it a sin to lay food, weapons, hammocks and other things in tombs?

A: Yes, and God forbids it because the dead will not come back until the end of the world.

Q: Is it a sin to accept the water which the *Sukias** have breathed out?

A: Yes, because God does not want us to have that water.[14]

According to the Capuchins' Reports, this system of Christianizing 'savages' — by giving them European names, and either rapidly indoctrinating them themselves, or making use of interpreters or of the kind of catechisms we have referred to — had excellent effects. The majority of convinced Christians would certainly not agree, if only because of the incredible distortions in the basic principles of dogma which took place during the course of such very hit-or-miss methods; this leads us yet again to note how little attention the Catalan Capuchins paid to the instructions of their own predecessors in the field, men like Fray de Carabantes, who had insisted in the seventeenth century on the need to know Indian languages if one were to understand Indian people and be able to teach them anything. And furthermore, as the Capuchins themselves admitted, they were only welcomed by the Indians because of the gifts they brought with them — which fact may also cast some doubt on the genuineness of the conversions they claimed to have made!

It is interesting to note just what those gifts were: the ac-

*In all Shamanic cultures there is evidence of the practice of a form of purification consisting in the Shaman's sprinkling those who are sick with a little water he has held in his mouth and breathes out over them.

counts for one of their apostolic excursions are illuminating:[15]

Purchase of foodstuffs	85.35 gold pesos
Medicines, etc.	59.80 ,,
Pieces of cloth, penknives and small mirrors for gifts	42.15 ,,
Small medals and crosses	12.00 ,,
Powder and ammunition	7.00 ,,

So the 'pieces of cloth, penknives and small mirrors' represented about twenty per cent of the expenses of the trip. Though gifts of that kind may have had a civilizing value in the eyes of the missionaries, it would seem that their recipients viewed them rather differently, at least to judge from the comment of one Indian guide who was engaged to try to approach the obstinate Tetete, a comment recorded by Fray Bartolomé de Igualada: 'Tetete no want clothes; machetes, axes, fishhooks, yes, Tetete like those.'[16]

Unfortunately Fray de Igualada does not make it clear whether the medicines on the list were intended for the missionaries' own use, or for the Indians they visited. It appears that the most commonly used remedies practised on such trips related more to sicknesses of the soul than the body, as in the strange case recounted by Fray Gaspar de Pinell, who was later to succeed Fray Fidel:

Amazing things still happen in these forests. One day I was called to bless a hut where they said the *Duende** was biting and tormenting a woman. Half-incredulous, half-curious, I decided to go and see what was happening, and what I could do for these neighbours. I was sure I should see nothing, and that it was merely a sign of nervous strain among these simple folk. But I was forced to admit that something very strange was going on, inexplicable by any natural causes, for in my presence and that of some thirty other adults, in full daylight, there were to be seen bites of various shapes and sizes all over this woman's arms and hands, and even saliva appear-

*An evil spirit frequently mentioned in Andalusian and Catalan folklore; it is often mentioned in the works of Lorca, but little is said of it in South America.

ing around them, without our being able to see anyone making the bites. I blessed the hut, and exorcized it; I urged the woman to leave, and apparently the matter ended there with no further trouble.

I have great faith in the exorcisms of Leo XIII against Satan and his spirits, and that is why, wherever we went during that trip, my first step was to carry out an exorcism, to rid these forests of the demonic influences which have for so many years been raging there in the absence of ministers of God to counteract them.[17]

There seems to be some discrepancy between this story and the formal statement in the Moskito Catechism that 'Catholics who assist at the driving out of a spirit are committing a sin, for these things are only done by the power of the devil.'

Be that as it may, it was in this fashion that the Mission bit by bit enlarged its area of influence in the Putumayo and Caquetá territories during the third decade of this century. Consequently, the missionaries could also get to know the central area covered by the Apostolic Prefecture, complete their adaptation to the local atmosphere, and bring back a rich harvest of experiences and anecdotes of a more or less exotic nature to fill their chronicles.

I will not say much as to the later stages of their evangelization of the infidels, both because there is already an abundance of missionary writing on the subject, and also because the methods and means used by the Capuchins did not change in any fundamental way, as is proved specially clearly by their continuing to use the Indian as a means of transport during their annual tours. If anyone finds this hard to believe, let me refer him to the photograph album of the Capuchin mission still kept at Sibundoy: in it, there is a photo dated 1965 of the present Vicar Apostolic crossing a bridge on a chair strapped to the back of an Indian – a practice condemned four centuries ago by the kings of Spain.*

*Transport on the back (or rather on the spine) of Indians is still a common sight in large parts of Amazonia, especially among the Peruvian Andes, where 'Indians' spines' replace – or complement – transport by rafts and trucks (cf. Bernard Lelong and Jean-Luc Lancrey-Laval, *Cordillère magique*, Paris, 1955).

Apotheosis and
End of a Reign

There are conservatives who have done such evil things that they should
rightly be called liberals, and liberals who should be at pains to get rid
of that ignominious label which does them such an injustice.

(FRAY FIDEL DE MONTCLAR, under the pseudonym Delfín Iza, 1927)

The noticeable slowing-down in the ambitious projects of Fray
Fidel de Montclar after the tremendous scandals aroused by his
colonizing schemes is most understandable. The reader will, I
am sure, recognize that even a man of his mettle could hardly
go through such trials without becoming profoundly disen-
chanted. But this discouragement was further aggravated by
the diminution of his physical strength which began to show
the strain of his incredible activity. Thus his operations became
less spectacular, and in the end he was forced to accept the
lesson of events; in other words: that the mestizos, long adap-
ted to working in the forest, and the Indians, incomparable
navigators, guides, hunters and walkers, together made up the
only human group which could, under present circumstances,
be effective in the development of Amazonia. So he abandoned
his idea of bringing in Spanish settlers, or any other Europeans,
and set about recruiting basic teams of Negroes, Indians and
mestizos for the small settlements that were founded along the
Putumayo and Caquetá rivers during the next few years.

The change was hard to accept, but did not actually involve
any alteration in the Capuchins' methods. This is clear from
the way in which the Father Prefect carried out one of his
oldest dreams: to found a village on the edge of Lake Guamués

as a staging-post between Pasto and the Sibundoy valley. To achieve this he had first 'to convince the lake Indians to settle in the desired spot'. But they, members of the old Sibundoy tribe, continued systematically to refuse to live together in villages, preferring to remain on their ancestral lands and protect them against the infiltrations of colonizers; at the same time they were utterly opposed to any settlement by whites, appealing to the Pasto authorities, asserting that the existence of their *resguardo* could not be ignored.

At that point, by a process well known in Indian America, the 'tenacious and bloody opposition' of the natives was conquered by law. The missionary chroniclers describe how the judge in Pasto in charge of the case established 'that the title the Indians allegedly had to these *resguardos* ... was illegal, inadequate, and not in conformity with the law'.[1]

A few months later Fray Estanislao de las Corts went into action, and wrote to the Father Prefect: 'They are coming next Monday to start cementing the church.'

For several years the missionaries attempted to create genuinely Indian or mixed villages, but fate was against them, and none of their projects came to anything.[2]

These few blots on their copybook did not prevent the situation as a whole from looking good, until two major reverses darkened the Capuchin horizon: the failure of the first attempt to establish a Colombian merchant fleet in Amazonia to break the monopoly of Brazil and Peru, and the revolt of the colony of Puerto Asís, so dear to the heart of Fray Fidel.

For a long time he had made appeal after appeal to the government to form a merchant fleet on the Putumayo, that enormous tributary of the Amazon which was the key to the economic development of the whole of eastern Colombia.[3]

At last, in 1921, Bogotá decided to import its first motor-powered boat from England. Fray de las Corts was at once sent to take delivery of the vessel from a port on the Pacific coast, and to get it brought back across the Andes to Puerto Asís. A year later the ship was floating on the Putumayo, but at the moment of launching a catastrophic discovery took place which stopped everyone in their tracks: the ship's motor was not strong enough to go against the current. Since the State had not the resources to remedy this defect, the project had to be delayed till times were better – which was not in fact until 1930.

The Puerto Asís rising caused the enterprising missionary an even greater disappointment. This colony, whose foundation I described earlier, had been largely settled by tractable 'coloured' or 'brown' people (a euphemism for Negroes) imported from the Pacific side of the Andes. It had developed smoothly, without any problems, especially as regards missionary establishments, until a sudden influx of settlers came to sow discord. These people, though chosen and registered by Fray Fidel's Immigration Council, at once began to criticize the missionaries, accusing them of limiting their freedom of action, and of preventing their reaching a level of development comparable with the Mission's own enterprises.

The situation was very reminiscent of the one we saw at Sibundoy. There too the missionaries owned weaving works, hydraulic mills, workshops of every kind, numerous buildings, ever-expanding cocoa and sugar plantations, and flourishing flocks and herds, while most of the settlers remained at a standstill for lack of money. And, like their counterparts in Alvernia, they held the reverend fathers responsible for the situation, accusing them of not paying them the State subsidies to which they had a right — an accusation which outraged the missionaries.

Who was in the right? It is hard to be sure. However, we can draw some conclusions from one of the Mission's account books.[4] The mission was never in debt, except during the first month of its establishment, and then to the tune of no more than 350 pesos. On the other hand, their credit balance, from the second month onwards, continued to grow until it reached 1,900 gold pesos. It is clear therefore that the Capuchins had, to say the least, used great prudence in their administration of the subsidies provided by the State.

These confrontations between settlers and missionaries became more frequent over the years, until they finally caused a fresh scandal in 1923. According to the Capuchins, 'thirteen heads of families were calumniating Fray Olot' and fifty-one attacking the entire Mission, accusing the Capuchins of having cheated them; the settlers were demanding that the government return them to their original homelands.[5] As on previous occasions, the leading spirit in the revolt had been the subject of special attention on the part of the missionaries, which increased their indignation.

It was truly the Alvernia affair all over again: once more the mission was being publicly accused of misappropriating State funds for its own use, an accusation all the more serious in view of the nation's crucial financial situation.

Fidel de Montclar opened yet another campaign to confound his detractors. From Pasto to Sibundoy the faithful were warned, from the pulpit and by means of public notices, that reading the 'evil press' – newspapers of liberal tendencies – constituted a sin.[6] But the Great Crusader had lost the vigour of his earlier days, and his uncertain health forced him to take frequent rests in Bogotá or Spain. This left the defence in the hands of Fray Gaspar de Pinell, as Capuchin Superior. His major manoeuvre was to publish[7] the accounts of how the money paid to them by the Council for the Missions in 1923 had been spent – accounts which showed expenses totalling 35,987 gold pesos and an apparent deficit of over 11,000 gold pesos.*

*In fact the Father Superior was neglecting to mention several additional sources of revenue:
(1) The mass offerings etc., tithes, first-fruits, *camaricos* and other religious payments.
(2) The ancient 'board-and-lodging' payment of 2,880 gold pesos from the State, as well as the emoluments paid to the Director of Public Education and the other religious employed in that field, of which the total for that year amounted to 17,000 gold pesos, out of the 20,240 allotted for the payment of the nation's teachers as a whole.
(3) Finally, he might have added the revenue from the Mission's *haciendas* which, according to Fray Marceliano de Vilafranca, was ploughed back every year into the 'Mission lands'.

Fray Gaspar's accounts may lead the reader to make two observations:

(a) That the annual support for each missionary was fixed at 600 gold pesos, whereas the salary of heads of schools (who received no subsidy for lodging, food, clothing, transport, medical care or holidays, and usually had families to support) varied between 500 and 600 pesos.[8]

(b) That the Capuchins listed as of major importance their own living expenses, then their investments in building and the cost of religious ceremonies; whereas 'help for the sick, aid to the poor, and the costs of visiting the Indians' were relegated to the rank of 'minor expenses'. These latter in fact were not even mentioned in the accounts, which gives some indication of their importance.

These glaring discrepancies could not fail to shock public opinion. Even the most convinced Catholics could hardly see any way to justify such a situation, while secularists continued to inveigh against the excessive proportion of the national budget allotted to the Capuchins: 100,000 gold pesos for education, and the building and upkeep of the road, as against 20,000 for the civil administration of the entire territory. This excessive aid provided by the government to the Mission did a lot to explain the imbalance between the two spheres of influence: compared with the rich buildings and *haciendas* of the Capuchins, the possessions of the State in the Putumayo consisted simply of a 'small post office' in Sibundoy, valued at 20 gold pesos, and a school at Mocoa, valued at 1,920 pesos.

The Capuchin sky, up to then so blue, became dark with clouds: protests came not only from the liberals on the opposition side, but from the conservatives in power as well. Fidel de Montclar had to think out a new line of defence quickly: leaflets and notices admonishing such 'traitors' suddenly appeared in all the towns and villages, signed by a certain 'Delfín Iza'. But the style left no doubt as to the real identity of the author; for instance, this:

We continued to read *El Pueblo* until, filled with indignation, we cast away that accursed paper which, in veiled but perfectly intelligible terms, is trying to sow seeds of doubt as to the honour and disinterestedness of the reverend missionary fathers of the Caquetá and Putumayo. We could not understand how a paper claiming to be Catholic could follow such a line. ... We then recalled that *El Pueblo* had been censured by his Excellency Monsignor Medina when he was bishop of this diocese, and recalled too something we had heard from the mouth of another important figure: 'There are conservatives who have done such evil things that they should rightly be called liberals, and liberals who should be at pains to get rid of that ignominious label which does them such an injustice.'[9]

Fray Fidel also published a fresh Report to strengthen his case. It shows the efforts made by the Mission towards the physical and moral development of the people of the Caquetá and the Putumayo, efforts that are roughly summed up in this table:

	1905	1910	1913	1916	1920	1924	1927
Churches	14	14	16	22	23	26	29
Residences	3	4	8	8	10	13	13
Hospitals	—	—	1	1	2	2	2
Dispensaries	—	—	1	3	5	5	5

This certainly made it clear to all Catholics how enormous had been the increase in churches and mission residences. It also gives some indication of a beginning in giving help to people, though the nursing offered by the sisters in these dispensaries was sporadic and not free of charge.

And here again the Capuchins' critics found objections to make. Why had the number of pupils enrolled in the mission schools not even doubled in fourteen years – 2,000 in 1927, as against 1,300 in 1913 – despite increasing financial assistance from the State?

Meanwhile, the activity of the Apostolic Prefecture in the Sibundoy valley was chiefly channelled into three practical operations: consolidating the ownership of the 'Mission lands', getting rid of the last of the 'Indians' lands', and draining the swampy parts of the Mission's *haciendas*.

As to the first objective, the missionaries refer to a great many lawsuits in which they fought Indians and settlers during the 1920s over both their seizure of new land, and the defence of land they had seized earlier – a defence which made use of methods which may seem somewhat surprising for preachers of the gospel, at least to judge from this statement we have from the settler Benjamín Caipe:

The first time I worked for the Mission for a year before returning home. When I got back to Sibundoy, Fray Andrés de Cardona, the Father Procurator, had a field sown with forty *arrobes* of maize, extending from the river Cabuyayaco to the Carrizayaco. [It was so enormous] that here by the Cabuyayaco the maize was already ripe, though it was barely beginning to shoot up by the Carrizayaco. The priest then appointed me to drive birds away from the plantations, but shortly afterwards he also said, 'If an Indian goes by knock him down and give him a thrashing or drench him with water.' It was as though they had already determined to take possession of the whole valley . . .[10]

On the other hand, information about the 'Indians' lands' is hard to come by: we know that at first the Capuchins took steps to get the State to unify those lands into *resguardos*, to prevent the Inga and Sibundoy from becoming too scattered. And the present Prefect Apostolic of the Amazonian Mission, Fray Marceliano de Vilafranca, adds:

But, since it took far too long to wait for our appeals to succeed . . . and on the other hand some of the Indians were continuing to sell off their land at very poor prices, the Prefect Apostolic decided to buy the land from the Indians on behalf of the Mission, simply in order to leave those same Indians there as tenants, so that they would be unable to sell them again and would be forced to remain there.[11]

This would seem not so much to indicate solicitude, as to be a pure and simple excuse to justify the incorporation of the Indians' land into the *Cofradía*s of the Blessed Virgin – yet another example of the total scorn in which the Catalans held the laws of the country. Indeed, it will be remembered that ever since the beginning of the nineteenth century natives had been regarded in the eyes of the law as minors, and thus unable to effect any transactions involving their own possessions without 'asking for a judicial authorization justifying the necessity or usefulness' of what they wanted to do: this condition, though imposed by law, has never been respected by the Capuchins.[12] But in their self-assurance the priests went further still: Fray Marceliano de Vilafranca writes:

The Mission then sought for legal bases by which to secure its land and that occupied by the Indians collectively. With this in view, it asked in 1926 for a judgment about all the land, including that let to the Indians. In this way the ground extending from the San Pedro to the San Francisco rivers could be kept as a single whole, where the natives could live.[13]

In other words, and indeed by its own admission, the Mission wanted the State not only to recognize it as the owner of the lands granted only a few years earlier to the Indians, but in addition to recognize its right to supervise the Indians themselves.

This new claim on the part of the missionaries led to increasing opposition from the settlers. They objected to the Apostolic Prefecture's demanding a judgment for over 3,500 hectares, since the greatest area allowed it by law was 2,500. Furthermore, they pointed out that, between their various sleights of hand and their buying and selling, the missionaries themselves had joined the ranks of the profiteers they were so loud in condemning.

Despite his poor health, Fidel de Montclar found himself once again forced to speak up in his own defence, and a notice signed by him appeared on walls everywhere. It contained the following declaration:

All over the Catholic world, dioceses and bishoprics, and even parishes and individual churches, own farmland to be used to provide suitably for the needs of carrying out religious ceremonies and good works, as well as for training the clergy in seminaries, and supporting God's ministers in a fitting manner, for as St Paul said, 'Those who serve at the altar share in the sacrificial offerings. ... Those who proclaim the gospel should get their living by the gospel.'[14]

But the weakness in the theological understanding of the Father Prefect's subjects led to their seeing not so much altar and gospel as *haciendas* — and this was the case with both Indians and settlers — so that opposition to judgment's being given in favour of mission ownership continued to proliferate.

The Capuchins had caused such an outcry that for a time they were forced to curtail their demands. The Marist brothers, on the other hand, given the modesty of their claims, were granted ownership of the twenty-two hectares they asked for in the Sibundoy area.[15] But this piece of ground was in fact later to become incorporated into the 'Mission lands'.

In conclusion we may note that the draining of land for the Mission (achieved by the natives' skill) provided additional fuel for those who supported the Inga and Sibundoy against the policies of the Capuchins. Both ordinary humanitarian principles and the law requiring that the Indians must be paid a fair wage for whatever work they did were used as a basis for numerous newspaper articles protesting against the obligation forced by the missionaries on their so-called protégés to do this job.

To these the Fathers replied yet again by, as it were, raising the bidding: anxious to show that they were indeed the Indians' protectors, they hastened to get through a law stating that 'Indians must not be committed to doing any work beyond their physical strength', that 'when their work was subject to contract, it must be a contract made before witnesses', and finally, that 'Indians must not be given any advance payments which could involve an infringement of their liberty': these, like so many other humanitarian measures adopted by Colombia in relation to the natives, were never actually put into effect.

These were the last incidents directed by the Great Crusader. In 1928 his health had become so poor that he went back again to Catalonia, this time for good. A year later, more fragile than ever, he finally resigned his post, and retired to live in the peace of the monastery of Arenys de Mar. Even from there his voice was still occasionally heard defending the achievements of the Putumayo mission, his own ideals, and Colombia's rights in Amazonia. The old campaigner never finally stopped speaking until he died. His death in March 1934 shocked the Colombian authorities who had delegated such enormous functions to him. The Senate of the republic paid a final public homage to him as a man whose place in history was that of 'apostle of Colombian civilization in the regions of the Caquetá and the Putumayo'.[16]

Fray de Montclar's death marked the end of an era: the time of the first transformations to take place along the Upper Putumayo. It is worth making a brief summing-up of the work achieved in the twenty-two years of de Montclar's reign as quasi-absolute lord of the fate of the area.

(1) As regards 'civilizing activity', two points stand out:

(a) The transformation in the racial balance which took place in the Apostolic Prefecture as can be seen from the statistics put out by the Capuchins:[17] in 1906 there were 32,600 Indians as compared with 2,200 settlers; by 1933 there were only 13,997 Indians as against 21,587 settlers. These figures give an overwhelming indication of how the aboriginal race was reduced during those years. The major causes of this were extortion by the whites, together with genocide, contagious illnesses brought from Europe, slavery, flight into the forests and suicides.

(b) The opening of the road from the east, and the various colonizing thrusts which are still going on.

(2) From the political point of view, the Mission had contributed to consolidating the national sovereignty of Colombia in Amazonia — a sovereignty which had until the 1920s been seriously threatened by Peru.

(3) In the area of education and evangelization, several thou-

sands of Indians and Creoles became fully literate, and far more were converted to Christianity.*

(4) As to the development of the Mission itself, the transformation here was effected on three levels:

(a) From being poor heralds of the gospel, the Friars Minor had become owners of *haciendas*, with cattle, crops, industrial operations and establishments for skilled artisans and building workers of all kinds – in brief, the foundation of a solid and stable ecclesiastical estate.

(b) Fray Fidel de Montclar left well established the political and administrative structures necessary for a further development of the Mission. A large part of those structures related to policies for and administration of native and agricultural matters, structures from whose consequences the Indians, especially those who once owned the Sibundoy valley, are still suffering. In short, the plans the Great Crusader had brought with him to Colombia were achieved almost to the letter.

(c) On the other hand, the former inhabitants of this 'heavily populated valley' had lost most of their land and their traditions (and consequently their reason for living) under the avalanche of western influence; so much so that, according to Fray Jacinto de Quito,[18] even the legend of Our Lord of Sibundoy has been touched up to make it a bit more Christian; it does not now recount that marvellous act of submission by Christ to the Indians, but instead tells of a punishment coming from heaven to strike a tribe capable of such sacrilege: 'Before they struck Our Lord', Miguel Juajibioy told me, 'the people of Sibundoy village spoke the same language as those of Santiago and San Andrés, which is Quechua; but as a punishment for the sacrilege they committed against his divine person, the Lord

*Here Fray Francisco de Igualada gives us the following figures:

	1906	1930
Schools	11	62
Pupils of both sexes	493	2,602
Baptisms	245	1,330
Marriages	125	223
Communions	9,600	84,979

took away from them the language of rational men, and gave them that of pigs . . .'*

It only remains to note that the highest authorities in the Church did not delay in recognizing the splendid apostolic work achieved by Fray Fidel de Montclar. On 31 May 1930 Pope Pius XI raised the Apostolic Prefecture to the rank of a Vicariate, at the head of which he appointed Fray Gaspar Monconill de Pinell, who had up to then been the local Capuchin Superior, as Vicar Apostolic.

*The Inga call the language spoken by their neighbours the Sibundoy *coche*, which comes from the Quechua word *cuchi*, meaning pig. This seems to date back to the old Sibundoy custom of raising pigs in common on the swamplands in the centre of the valley.

PART THREE

A State within a State (1930–70)

CHAPTER 14

The 'Agrarian Reform' of the Capuchins

If they refused to work on the Mission farm, then off to the *cepo*! ... If they refused to marry when they were supposed to, then off to the *cepo* without more ado!

(BENJAMIN CAIPE, settler, 1969)

I weep in my heart. I am poor, though I do not know why, for the Mission has taken everything from me and thrown me out into the street. I weep in my heart.

(SALVADOR CHINDOY DE MERCEDES, 1970)

The creation of the new Vicariate coincided with that crucial moment in Colombian history when, for the first time, a member of the liberal party became head of government, thus bringing to an end a conservative hegemony which had continued uninterrupted for almost fifty years. A series of reforms directed to modernizing the interior of the country was to follow this event – at least as regarded 'civilized' society.

For the missionaries, on the other hand, Fray Fidel's fears proved unfounded. In fact the rule of his successor, Fray Gaspar, whose appointment was only announced after the victory of the liberal candidate, began very hopefully indeed. The new president, 'who had always counted him among his closest friends', agreed to stand as his sponsor at his episcopal consecration.

In his first pastoral letter, given that same day, the new prelate included several passages in which he defined his native policy.[1] He began by noting the need to develop the Christian spirit 'so that all our faithful may be able to satisfy their hunger and thirst for supernatural justice, thanks to the good shepherds who work hard to administer to them the divine food of God's word . . .'

He goes on to stress the need for white colonization, whereby 'the natives have learnt by example how to work honestly, and at the same time to replace their ridiculous and brutalizing customs with Christian and civilized ways'. Finally, Fray de Pinell makes clear that public education must be developed in order to educate 'Christians strong in faith, and firm patriots', in accord with the Holy Spirit's advice: 'Hast thou children? Instruct them, and bow down their neck from their childhood' (Ecclesiastes, vii, 23).

Such were the traditional standards of the Capuchins, and Gaspar de Pinell was to direct all his activities towards their achievement thoughout the whole of his life as Vicar Apostolic. We may try to reconstruct that period clearly, using both the official archives which go on getting more detailed and better organized, and the evidence of a number of those involved who are still alive today.

Colonel Amadeo Rodríguez, a Catholic and a conservative, who was at that time the officer-in-command of the southern frontiers, provides us with a first impression of the way in which Fray Gaspar exercised his authority over the natives, and forced the local officials to grant him certain privileges. In a confidential letter to the Minister of Industry in June 1932 the Colonel complains of 'the appalling persecution by that Mission which calls itself Christian . . .' To support this letter, he gives an account of an interview he has had with the new head of the Mission, of which the following paragraph is an extract:

We were discussing the Jacanamijoy Indians, who had left Mocoa to settle beside the river Yurayacu. The Bishop declared that those Indians should not have left the place where they had been living in a settlement with the benefit of religious education, and that they should return to Mocoa, even if it meant leaving their homes and selling their plantations and canoes. He added that these Indians had defied his rightful authority because the national government, by earlier laws and decrees, had decided that they must not leave the place where they were living but should remain in the areas assigned to them by the Mission.

Colonel Rodríguez explains why the civil authority was giving its support to the Jacanamijoy:

(1) The Jacanamijoy alleged that they had left Mocoa in order to be left in peace, and that the priests of the Mission made them work without payment, doing domestic chores, and clearing their private paths and gardens, without any form of remuneration, and forced the women to do the same hard work as the men.

(2) When Apolinar Jacanamijoy went to visit members of his family still living in Mocoa, Fray Bartolomé had him put in the *cepo* for eight days, as a punishment for crimes he had not committed; and then, to keep him there and prevent his leaving the group, he married him to an Indian woman he did not even know.

Having given his evidence for these statements, and also reported that when the Indian governor refused to carry out the punishments ordered by the friar who was president of the chapter he was himself subjected to those same punishments, the Colonel closed his report with these words:

The officer-in-command pointed out to His Lordship the Bishop that the larger part of the natives can read and write, that a number of them have given up wearing the *cusma*, and that a great many use their right to vote – in other words they may be considered full Colombian citizens (in some areas at least, if not in all). To which the Bishop replied that none of this was relevant, since the law considered them as having the status of minors as long as they were under the authority of the Mission. The Bishop concluded by saying that though he had no wish to break off relations, if the officer-in-command persisted in protecting and favouring the Indians, then relations would automatically cease.[2]

This dispute between the military and religious authorities did not however develop, because an armed confrontation with Peruvian forces intervened, forcing the two to collaborate. And though Law No. 5 in 1931 had declared the use of the *cepo* 'abolished once for all' all over the country, the missionaries informed the minor local authorities that 'serious consequences would result from its abandonment', since 'there were no prisons for criminals to be shut up in and, as none of the houses had locks, none could be improvised'. Thus, the law notwithstanding, the Capuchins were to retain their 'power to punish'.

People now living in the Sibundoy valley have provided details on this point. The native Juan Manuel Chindoy has provided us with a drawing of the instrument used: real criminals were held by the neck in the central hole, whereas minor delinquents were held in the other holes by the legs only. According to the same informant, Indians guilty of fighting were considered by the tribes to be 'real criminals', and offenders would be put in the *cepo* for a period of time proportionate to the offence. On being freed, they would receive two strokes of the whip from the offended party to remind them not to do it again.[3]

One white informant, the settler Benjamín Caipe, gives us the following indication of the offences considered as most serious by the Mission: 'The natives had to provide the monastery with wood for fuel, otherwise off to the *cepo*! They had to work on its farms, otherwise off to the *cepo*! If they didn't pay their first-fruits (eighty *paires* [about 200 kilos] of maize), then off to the *cepo*! If they didn't marry when they were supposed to, then off to the *cepo* without more ado!'

It is noteworthy that in the last-mentioned instance the punishment followed a certain ritual pattern, as described by the Indian Salvador Mavisoy when he was *alguacil*:

In those days the whip was certainly no light matter. No, indeed it was not. Those accused of sleeping together without being married were both brought before the Chapter. The man was put in the *cepo*, and, if he agreed to marry, well then, he was freed, and they were married. But if he refused, he would be given thirty strokes of the whip at five in the morning and then put back in the *cepo*. The next day he got another thirty strokes. And so it went on until he agreed. Yes, indeed, there was far too much whipping, far too much indeed.[3]

At the risk of over-stressing this point, I must mention one fact not hitherto reported which proves – if proof were still needed – that the Capuchins were those who stood to gain most from the 'power to punish': the use of the *cepo* had long been carried over into their schools, providing them with just one more means of subduing even quite young children. Sibundoy now aged over thirty-five number this among their childhood memories.

The missionaries were quite mistaken in their apprehensions about the liberal government. The Vicar Apostolic and the Mission retained all their privileges; the Council of the Missions continued to receive yearly payments from public funds; and the government was quite ready to leave conservative officials in place throughout the territory. However, as in the past, criticism of the Catalan fathers still continued sporadically to blacken the national press, each time to be refuted. Though these episodes are largely forgotten now, they do still indicate how little the arguments used by the missionaries to defend themselves have altered over the years. For instance in 1933 a native delegation visited Bogotá, which led to the appearance of a series of articles and reports about the valley. The missionaries had to step in with a categorical and total denial of all the journalists' assertions about their 'vast landed estates', on the ground that 'these belonged not to the Capuchins but to the Apostolic Vicariate', and had been established only in order to provide the Indians with the land they needed. Again, when accused of having done nothing to contribute to the nation's defence against Peru, they were indignant; and they refused to provide any explanation of how they had made use of State funds, giving as their reason an opinion put forward twenty-five years before by a revenue official.[4]

But these were the merest flea-bites, causing barely a ripple on the calm surface of the tranquillity in which the liberal régime left the Capuchins; and they were able to go on quietly getting title deeds to more and more of the land in the Sibundoy valley.

It will be recalled that when the conservatives were in power they refused, for juridical reasons, to grant the Church the land of the *Cofradías*. They could hardly openly violate their own law whereby 'the unused lands on which the natives lived belonged to them', and the greater part of the 'Mission lands' in fact came under this head. The fathers were left with no other solution than those advised by their lawyer: to drive off the Indians wherever possible, or to get them to sign 'rent contracts' as worked out by Fidel de Montclar, or, finally, 'to give up those lands to the Indians while making them pay for improvements made there'.[5] What was involved was a redistribution of the land, affecting the greater part of the Indian population, but in precisely the opposite direction to that envisaged by Fray Fidel: instead of establishing the Inga and Sibundoy within the bounds of the 'Mission lands', they must be moved out. According to Fray Bartolomé de Igualada, this new plan began to be put into effect in the same year as the Vicar Apostolic's 'close friend' became President of the republic. During the next ten years the Putumayo Mission was to become a kind of land agency, generally using the same means used by colonizers in similar situations: everything from highly advantageous contracts of sale to usurpation pure and simple. It was in fact the final attack on the last few possessions of the Indians.

We may remember how the intensive legal actions to defend their inheritance brought twenty years earlier by the Inga had put a stop to the territorial expansion of the Capuchins in the area around the village of Santiago. This did not however prevent the *Cofradía* of Carmen from quadrupling its size to the cost of the less powerful natives; those who were more powerful, led by Francisco Tisoy and his son Diego, continued obstinately to defend themselves, and even succeeded in increasing their estates, at the cost of the poorer settlers and their own fellow-Indians, to whom they thus 'gave a bad example'.

For that reason, Benjamín Caipe tells us,

the parish priest put Francisco Tisoy in the *cepo* one day. But the old man at once appealed by letter to the President of the Republic, and the *Corregidor* received a telegram from the capital reminding him that the contract agreed between the Church and the Mission was intended to assist in the subjection of savages, and not in maltreating people living in a perfectly civilized way a stone's throw from Pasto. The following Sunday the priest summoned Francisco Tisoy and said to him: 'Don't worry, *Taita** Francisco, you'll still live many years, and this business of the *cepo* was really just a little joke' . . .[3]

However, such instances of self-defence were the exception. The Santiago Inga, for the most part, found themselves reduced to owning only tiny pieces of land, and condemned to become *peones* on the large estates of the whites, or else to depart, in ever-increasing numbers, to peddle Indian medicines and magical cures – for which they have become famous not merely in Colombia, but also in Venezuela, Ecuador and even further afield.

The other Inga, those from San Andrés, were still less fortunate. Less clever and less educated, they had accepted the missionaries as guardians of their communal lands. Father Lino Rampón tells us what happened in their village when Bartolomé de Igualada became its parish priest: he immediately got his parishioners to sign 'rent contracts' (drawn up by himself) for the land on which they lived, as though that land belonged not to them but to the Church.

But one day the Indians who had signed the rent contracts began selling their land to the whites. Then Fray Bartolomé, deciding that it was pointless to let out land if the Indians were going to sell it, said: 'Let your land to the Church, and it will help you to educate your children; we will get Missionary Sisters from Mother Laura, and provide them with a church and a house.'[5]

This notion, Fray Bartolomé tells us, came from the more intelligent among the Indians, who realized that that was where their own best interests lay.

But the Indians saw things somewhat differently:

I remember the affair very well [declares Diego Mavisoy, the pre-

---

*Taita is a familiar form of address to elderly people, meaning 'Father' or 'Papa', but without indicating any blood relationship.

sent governor of the place]; it happened when the late Fray Gaspar Monconill was Bishop. He came here one day to question all the inhabitants. We gathered everyone together down there in the centre of the village. We were asked whether we would agree to give up our land of our own free will, for the good of the village. So people said, 'Fine, we'll give it up.' But in return, Fray Bartolomé would be obliged to give each one of us a pair of animals of some kind from elsewhere: chickens, pigs, calves. . . . Do you follow me? We finally *saw* a few hens, but nobody actually received anything. . . . And the documents were already completed and signed! No claims could be made.[3]

On the other hand, a very few villagers say they did receive sums up to forty pesos in return for their pieces of land. And a few others, such as Salvador Mojomboy, still continue to hope that they will get something: 'I am still waiting for a heifer which Fray Bartolomé promised me in return for my land.'

So the final *Cofradía* of the Sibundoy valley was formed in the little village of San Andrés. Once again having received the consent of his parishioners with no great difficulty, Fray de Igualada set about unfencing and clearing the gardens of the Indians, turning them into pastureland, apart from a few hectares of swampland alongside the river, upon which he tried to establish a native cooperative. But this modest attempt to cope with the unemployment created by this brutal theft of the Inga's lands was not to last long: the excessive moisture of the land, combined with deaths from an epidemic of dysentery in 1934 and 1935, soon made it no more than a memory. The missionaries, to give their subjects work, then got some of them to sign 'rent contracts', which they described as 'free'. These documents, which can still be seen, contain clauses identical with the first farm-rent contracts worked out by Fray de Montclar, as is clear from this paragraph taken from a contract signed on 25 March 1935:

Art. 2: The farm rent contract is to be valid for a period of seven years from the date of the signature of this document, and to be renewable by tacit continuation of tenancy. Nicolás Mojomboy, son of Bárbara Mojomboy, binds himself to cultivate the existing crops, to fence them in to secure their protection, to keep them in good condition, all at his own cost, and, if he builds a dwelling, to hand it over with the rest to the ownership of the Church; to contribute to the construction and repairing of the fences between the Church lands and the land of individuals; being careful to keep clean and well-tended the land he receives for farm-rent, when this contract expires, without being allowed to sub-let it. Since the improvements he may make provide the basis for working out the annual payment, fixed at a sum of fifteen pesos, and since this land is already under cultivation, he has no right over those improvements, and freely hands them over forthwith. . . . The contracting party binds itself to pay a sum of thirty gold pesos to guarantee the fulfilment of this contract . . .[6]

Passing over the fact that the signatures of the contracting party and the witnesses to this document are curiously similar – in handwriting, ink, and pen – to that of Fray Florentino de Barcelona, whose signature figures on behalf of the church; passing over, too, the fact that to rent out unused lands (*baldíos*) is in itself illegal; it still remains that these farm-rent contracts were far from being as 'free' as the Fathers claimed. One may even say they were extremely costly to the wretched farmer, since he had to hand over to the church whatever improvements he had made to his land during the seven, fourteen, twenty-one or even more years during which he worked on it: this can only be called legalized slavery.

The Putumayo Capuchins took an animated stand against this kind of interpretation, and through Fray Francisco de Igualada they defended themselves thus:

Starting from a position which could well be better informed and less fanatical, people have accused the Mission of giving back to the Indians land that is completely uncultivated, and then demanding that they hand it back in good condition. Nothing could be further from the truth: from the fact that the state in which the land is let out is not mentioned in a single document, one may deduce either forgetfulness arising from a lack of practice in the formulation of such deeds (and we missionaries are after all not specialists in civil law), or what one likes; but it is not logical to deduce that if something is not mentioned in a document drawn up by non-specialists it does not therefore exist at all.[7]

The only comment to be made on this particular argument is that, by their own admission, the missionaries had always had the legal assistance of qualified lawyers.

This 'agrarian reform' by the Capuchins was of enormous importance to the Sibundoy area, both because it affected all the members of the largest tribe in the valley, and because it was to lead to the fullest official inquiry ever undertaken into the abuses they had suffered.

Pressure from the white man on the former owners of the valley was such that in 1934 the Chapter of the tribe sent the government a petition asking for official recognition of their ownership of the eighteen hectares which constituted Sibundoy Grande, 'to prevent the whites from despoiling us of the said land which we have occupied from time immemorial; if they did so we should be forced to leave and go elsewhere, grieved at having to leave our little homeland'.[8]

It was at this critical moment that Fray Andrés de Cardona, parish priest of the village, reappeared on the scene. This priest, also a great huntsman, had gained a certain notoriety by having recovered the payment he was owed for masses with the help of the police, whom he had actually got to fire on the Indians. He set about the reorganization of the *Cofradías* of the Blessed Virgin, planning to settle the Indians he wanted to move out in the swamplands and mountains where the climate was insupportable and the soil useless. But he counted without the watchfulness of the white settlers, who also wanted the land. They denounced him to the authorities, accusing him of trying to settle Indians there 'on the pretext that the national government has granted all the unused lands [*baldíos*] of the Sibundoy to the missionaries'.[9] And the civil governor of the Putumayo upheld their claim in these terms:

I must, though it goes against the grain, admit that the Mission is at the root of these disturbances, solely, as far as I can see, because of its anxiety to prevent the white settlers having the unused lands; this is its nightmare, for it is fully aware that by keeping the natives the government's ideal – that of white colonization – will never be achieved, since the native is quite happy to occupy himself with no more than a hectare of land which will provide the maize he needs for his own yearly consumption.*[10]

From another point of view, Fray Marceliano de Vilafranca, spokesman for the Capuchin community, makes this comment:

The Reverend Fray Cardona then began to ascend the Calvary on which he was to die crucified. Since this step put a stop to the ambitions of certain whites, objections rose loudly against this Father, accusing him of wanting to take possession of everything for himself, of being a foreigner come to steal the goods of Colombian citizens, etc. A lot of ignorant people were added to the ranks of his persecutors, prepared to fight in what they believed to be a holy war for the poor Colombians, against a foreign invasion.[11]

The initiators of this 'holy war' were the settlers Manuel Silva and Benjamín Caipe, who, with the advice of Diego Tisoy, managed to persuade some of the Sibundoy that they must actually go to law against the missionaries. One of them, Salvador, from the Mavisoy clan, who still recalls the whole affair, has explained recently the methods used by the missionaries to 'round off' their lands:

The late Fray Andrés, who was our parish priest and our friend, had lent us a small piece of ground which we farmed, on the edge of the *Cofradía*. But animals from the Mission kept destroying our crops. So he called us and said: 'It is certainly our animals which have caused this destruction. So we will settle you somewhere else, on a piece of empty land where you can farm in peace.' And certainly he did resettle us. Years later, Fray Andrés died, and Fray Pascual de Castellar succeeded him. And he came to inform us that he had found papers proving that the ground we were farming was not *baldío*, as Fray Andrés had said, but had been bought by the Mission from Ventura Chindoy, for forty *patacones* (ounces of

*In other words, for this official, as for so many others, there was no call for the State to protect the Indians since the government's 'ideal' was something very different. But later on he contradicts himself. Though he denies that the Indians have any interest in agriculture (despite their having once been the only people who farmed in the valley) and forgets their position as tiny landowners, he stresses the high degree of education and skill of their leaders when it comes to defending their tribal lands, 'lawbook in hand'.

silver). But we had now been settled there for ten years; we had plantations on it, and had five houses there.

And he had us summoned by the governor, who was our uncle, Cipriano Jacanamijoy, and through his intervention made us sign a contract of loan. We replied that it was not fair to ask us to recognize this land as being 'loaned' to us after so long a time. But our governor-uncle told us to sign it to save trouble. And we signed it. But we then grew more and more convinced that it was not right, especially when a brother of that same governor began a lawsuit against the missionaries because he refused to sign, and demanded instead that the government recognize his ownership of his piece of land. Then a friend came and said to us: 'Why did you sign to say that it was a loan when it was a piece of unused land? What you did was wrong. You too should ask the government to reconsider the case.' So we asked for a judgment to be given in our favour, because we signed at the demand of the governor and the *alguaciles*. For doing this they tried to say we had perjured ourselves. We went to Pasto to defend ourselves, and since the whole thing was so recent, we could prove it all. And we got a lawyer to defend our land. The case lasted for four years. When we had won in Pasto they took the case on to the Council of State, while Fray Marceliano de Vilafranca got us to sign one agreement after another . . . until at last he won — or, rather, came to own us! For while the case was dragging on before the Council of State, we were forced to buy back our own land. That is how the whole thing happened.[3]

These first Sibundoy plaintiffs set an example to others. Some objected because the Capuchins had paid for their land with the meat of dead animals, and others, following the example of the first group, went to law against Fray Andrés and his successor. It was rich ground indeed for lawsuits, in which the Indians 'suffered more than anyone else'. For in fact various unsuccessful lawyers from the Nariño saw defending the Indians' land rights as a quick way of dispossessing them: 'The system used to get rid of the Indians', reports the Special Commissioner, 'was to egg them on to bring a case against the Capuchins, with or without good cause, for whatever happened the Indian would soon be forced to sell what little he had to pay the fees of the charlatan who had urged him to appeal.'[12]

However, the missionaries and the State official reached

different conclusions on this matter: whereas the official ordered the setting up of a new *resguardo*, the priests saw that as a thoroughgoing liberal anti-Capuchin conspiracy. And so sure of this were they that Fray Marceliano de Vilafranca described it as 'well conceived, because they carefully chose the natives with the best flocks of hens, thus enabling them to provide the kitchens of all the small lawyers in the valley with eggs'.[13] To prevent the bad example of the Mavisoys from being followed by all the other clans, the Vicar Apostolic sent a stern pastoral letter about 'the ease, the thoughtlessness or the malice with which some of our sons have let themselves slip into the crime of perjury'.[14]

It is worth pausing for a moment to study Eduardo Canyes, better known as Fray Marceliano de Vilafranca, whose career in the Church has left its mark wherever he displayed his talents. He came of a convinced Catholic family (five brothers became priests) and his life passed peacefully in Barcelona until the Franco uprising of 1936. Appalled by the 'red tidal wave' which submerged the town, and still more by being called to join the army, his brother Father Marcos says that thenceforth he had but a single wish – to desert: an understandable attitude if one recalls the treatment to which ecclesiastics were subjected when caught fighting on the side of the rebels. Both brothers therefore tried to get passports from the Spanish authorities, and when these were refused, Marcos planned the following stratagem:

. . . Fray Marcos de Castellví (that is myself), as Director of the College of Theology of Sarria, signed a declaration to the effect that the two Brothers Prats Gómez were Colombian nationals, and that they had lost their identity papers in the fire at the Sarria Monastery. Though he knew quite well who we were, the secretary of the order of lawyers in Barcelona countersigned the statement.*

*This extract comes from an unpublished manuscript, the 'Tragedy of the Canyes Family and the Flight of Frays Marcos and Marceliano', dated 29 December 1936, written by Fray Marcos de Castellví in Catalan and translated into Spanish by Ramón Lombera Gómez. The original is still in Fray Marceliano's house in Bogotá. (A photocopy is in the possession of the author.)

With this document in hand, the brothers presented themselves to the Colombian consul in Barcelona, having darkened their hands and faces with an iodine solution 'to make ourselves look more American'; and so successful were they that they actually managed to be 'repatriated' at the expense of the Colombian government. 'We went in Spaniards, and came out Colombians, as though by magic,' notes Fray Marcos; to which he adds that as soon as they arrived in Colombia he and his brother '*ipso facto* dropped their Colombian nationality without breathing a word of the story to anyone'. However there can be no doubt that the fact of having abandoned their nearest and dearest preyed on their consciences – to such a point that they developed a genuine hatred for the Spanish republicans, a hatred which was to be shown in the Vicariate Apostolic of Fray Gaspar to which they became attached at the end of 1936.

Discreetly spread in pro-Capuchin circles, the adventure of Fray Marceliano rapidly took on a tinge of heroism. Instead of merely a recruit, he became a hardy fighter of the Falange – a story he never denied. Thus was born the legend of his having taken part in some of the greatest battles against the republican forces, which obliged the stronger-minded of the inhabitants of the Sibundoy valley to take up a position on matters as far removed from their lives as the differences between Franco's party and republican Spain. The whole story became so fixed in their minds that the settlers ended by describing Fray Marceliano in such terms as 'the monk who, swallowing all shame, fought alongside Mahomedan Moroccans against the forces of the republic'.[15] His reputation as a warrior was so great that he was nicknamed 'Fray Manga' (Brother Strongarm) – a name still used of him in the valley. Such was the situation when, in March 1938, Fray de Vilafranca was appointed parish priest of Sibundoy.

The Capuchins' programme of agrarian reform had now reached an impasse. The first problem was the legal protection obtained by the Mavisoy clan, which seemed to carry the risk of leading to other equally troublesome situations; another was that the government had just been so bold as to appoint as

head of the civil administration of the territory a liberal commissioner, thus for the very first time breaking with a long
tradition of conservative officials. This was all the more serious
in that the new commissioner, from the very first, set himself
apart from the religious administration: he began by refusing
to be officially installed as ruler of the capital of the Vicariate,
so as to avoid having to take part in the religious ceremonies
which were normally involved; he went on, outraged by the
activities denounced by Diego Tisoy, to burn the Santiago *cepo*
in the public square.[16]

Fray Marceliano himself throws some light on the first
element of this impasse:

The Reverend Father Pascual – the successor of Fray Andrés –
had, as I have said, given part of the land over to the ownership of
the Indians; others, upon which a band of thieving Indians had
settled, remained in a farm-rent situation, and the Mission could not
get rid of them, not having the needful stamped paper provided for
doing so by the government . . .

It became more and more difficult to get judgments of ownership
given. . . . However a map of La Granja, an area where few Indians
were settled, was made, as well as of San Pedro, San Félix and El
Sauce, where there were still a good number of Indians.[17]

With the 'Mission lands' thus clearly marked out, Fray de
Vilafranca set about getting 'judgments' – in other words, getting rid of the Sibundoy settled there, around the marshy
centre of the valley, on land formally divided up and sold to
them by him.* And, to prevent those Indians without any
money from leaving the area, he once again asked the government to consider establishing a *resguardo* on the wooded and
chilly hills north of Sibundoy.

The energy with which Brother Strong-arm set to work was
not very popular. The 'thieving natives' began once again to
utter complaints, and, with the support of José Pajajoy, they

*It would seem that prices varied. Some Indians say they bought areas
of swampland at ten gold pesos per hectare; according to Fray Bartolomé
de Igualada, the scale was twenty-five pesos; and there are contracts still
in existence referring to a rate of seventy-five pesos.

appealed to the State against the Capuchins, accusing them of selling to whites fertile lands not shown as theirs on the map. Among those thus favoured they mentioned 'the Mission's lawyer, to whom they made a present of some fifteen hectares taken from the natives who were the legal owners', the Indian woman Andrea and her brother Matumbajoy. Whereupon the settler Benjamín Caipe spoke in support of their action, demanding that the State send an investigator to deal with the question of land ownership on the spot, and also to make certain the *cepo* was abolished once and for all. For, according to Fray Marcos de Castellví's personal evidence, this instrument of chastisement was still being used in the villages of San Andrés and Sibundoy, with all the old ritual trimmings:

Today, 23 January 1939, I went to the residence of the governor of San Andrés. . . . The *cepo* was once again covered in flowers, having recently been brought there from the house of the previous governor. It was further adorned with a wooden cross, with a whip hanging from it, and a lighted candle at the bottom.[18]

This piece of evidence is the most recent we have of the survival of this feudal custom. For as soon as the missionaries learnt of the government's decision to send an investigator, they hurried to dispose of all *cepos* for adults. As to the one designed for children, it is said on good authority that it was buried secretly, under cover of darkness, under the floor of the seminary being built at the time.[3]

The government investigator arrived among the Sibundoy in June 1939: he was Adolfo Romero, a lawyer, and his official mandate was to look into the legality of the constitution of the new *resguardo* demanded by the local officials, both native and Capuchin. But his report extended beyond this rather narrow limit:

When the farm-rent contracts come to an end the Mission almost never needs to apply to the authorities to get rid of the contracting parties, since they leave of their own accord; the subjection of the Sibundoy natives is so complete that they would not dream of showing the slightest resistance. Once a farm is abandoned, it soon becomes pastureland for the Mission. According to Fray Marceliano de Vilafranca's own admission, there are something approaching a hundred such farm-rent contracts. But it appears from a great many private sources of information I have been in contact with, that virtually the entire native population of Sibundoy are in a situation of bondage to the Mission through contracts of this kind – contracts which violate principles sanctioned in all land legislation, and most especially those relating to the ban on unnecessary enrichment.[19]

Furthermore, he denounces the disadvantages of keeping public education in the hands of foreigners, arguing, amongst other reasons, that he himself had seen 'with patriotic distress, a Colombian schoolmaster, instead of teaching children about the virtues and heroic bravery of our own great men, occupied in exalting the figure of Francisco Franco'.

The publication of this report produced the greatest newspaper scandal ever to touch the Putumayo mission.[20] As one might have expected, the Apostolic Vicariate produced one denial after another.[21] Ultimately the government found itself forced to respond by publishing two decrees.[22] In the first, it established the 'upper *resguardo*', containing 6,445 hectares of uncultivated mountain land, of which 400 were 'yielded up' by Fray Marceliano 'on condition that he retain his title of permanent president of the Sibundoy area'. In the second, a 'national reserve' of some 5,000 hectares was set up in the centre of the valley. But these two measures were never put into effect: the hostile climate of the mountains – even apart from the Sibundoy's attachment to their valley – made the large majority of them cling desperately to the tiny pieces of land sold or rented to them by the Mission, thus making them what one might call *microfundiarios*. On the other hand the 'reserve' remained as before, occupied partly by Capuchins, partly by settlers and partly by Indians, until even the government finally forgot what it had itself decreed in the matter.*

*The subordination of local functionaries to the authority of the clergy dated from the first outlining of the *resguardo*. What in fact happened was that the engineer whose job was to make the plans, before sending his report to the government, sent 'Brother Strong-arm' a letter in which,

This storm over, Fray de Vilafranca concluded that 'as long as there are natives within our lands, the battle will continue indefinitely'. So he decided to sell to a few of the more recalcitrant of them (such as the Mavisoy) the pieces of land which they refused to let him have. In exchange for this, he dealt with the less forceful of them in a single sweep:

> In September 1939 [wrote Benjamín Caipe to the Minister of the Economy] the missionaries brought along the judge, the secretary and the treasurer. At the same time, they told the Indians that they must come to mass, bringing all they could afford for the collection, to say special prayers in view of the fact that there seemed likely to be an invasion of insects very soon which would eat all the crops. The obedient natives brought their pennies, and Fray Marceliano ordered the Indian governor, Juan Chindoy, and the *alguaciles* to take them all to the seminary to sign the papers he had waiting there prepared, for the sale, or rent, to them of supposed improvements made by the Church.[23]

That there should be no doubt as to the willingness of the Indians, the Capuchins quoted witnesses like this, from Ramón Juajibioy:

> As soon as we had a permanent school, our children went there, and just like their parents, they complained, 'The Mission has kept my land, the Mission has kept my land.'
> But it was not the Fathers who took our lands. It was our own fault . . .
> In my case, for instance, the Mission told me: if you wish, we will make an exchange, and we will give you more than you now have. I saw that in fact they were giving me more, so I said, 'All right Father, I accept the exchange.' The matter was settled. I gave them a

---

having assured him of 'his most respectful homage and admiration, gratitude and support', he added: 'I beg to solicit Your Reverence respectfully for your valuable and effective cooperation on this occasion. I am trying to present to the Commissioner General of the Putumayo a total report dealing with the work I have done in this matter, to which I have given special care and attention. . . . It is my wish that the contents of that report be totally in accord with Your Reverence's views, and for that reason would be highly grateful if you would assist me in working it out.' (M.G. Archives, 1939.)

piece of land left me by my ancestors, and received three times as much, which I still have today. True, it is lower-lying and swampy, but it was my own choice.[24]

From his point of view, Fray Marceliano justified the sums extorted from the docile natives in exchange for scraps of swampland in a manner which complements the evidence just quoted:

While it is true that we fixed a price for the land we gave them, it must also be pointed out that it was a modest one, and that they were given a year in which to pay it. The Mission was free to sell or give the land, for it belonged to us. We should have liked to offer it to the Indians for nothing; but we thought that it would have been imprudent to have done so, since those people of ill will who had had no hesitation in labelling us thieves and cheats would then have been quick to see it as simple restitution.[25]

Finally, to get rid of the final recalcitrant few, Fray de Vil-afranca used his influence over the minor local functionaries. One letter sent by a group of Indians to the national Senate contains some interesting points in this connection:

They can act with impunity, alleging that they have been given the legal authority to act as police over us all. Once a Capuchin has spoken, the official names a fine and we must either pay it or go to prison. For these officials have the bad habit, from the day of their appointment, of running to the Capuchin monastery full of pro-testations of cooperation, and drinking themselves sick there.[26]

In another letter to a minister Benjamín Caipe speaks of 'the devilments of Fray Manga, the Falangist':

It is appalling to realize that we are still afraid of men whom our ancestors defeated in all the battles for independence! You should just hear this Father shout – and he has a fine loud voice – 'There can be no question of the liberals coming here to order us about. Here it is the Church that gives the orders!' And he comes into the local government offices, clashing his spurs and waving his whip, without a soul's daring to put him in his place.[27]

Thus, by use of intimidation, this energetic Capuchin achieved his goal in three years: all the Indians were removed

from the 'Mission lands'. For thirty-five of them the most
extraordinary reasons were given – as, for instance, for Miguel
Chindoy, 'that his land had already earned him quite enough
profit', and for Juan Chicunque 'that he was living in concubinage',[28] and so on.

Caipe himself finally saw some of his own land fall into the
hands of his neighbours at the Mission. Still now, in 1970, he
recalls how on 28 September 1940 Fray Marceliano took advantage of his absence to effect a decree of expulsion against
him. At the head of a small band of *peones* and local officials,
the priest destroyed his house, took his wife (though 'suffering
from lung trouble') to prison, and left his invalid son lying in a
field; after which he left fifty calves loose among his plantations, which were later sprinkled with salt.[3]

Fray Marceliano himself has written the epilogue for his
work as a land reformer:

Finally there came from Bogotá the Act of 10 July 1916 which
recognized our ownership of La Granja. The area of the piece being
some 232 hectares, which together with 50 others previously
adjudged to us, the 27 hectares adjudged to the Marists and the land
bought back by the Mission provided the parish of Sibundoy with a
total of 309 hectares.[29]

On 1 October of that same year, the government similarly gave an
adjudication in our favour of the piece of land claimed by the Vicariate Apostolic which, as was said before, covers 886 hectares of pas-
ture and swampland.[30]

. . . To put a final stop to the suggestions of political manoeuvring
which have been made about these decisions, it is worth pointing
out that the act relating to La Granja was signed by a conservative
Minister, under the liberal administration of President Lleras Camargo (1946); while it was a liberal minister who signed the adjudication of the land for the Vicariate, under the conservative
government of President Ospina Pérez (1946).*

. . . Thus was concluded a matter which had been an object of
struggle for the Mission for over twenty years, and which had caused

*It was during that year that the liberal party, weary perhaps after
fifteen years in power, split and lost the elections to its traditional opponent.

our missionaries to suffer a lot, to make sacrifices, and to be mis-
understood, abused and calumniated by enemies of their religious
work. May God forgive all that wickedness, and accept all the
sufferings we have undergone for the good of this region as a
whole.[31]

These adjudications, to be completed in 1954 by further
governmental decisions recognizing the Mission's ownership of
the *Cofradías* of San Andrés and Santiago (212 hectares), en-
croached on the 'national reserve' established by that very
same government. But Fray Marceliano saw the problem in a
different light: what concerned him was that the State was still
only satisfying a minor fraction of the Church's territorial
demands. So he consequently proceeded with all speed to sell
all the lands of which he had not been granted ownership,
describing them as *baldíos*. The lucky beneficiaries of this
windfall were the members of some of the important families
of the interior, as well as one Swiss immigrant, who was
granted an estate of 500 hectares.

Hardly could there have been a more overt mockery of the
law, especially that part relating to the 'national reserve'. As
might have been expected, this further initiative on the part of
Fray de Vilafranca aroused one final wave of enraged protest
from the most underprivileged of all the valley's inhabitants.
Poor whites and Indians found themselves in the same leaking
boat: the first, because they could not even buy as much land
as they could afford, and the latter, because they were wit-
nessing the final disappearance of the last traces of their traditional patrimony which twenty years earlier even Fidel de
Montclar himself had not dared to touch. But all protests were
in vain.

The Capuchins' thirty years of fighting on the agrarian plane
thus closed with a final adjudication of their ownership of
1,407 hectares, to say nothing of the profits earned by farming
a large part of the valley while the battle was being fought, and
the sums earned by selling thousands of hectares. In comparison with the scale of the battle 1,407 may not seem a large
figure; but it is enormously important:

(1) For the Sibundoy, because the hundred or so tiny strips of land sold to them did not among them add up to even half the area granted to the Church;

(2) For the Mission, because in the eyes of the priests this official recognition of their establishment in the valley as land-owners constituted official approval of the rightness of the methods whereby they had carried out their evangelical work. That was why, as soon as the government's decision was made public, 'Brother Strong-arm' hastened to give a talk[32] to all his flocks, to make clear to them that 'those who declared that the government would never recognize the property of the priests had lost their bet!' This triumph was all the more glorious in that it was achieved under the liberal régime so execrated by the clergy.

No longer even able to abdicate freely, most of the Inga and Sibundoy were left with no option but simple submission. Well aware that there was no effective authority apart from that of the Mission, which was really a state within a state, they set themselves to draining the swampland which was all that was allowed to them. They did not even dare argue the principle whereby the missionaries were allowed to preside over the Indian Chapters, still less that whereby they could force the Indians to work every Monday for nothing on their *haciendas*. Fear of the supernatural supplemented what was lacking in fear of authority . . .

The missionaries were very skilled, when the need arose, at playing on this superstitious fear, as we see in the request presented by the old man Salvador Chindoy de Mercedes and his son in 1968 to the Minister of the Interior, for the return of an eight-hectare lot 'which Fray Marceliano de Vilafranca took from me by a trick, and without any payment, in 1942', wrote Salvador. Having described how he found himself 'thrown out into the highway', he added, 'I have spoken to Fray Marceliano several times about getting my land back, and the last time he replied, "If you continue with your demands, then instead of burying you in the cemetery when you die, we shall throw you into the swamps for the vultures to eat." And for fear of this, I have stopped demanding what is mine until now, because I really need it, having several sons but no land for them to work.'[83]

None of the other claims presented by Indians since 1960 have been considered: 'Too late', was the Capuchins' reply; 'the final date for making claims is past – though that did not prevent their continuing to declaim from the pulpit 'the obligation of making restitution of all ill-gotten goods . . .'[84] Evidently, then, the older Indians still smart from their wounds, but years of struggling have exhausted their will to fight. Or so at least it seemed to me at the beginning of 1970 when I visited the old man Salvador Chindoy de Mercedes, to find him repeating over and over the fact that the Vicar Apostolic 'doesn't dispense a very attractive kind of justice'. But inwardly his consciousness of painful injustice produces an incurable torment:

You might say that the Colombian is in the street while the foreigner is in his armchair. . . . Or, perhaps, that the foreigner came into the house to drive the master out. . . . That is why I weep in my heart. I am poor, though I do not know why, for the Mission has taken everything from me, and thrown me out into the street. I weep in my heart.*

*This fine old man today lives on a smallholding of three quarters of a hectare 'which the late Fray Bartolomé gave me to stop me from living by the roadside on public charity'. This is perhaps a good point to note the special style to be found in all these contemporary statements, especially those of Salvador Chindoy de Mercedes, Benjamin Caipe and Diego Mavisoy; it gives us as close an approximation as we can get to their actual tape recordings. It is a tone very different from what one finds in other 'quotations' from natives, because the latter are all taken from official documents.

CHAPTER 15

Belated Fruits of Roman Imperialism

Blessed be God, and blessed be Franco.
(*Amazonia*, the Capuchins' review, n. 1, 1940)

It emerges from the inquiries made by this embassy that over 100 Protestant churches and chapels and about 150 schools have been closed by violence.

(JOHN CABOT LODGE, US ambassador to Colombia, 1958)

Agrarian development was not the sole concern of all the members of the mission during Fray Gaspar Monconill de Pinell's apostolic administration. Some really longed for the day when they would be able to extend their evangelizing work to the whole of the area entrusted to them, an ambition hampered by lack of 'seraphic labourers'. They determined, therefore, to fill this lack by training native clergy on the spot.

Despite immense criticism, some of it actually from within the Church, the seminary of Sibundoy was begun. Fray Marcelino de Castellví was put in charge of teaching the few young men, white and Sibundoy, who were delighted by the chance thus offered them to extend their education beyond the minimum provided in the existing schools.

But the Indians do not seem to have felt a very strong vocation to evangelize; as soon as they felt sufficiently prepared to cope with the world outside, they left to fight for their future elsewhere. The most persevering among them was finally – twenty years later, and against major opposition from the Capuchins – to get a degree in anthropology.

Apart from this single success (of a somewhat unforeseen kind) the final balance sheet was not very encouraging to the

Capuchins: only one of their students, a Creole from the Nariño, actually reached major orders, and the one Sibundoy who emerged from the seminary opted to join another religious community as a lay brother.

The efforts of Fray Marcelino de Castellví, however, were not wholly in vain. He was a man of immense intellectual capacity and insatiable scientific curiosity, and these led him to set up a 'Centre for Linguistic and Ethnographical Research in Colombian Amazonia' (CILEAC) – an enterprise well worth saying something about, not only because it was the first and the greatest scientific undertaking by the Putumayo missionaries, but also for its repercussions on the world of anthropology.

The object of CILEAC's founder was to study the vast area entrusted to the Mission, applying to this a new method, consisting of studying it under the head of forty-five 'Colombian studies' which he himself defined and classified: 'Colombian hierology', 'Indo-Colombian glotology', 'Amazonian museography', ethnomorphic aesthetics', 'ethno-pharmacology', 'ethno-therapeutics', etc.[1] The work began with the collaboration of missionaries of both sexes, and also of seminarians, for whom the infectious enthusiasm of their leader amply compensated for their lack of scientific training. With them, and later on with the help of Indians and independent researchers, Fray Marcelino managed within a few years to get together the most interesting collection of anthropological and folk material gathered by the Catalan Capuchin Mission during its entire history; Fray de Castellví completed this work by producing a list of the various Indian languages used in Colombia, and certain other information, all of which he presented at the numerous scientific conferences in which he took part.*

*The international conferences at which Fray de Castellví represented Colombia are not easy to enumerate, but we know for instance that there were ten during the period between June 1948 and September 1949. According to some missionary sources, he would seem to have been a 'member of thirty-three scientific societies and academies all over the world, and in touch with some fifty-three others' – figures which Fray de Vilafranca reduces to twenty-one and thirty-nine respectively. The dis-

The most important single thing Fray de Castellví did in support of the Sibundoy culture was to change their name to *Kamsa* – a mistake in identification which, once imposed, deprived the tribe of its ancestral title.

We are also indebted to the CILEAC for the five numbers of the review *Amazonia colombiana americanista,* in which documents of considerable scientific interest are interspersed with exhaustive apologetic studies of the work of the Mission;* we also find mention of a 'bibliographical and classificatory file' whose content is estimated by the Capuchins themselves – depending on the situation – variously at between ten, fifty and up to a hundred thousand items.²

For the CILEAC has always remained an institution inaccessible to anyone who does not share the viewpoints of the Capuchin community. Thus when in 1945 the historian Juan Friede, who had just published *El Indio en lucha por la tierra,* tried to do some research there, he found himself denied access to the special material and even to the library because 'he had got hold of a book without the director's permission'.

He wrote to Fray de Castellví on this occasion:

Your Reverence's attitude has been guided by your lack of sympathy with the direction my work is taking; by your fear that it may eventually prove unfavourable to the Mission; and, above all, by my membership of the Colombian Native Institute, which you look on as a fictitious body created as a cover-up for 'communist' activities. . . . Though legally you have the right to close your doors to me, that right seems to me, to say the least, questionable from a moral point

---

crepancy does not appear to worry either the missionaries or the inhabitants of Sibundoy who venerated Fray Marcelino as a scholar and a saint.

*The first number of the review is wholly devoted to lauding the character of 'Monsignor Gaspar Monconill Viladot de Pinell, titular bishop of Cadosia and Vicar Apostolic of the Caquetá and Putumayo, on the occasion of the silver jubilee of his ordination'. It contains all the speeches, the praise from scholars, and the poems, as well as a photograph of the gold card presented him by the government, and a brief biography. The latter, be it noted, contains this invocation: 'Blessed be God, and blessed be Franco.'

of view, for the Mission, and *a fortiori* the CILEAC, which has already received most valuable assistance from the State, is economically supported both directly and indirectly by the government and people of Colombia.[3]

Such a policy of discrimination was bound to lead to difficulty in establishing any real bond between the missionaries and the world of anthropological studies. The Centre further suffered a serious blow with the death of its founder. The emotion resulting from this was tremendous in those national scientific circles where he was well known and they were loud in his praises. Here are some descriptive words from the Franciscan scholar Gustavo Huertas, which will give the reader some idea of the debt owed by science to Fray Marcelino de Castellví:

We shall not say that the unforgettable Capuchin scholar was indescribable, but we can say, without wishing to play to the gallery, that it is rare to have the privilege of meeting a character at once so happily and loftily endowed. ... With the original and rich intuition of a research as keen as it was thrilling, this young missionary plunged into his research with urgency and fervour, and soon realized that it would be necessary to launch a comprehensive voyage of exploration of Amazonia; the venture, which would take him across virgin territory and down unexplored avenues, captivated him from the start. This flight of genius led him to such exciting theses that he soon created his own original anthropological system which confirmed his imperishable reputation in the world. ... He christened it the 'Pan-anthropological Method', and described it as the 'maximal fertilization of the study of man, through the total coordination of the sciences – physical, natural, physiological and psychological – in convergence on three specialist studies: (1) an adequate racial study = panethnio-panthropology; (2) vocation = pancleseology; (3) work = panergology' [sic].

Further on, our commentator speaks in these terms of the enthusiasm about which Fray de Castellví set about his classifications:

When it came to concrete application, the scholar seemed as determinedly original as he was outstandingly careful, for when, discovering the inadequacy of the divisions and subdivisions in anthropology and its related sciences – already complex enough – he laid the bases and opened the way to the objectives which his method was seeking, with the incredibly bold and lucid creation of wholly new speculations. For instance, we have the unfolding flower of eclogotechnology (scientific synthesis derived from cleseology or the science of the personality): to define the purposes and characteristics of this discipline, the author chose as his paradigm the magnificent face of the Sovereign Pontiff.[4]

Fray de Castellví was a self-taught man, as his panegyrist stresses. And he concludes by mentioning his even more outstanding merit of having managed to get to know the whole of Amazonia better than anyone in the world without ever having left his monastery!

But the epilogue of this Capuchin scientific work was rather less glittering. On the basis of such incontestable proofs of the 'irremediable loss to Colombia' of the death of his brother, Fray Marceliano de Vilafranca, as the dead man's spiritual heir, demanded in 1951 that the government devote a section of the national budget to the support of the CILEAC, to be paid to him personally. This having been refused, he removed to his Vicariate the library, the archives and the collections of the CILEAC, which he divided into two sections: one was sent to Catalonia, and the other to the attic of his personal residence in Bogotá. Since then, sheltered from the gaze of the imprudent, and as the private property of 'Brother Strong-arm', the remains of the Scientific Institute of the Capuchins in Amazonia have lain permanently hidden.

We have no precise information about the situation of the Sibundoy natives during the last period of Fray Gaspar de Pinell's vicariate, since the publications of the Capuchins covering those years are purely apologetic in nature, and all government documents for that period have vanished. The only scrap of evidence we have to compensate for this is an article by the chaplain to the national police force, who visited the valley in 1945:

There exists a fine building in Sibundoy which the Capuchin fathers built to house a native seminary. However it stands empty today, because there are no longer any Indian students, and the very few sons of settlers who have shown a wish to take holy orders are now studying in the seminary of Yarumal. The cathedral is made of wood; there is also a boys' senior school, run by the Marist Brothers, and a girls' school administered by Capuchin Sisters. Though these two schools are also attended by settlers' children, there are periods during which Indian and white children have to be separated, to let the former talk in their own language and behave with greater freedom: for the presence of the whites makes them shy and withdrawn. All of them demonstrate a certain sense of depression . . .

The Sibundoy Indian lives in intense poverty, because he has neither the land nor the means to work. . . . They cultivate maize, that is all; they make *chicha*, and that is the only drink they have. This race, though still strong and indeed handsome, will ultimately destroy itself and vanish of its own accord; they have no doctors, no medicines, and though the Capuchin fathers have a dispensary, it does not seem to me to be of much use.

I greatly admired the Indians' piety: they kneel on both knees when they meet a priest, and are humble and obedient; they sing with artistry and feeling.

The poverty of the Indians can also be seen in the schools. I visited the girls' school in Sibundoy with His Excellency Fray Gaspar Monconill: there is virtually no equipment for study; I saw no maps or books, and when the sister wanted to get some of the girls to read, she gave them scraps of printed paper, each a few lines long, cut from journals. I cannot say whether they had any reading books, but I certainly saw none; they write on slates, but I only saw a few who had even tiny ends of chalk.

Having noted the absence of running water and drainage, and the fact that 'in Sibundoy it is only the Capuchin fathers who have electricity in their houses', the police chaplain concludes: 'In brief, the impression left upon me by the Sibundoy Indians was one of profound depression.'[5]

This commentary, which demonstrates among other things that the Capuchins had succeeded in getting the Sibundoy to go on their knees to white men – 'a humiliating custom' condemned in relation to the Mocoa a century earlier – was rejected and condemned by the Catalan missionaries. But it deserves respect because of the author's own standing, and also because it was published by the official organ of the metropolitan curia in Bogotá. What is quite clear from its conclusions is that the situation in the Sibundoy valley was not very admirable when Fray Gaspar Monconill de Pinell suddenly died in February 1946.

A few months later the Vicariate was handed over to Fray Plácido Crous de Calella, who is still Vicar Apostolic as I write this. The Mission then met with rather more luck: it had just had its ownership of its *haciendas* recognized, and the conservative party was once again in power. This change of government occurred in the nick of time for the Capuchins, enabling them to blame the liberal – if not 'communist' – atmosphere prevailing under the previous régime for all the criticisms still being levelled against them. Perhaps chief among them was the rumour that they had sent tens of millions of pesos to Spain to support the Franco régime's military effort and expenses of reconstruction.

Encouraged by this hopeful omen, Fray Plácido Crous had the idea of hastening the setting up of some farming cooperatives, so as to allay the disastrous consequences of the minifundist policy forced on the natives in the Sibundoy valley. There was not just poverty but abject destitution there, with the inevitable result of a growth of small-scale delinquency, and especially of cattle-thieving, which affected the missionaries more than anyone. Fray Marceliano, the 'strong-arm man', had often had to deal with this type of robber, as Juan Manuel Chindoy tells us:

This happened when I was ten or twelve. The thieves would meet together, four or more of them, perhaps ten, and cut up an animal to divide among them. But since there were many of them, the meat would only last for two or three days. So Fray Marceliano paid a man to find the thieves, and when his spy came to tell him that they were in the act of eating the animal in such and such a place, he would send the *alguaciles* round the homes of the suspects at five a.m.; and when they saw people coming home with the meat hidden under their clothes, they would arrest them and take them to the village. There they would be whipped if they admitted their crime; if not they would go on being whipped until they were ready to confess.[6]

In other words, despite the abolition of the *cepo*, the Capuchins still applied punitive measures. Here the evidence of white and Indian is unanimous, listing the traditional causes for punishment, and stressing the fact that adults were flogged for breaking the sixth commandment, while guilty women had their heads shaved. Furthermore, the missionaries' well-tried policy for preventing immorality remained in force:

I remember [declares Diego Mavisoy,[7] who was governor of San Andrés several times] their marrying people by force. They would even lock them up until they agreed to get married. That was their law. They would even make children of thirteen or fourteen get married. The poor little things weren't even old enough to handle a machete, a shovel or an axe, but the priests still insisted. ... Ah, it was Fray Bartolo (de Igualada) who was the worst: 'Get married,' he would say, 'and then live in peace with your wife; that is God's law which he has given us ...'*

Though Fray Marceliano had now completed his programme of agrarian reform, he did not therefore settle into inactivity. His major occupation was now to increase the profits from the Mission's farms and livestock; at the same time, he was demolishing (for the second time in thirty years) the mission's buildings, in order to rebuild them 'in a really thorough way'. Thus, with the help of generous gifts from the State and from pious Christians, modern monasteries began to appear in Sibundoy, San Francisco and Florencia, and churches and presbyteries in the smaller villages. Lastly, to support the day and boarding schools being set up in these hitherto untended areas, the Mission brought new groups of religious over from Europe: De La Salle brothers, Handmaids of the Sacred Heart, Sisters of

*As we shall see further on, this particular Indian had considerable esteem for Fray Bartolomé, as 'the best of all the missionaries', because he used to do small favours for him.

Charity, two groups of Franciscan sisters, and three of Sister Servants of Mary Immaculate.*

This huge increase in religious staff gives some indication of the power wielded by the Capuchin mission; for it now had under its authority some seventeen lesser communities; and in one statement, the proud claim appears: 'The life of the place was clear from the magnificence of the churches, the numbers receiving the sacraments, and the growth of pious societies.'†

Meanwhile, the change brought about by Creole settlement at the foot of the Andes became more and more marked. The stream of immigration following the two roads which linked the interior of Colombia with Florencia and Puerto Asís continued to grow: there were now quite a number of motor-driven boats travelling the waterways; regular aircraft landings were taking place on several landing strips, and large-scale livestock-raising prospered. The Capuchins' apostolic work was quite inadequate to cope with this rapid development, and the head of the Mission was actually quite relieved when, in 1951, the Vatican decided that the Vicariate be split into two. The Caquetá region became an autonomous Vicariate, while the enormous territory ending only at the Amazon was now the Prefecture Apostolic under the authority of a man already well known to my readers – Fray Marceliano Canyes alias de Vilafranca. The new prelate now installed in Leticia presided with

*Thus, according to the missionaries' statistics, the progress in education throughout the Vicariate over the course of eighteen years resulted in considerable growth from 1933 (65 schools, with 2,700 pupils) to 1951 (102 schools, with 7,580 pupils).

†From now on the administration of the sacraments was strictly checked on. Two of the required conditions were these: 'When the patient is seriously ill: *if he is an adult*, call the priest to give him the sacraments. . . . Those who have not yet reached the age of reason do not need a priest, and there is no point in disturbing him. When the patient is not seriously ill: do not call the priest, unless the person is actually in the village and living near the presbytery, and wants to receive communion on the first Friday of the month because he usually does so.' (*Bol. Cat.*, Nos. 130–31.)

his customary energy over the spiritual and economic fate of Colombian Amazonia, while the Upper Putumayo and the eastern part of the Cauca province, which had always been the area most beloved of the Capuchins, were brought together under the symbolic title of the Vicariate of Sibundoy.

The Vicar Apostolic, Plácido Crous, drew attention to his problems as an evangelist. One of his publications tells us:

At this period the Mission had to defend itself against infiltration and attacks from Protestantism, which threatened to undermine the foundations of both religion and nationhood in some sectors of the territory. Faced with this danger, the Mission got the Church's rights, especially in relation to education, recognized in agreement with the national government.[8]

This statement calls for a little explanation. Colombia was at the time undergoing bloody confrontations between conservatives and liberals, people's guerrillas and the dictatorship, known, especially between 1949 and 1957, as *la Violencia*; one of the aspects of this unacknowledged civil war was a persecution of the Protestant minorities in the country. A great many churchmen took an active part in this, always in the name of the real or imagined right to do so conferred on them by the Church. The result was a veritable witch-hunt, carried out quite openly though without any justification in law up to 1953, and continued after that on the basis of an interpretation of the new Convention of the Missions which had just been extended for a further twenty-five-year period. Following this agreement, the Prime Minister sent out to all the regional authorities a series of five circulars and a pamphlet, prohibiting anywhere on the nation's soil all religious worship and proselytizing other than Catholic.[9] Furthermore, he declared: 'the presence of pastors and missionaries of any religion other than the Catholic church is to be banned in all the Mission lands of the country'.

This official defence of the Catholic monopoly of missionary activity obviously resulted in an immediate and extreme increase in the persecution of Protestants. John Cabot Lodge, then US ambassador in Colombia, commented on the resulting situation:

> There have been Protestant schools and churches in Colombia for the past hundred years, most of them affiliated to the United States. Until 1948 they seldom came across any difficulties with individuals or public authorities in Colombia. But since then, these establishments and their work have been faced with increasingly violent attacks – sometimes, though not always, in places where political violence was the order of the day – which has resulted in many of them having to close down. Under the dictatorship [of General Rojas Pinilla], following government regulations sent out between 1953 and 1956, an even larger number of Protestant schools and churches were closed, over a wide area of the country. Inquiries made by this embassy have shown that over a hundred [Protestant] churches and chapels and about 150 schools have been closed by violence, following steps taken by the government. . . . Most of the churches and schools closed were on Mission land.[10]

Since this *Violencia* was unknown in the missions of Amazonia, it is clear that the Capuchins' battle against 'infiltration and attacks by Protestantism' was based solely on the reason put forward by the Catalan missionaries: their unshakeable resolution to pursue to its ultimate conclusion the religious radicalism inherited from their predecessors.

It is also worth a glance at the so-called 'white' population, and the economic development they brought to the former kingdom of the Sibundoy. We know that the core of that population consisted of Creole farmers – small landowners and officials, who together made up some quarter of the valley's inhabitants. On the other hand, owners of over fifty hectares – barely thirty all told, a number being officers – went on improving their situation, by taking advantage of the appalling cheapness of Indian labour to get more and more of the 'national reserve' land drained, and to clear hillsides for pastureland.

But in the 1950s there came a new wave of immigrants, and the whole colonization process took on a new impetus. Livestock raising increased to such a point that in 1954 the Cicolac-

Nestlé Dairy Produce combine considered building a factory in the valley. But the preliminary examination made by the society's experts and government agents led to the conclusion that the time was not yet ripe for such an enterprise.[11] In their report we find some interesting information:

The cattle in the area numbered up to 14,000 head, almost all of which belonged to the white population. Selling of meat to be eaten in the large towns in the interior was the main object.

The major producer was the Capuchin Mission, which also sent to the interior a large quantity of butter and cheese, while keeping the skim milk for feeding to their pigs.

The human consumption of milk in the valley amounted to no more than 800 litres a day – among over 1,000 families.

Five hundred families, with no land to cultivate at all, lived in conditions of quite appalling hardship.*

This interest on the part of private business in the Sibundoy valley led the government to look at it further. It therefore set up a branch of the Crédito Agrario, and a central livestock-breeding service. It was at this point too that the first industrial enterprise made its appearance: a Swiss immigrant managed by growing and processing mint to supply most of the demand of the Colombian market.

A final major event occurred to favour the increase of white settlement: the geological testing carried out by Texas Oil at the foot of the Andes, around Puerto Asís, resulted in the discovery of rich deposits of oil, the exploitation of which was to lead to an upheaval in the traditional economy of the entire Putumayo.

*Among the conclusions to be drawn from these facts, do not forget that the movement of produce out of the valley to other, richer areas made Sibundoy a typical example of the kind of internal colonialism from which so many countries suffer. It is obvious that that kind of systematic exportation can only reduce the food available for the local population, thus impeding still further their chances of improvement, since the profits of all this trade only went to the large landowners, who themselves lived in the large towns and reinvested the money they made there.

This fresh wave of Creole newcomers met with some obstacles. For instance in 1953 the government sent a commission to what had once been the territory of the Sibundoy to study the new territorial conflicts arising from it. This new deputation from the central authority could, once again, ascertain just how poor the Indians were. Their report makes clear that they found them reduced to eating carrion, and that the parish priest of the former capital of the valley had granted the right to use the forest land of the 'upper *resguardo*', founded in 1939, to the settlers.* The cause of this state of things is explained as 'the poor use being made of the land' – since the four hundred families studied, with their rudimentary implements, could only cultivate a very few hectares each. Consequently, the commission recommends disposing of that *resguardo* altogether 'in the object of seeking solutions which would give the natives greater economic stability, and provide them with the necessary means to raise their standard of living'. It was the commission's view that once each family had been granted a piece of mountain land the natives would have the means, since that would give them the ability to sell or mortgage it to finance the needful work.[12] Curious reasoning indeed, which can only be explained in the framework of a national policy directed to suppressing the native *resguardos* once and for all. The effect of the report was not slow in coming: three weeks later the *resguardo* was divided into smallholdings.[13]

As might have been expected, this suppression of the 'upper *resguardo*' ended in utter disaster. The sufferings of the Indians became so much worse that, given their ever-mounting protests, the government was forced in 1956 to think of some palliative measure: the 'national reserve' (constituted, we may recall how, years before in the centre of the valley) was raised

* 'Exploitation of the forest,' declares the report, 'is now taking place as a result of contracts made between the Rev. Fray Lucas de Batet (Capuchin), President of the native Chapter, and white timber men. . . . The sums paid on the signature of these contracts are now in the possession of Fray Lucas.'

to the status of a *resguardo*. But, as we have also seen, the major part of that 'reserve' was by now occupied by the Mission, by former officers, by settlers, some rich, some poor, and the tiny patches of land for the Sibundoy resulted from Fray Marceliano de Vilafranca's 'agrarian reform': consequently all that could be done was to settle those natives who had no possessions of any kind on barely nine hundred hectares of pure swampland.[14]

In short, the creation of this new and wholly illusory 'central *resguardo*' changed nothing and provided no solutions; all it did was enable the voracious small-time lawyers in the valley to tempt the dispossessed Indians to open further court cases to claim back the possessions of their ancestors – cases that would inevitably fail, and could only impoverish still further the unhappy plaintiffs, thus bringing their sufferings to hitherto untouched peaks: they even lost their daily wages as *peones*, which might be worth something in the region of 20 cents (US) per day when they could get work.

The relative calm which ensued made it possible for that veteran missionary Bartolomé de Igualada – parish priest of Sibundoy, bursar of the Mission and president of the Indian Chapter – to demonstrate his dynamism yet again. He gave enormous impetus to the construction of Church and State buildings in his area: churches, monasteries, dispensaries, colleges and schools. His silhouette, riding a magnificent horse, and often preceded by a couple of Indians and a few dogs, soon became well known to all those living in the valley.[15] They would see him inspecting work-sites, encouraging the Indian *peones* and small farmers, or bargaining over the sale of hundreds of pigs, oxen or cows from the Church's herds.

In addition to these labours, Fray Bartolomé also carried on his missionary work, and kept a close watch on the daily lives of the native population: he was never slow to intervene when order or morality were at stake, not just in public places, but inside the home too, 'advising' – as the Indians called it – his rebellious flock when guilty of sins of the flesh with twenty or thirty strokes of the lash. In effect, he presided so totally over the fate of the Indians that no one could even leave the valley without his permission.[16]

Despite all this chastisement – some of it traditional, some an innovation on the part of the missionaries – Fray de Igualada still enjoyed a quite special popularity. For what set him apart from the other Capuchins was the fact that he was able to respect certain elements in the culture of both Inga and Sibundoy to which they were peculiarly attached, notably their pharmacopeia.* For that reason, and those given by Diego Mavisoy, the Indian governor of San Andrés, the natives have preserved grateful memories of this priest:

Fray Bartolo was a good man, he was. He stayed among the Indians from his youth, and helped us in a lot of ways – a few pence here, some piece of clothing there, or a little maize, or flour or milk (the powdered kind that come from the US).

And Diego added, with a slightly malicious grin:

I remember how once Fray Bartolo brought a cow here, one of those just about to die, so that the village could have a bit of meat to eat.[7]

This humanitarian concern on the part of Fray de Igualada, though it hardly compensated for his belief in the lash and in forced marriages, meant that he did win for himself more affection than any other religious ever got from the natives in the valley.

This, then, was the day-to-day life of the Capuchin mission at the end of the year 1959.

On the national level, it may be briefly said that during that

*A great many Indians were able to bear witness to Fray de Igualada's reputation as a healer. But there was unfortunately at least one case in which his good advice came too late. 'Seven years ago,' records Dolores Juajibioy, 'my children were among those struck by the terrible epidemic of chicken pox, and I went to see Fray Bartolomé, who advised me to use the flower of the *yarumo* (*Cecropia peltata* L.). But since it was only to be found in Mocoa, two of my children died in the night, and the third the next day. A lot of families woke to find their children dead that morning.'

decade, Colombia had reaped the belated fruits of the 'Caesaro-Papism' (Church–State alliance) introduced seventy-five years earlier in the nation's Constitution, as well as in the Concordat and the series of Conventions of the Missions signed with the Vatican. That the Church's political and economic power had reached a quite unparalleled scale, is borne out by the fact that the Protestant minorities (amounting to no more than 0·5 per cent of the population) were subjected to bloody persecution.

And on the local level, though the valley we are looking at here still contained 5,425 Inga and 2,125 Sibundoy, the once huge tribes at the foot of the Andes had been reduced to 350 Siona, 290 Cofan and 20 Huitoto. As compared with this, the numbers of settlers now established in these areas had reached some 32,500.[17]

In other words, while the white population of the Putumayo had tripled in thirty years, the native population had actually become only a quarter the size it had been. This demonstrates the triumph of white over Indian, of 'civilization' over 'nature' – which is clear too from the new impetus to the economy of Colombian Amazonia. It was also the triumph of Western cultural ethno-centrism over the policy of protecting Indian cultures: from now on, if the aboriginal, once master of all those lands, wanted to survive physically at all, he could only do so by becoming integrated at every level into the only permissible civilization: it was the survival of the fittest with a vengeance.

CHAPTER 16

Confrontations

Sibundoy . . . is a classic case of the Church's having yielded to the temptations of economic and political power.

(CAMILO TORRES ex-priest and guerrilla, 1965)

. . . If they trust us, let them support us, and we shall be only too pleased to work for the good of the Indians and their country; if they do not trust us, let them send us away.

(FRAY BARTOLOME DE IGUALADA, Capuchin, 1966)

The unprecedented stream of migration which brought Colombians into Amazonia during the 1950s was not caused only by economic considerations. A large part of the new settlers consisted of peasants from the interior of the country, driven from their own land by the *Violencia* ravaging the countryside, and also by members of the urban sub-proletariat moving out of the towns in search of somewhere to live and support themselves unmolested. Though this phenomenon contributed to relieving the pressure on areas of high population density, it had the corresponding disadvantage of increasing the incessant requests for help from the central government from those living in these forgotten regions. The State was in a strong position, politically because of the two-party coalition, and economically because of the general development going on all over the country. But the moment it decided to act, it found itself face to face with a power hitherto unreckoned with: the missionary Catholic Church to which it had handed over three quarters of the country. The confrontation which ensued was, in the Putumayo at least, to bring the two opposing powers to grips on three fronts: native affairs, education and agrarian policy. In this chapter we shall consider them all.

In 1960 the Colombian government decided to undertake a programme of aid and protection for the surviving aboriginals, by means of an integration-oriented native policy. I speak of 'surviving' aboriginals, because natural selection, miscegenation, proletarianization, and the persecutions to which our natives had been subjected had over the past hundred years fundamentally changed the ethno-cultural scene in Colombia. The country then had over sixteen million inhabitants – as against only twelve million a decade earlier – but the Indian population, strictly speaking, including the tribes brought together in the *resguardos* as well as those still living scattered in the forests, did not exceed 350,000. I speak here of a native 'policy', because up to then the various bureaux for 'native affairs' had been no more than sub-offices – some existing only in the imagination – handed on from ministry to ministry until they were ultimately combined with *agriculture*.* Their activities were generally limited to recording complaints about land-ownership decisions, and to suppressing those *resguardos* where the tribes had become physically or culturally extinct and those held to be economically unprofitable, so as to pave the way for the so-called integration policy. This system was to become more and more clearly defined in the mind of the Colombian government which finally decreed a new law, the first law of 1968 (still in force) to speed up the removal of the remaining *resguardos*.

This policy was not even a palliative. To the State, 'integrating' an Indian simply meant making him abandon his traditional customs – despite their being ideally suited to the situation he lived in – in the hope that he would adopt the

*The administrative situation of the all too notorious 'Indian Protection Service' in Brazil was equally wild, and that too was put under the general authority of the Ministry of Agriculture after its establishment by General Rondón.

pattern of western society, both culturally and economically. But the result turned out to be the precise opposite. First of all, because the segregationism universally practised meant that while the government was quite ready to spend 3,650 dollars (1970 value) on the education of a middle-class professional, it felt that to spend just over three dollars on the integration of an Indian compatriot would be excessive. Secondly, the fact of becoming 'dis-integrated' from his own society and culture did not automatically make an Indian integrated into the rest of society. He was merely transformed into an alienated and undefined being, condemned to take the lowest place in a society which could only see him as an inferior kind of person.

That is why, contrary to the claims of some South American governments, one cannot look to a speeding-up of the inevitable process of trans-culturization for any improvement in the life of the Indians, any profit to the nation's economy, any modernization or any progress towards a hypothetical 'national unity'. This 'programmed integration' of Indian minorities would seem in Colombia, as elsewhere, to be no more than at best a Utopia – with the hope of opening new consumer markets to industry – and at worst merely an excuse for taking the last scraps of their land away from them; or then, again, it might look like the result of the childish attempt of the Indo-American majorities to gloss over the fact – which they so hate to recognize – that most of us have Indian ancestors.

Thus in 1960 there was set up the Department of Native Affairs (División de asuntos indígenas, or DAI), linked to the Ministry of the Interior. This new bureau came to do its first work in Sibundoy by securing for the Indians a century-old right of way across a *hacienda* sold by the Mission to one of the settlers assisted by its dealings. But when the Director of the DAI asked Fray Bartolomé to show him the Deed of Sale for the land, the missionary refused, and accused him of 'abusing his power'.[1] The Mission held the trump card, for the settler in question was a member of the Council of State.

During the following months the Capuchins went further

still. According to the report of one official commission, the Vicar Apostolic personally stepped in to prevent the Indian landowners from accepting the title-deeds the government wanted to give them to secure their property.[2] It was a clear indication that the missionaries had no intention of allowing any interference from government representatives in what they considered to be their domain.

The director of the DAI, fully aware of the implications of this challenge, was determined to deal with it when, at the beginning of 1961, the affair of the Indian Chapters provided him with just the opportunity he needed. In exchange for the tours the missionaries obliged them to make, to see that order and morality were preserved in the villages, the native governors and *alguaciles* were supposed to receive a (modest) payment from the State. That year they began making complaints that these payments were only coming to them partially, if at all, and that the missionary-presidents of their Chapters were not helping them in their attempts to receive their money.[3] To strike at the very core of missionary power, the director of the DAI ordered that these payments be simply stopped, and that with the money thus saved medicines, seeds and tools should be bought and distributed free among *all* the Indians: there could hardly have been a more open way of showing the Indian masses how they had been being taken in by these governors and members of Chapters chosen by the Capuchins.

The reaction of Fray Plácido Crous, the Vicar Apostolic, was at first temperate. In a letter to the Prime Minister he simply alleged that such steps were likely to 'disorganize' the Indians who 'would not willingly accept this kind of attitude to their Chapters'. Fray Bartolomé de Igualada hastened to give his superior his full support; but the latter, probably in fear of being surpassed in energy by his own administrator, decided to adopt a more belligerent attitude.[4] He now accused the government 'of opposing the Church because her activity in the sphere of national education and the government of the Indians goes counter to the views of the State'.[5] In other words, so sure was the Capuchin Mission of the legitimacy of its established theocratic rule that it had no hesitation in playing the part of the innocent accused turning the tables on his accuser.

The director of the DAI, in view of this warning, took a very wise step: at the end of 1961 he asked the Salesian Lino Rampón, representative of the Catholic Missions in the Colombian Native Institute (a non-confessional organization) to make an inquiry into the dispute. Rampón's reply confirmed the Capuchins in their position:

There is one point at which civil and missionary activities meet: the Indian Chapters. These constitute the Church's instrument for preserving her system of moral and religious organization among the natives. It is thus quite understandable that when the government tries to touch their payment, the bishop should arise at once to defend it.[6]

However, the Salesian's report was not limited simply to justifying the Capuchins' attitude to the matter of the Indian Chapters; he further praised their achievements in the sphere of colonization and teaching, and offered no protest as to the legality of their acquisition of their land; in addition he made some neutral comments:

The teaching religious feel it to be unjust that the age of the children should be the only criterion for determining when their education should end, without reference to the actual stage of development they have achieved. For they all leave school at the age of fourteen, and are given the 'certificate of young unmarried people' which marks their entry into social life.
... Here, in the Chapter's meeting room, a cross covered in red, white and green paper draws one's attention. At its foot is a low table with a whip on it. In front of the cross, Indians guilty of crimes are given the ultimate punishment of flogging with the whip.

But finally, he does make a few rather more critical remarks on the work of these present-day *doctrineros*:

The Catholic Mission of the Putumayo is not carrying out any consistent social programme, but only sporadic action, arising from the needs of the moment. We are still faced with virgin land . . .

The whites occupy the largest part of the missionaries' time . . .

The Mission is considerably taken up with the problem of dividing up the land. This cannot be ignored, and is linked with all its economic activities . . .

I wonder whether here, as alas in other Catholic Missions, there is not a prevailing assumption that the Indian race is one destined to disappear.

And Father Rampón concludes his report by recommending that the government should establish a commission for assisting the natives in the Putumayo. For daring to make comments of this kind the poor man was to undergo sufferings bitter indeed: he was calumniated and condemned by the Catalan Mission, expelled from the Native Institute, actually held by the police in another Capuchin Vicariate, and finally subjected to so many outrages that he was forced to leave Colombia and return home to Italy.

However, for the DAI the results were encouraging, and an official was at once sent to have talks with Fray Plácido and consider the possibility of setting up in the Vicariate the native commission recommended by the Italian priest. It was to him that the enraged Fray Bartolomé, ignoring the presence of the Vicar Apostolic, made clear his views: on Father Rampón: 'he is a freemason in a cassock, in the pay of the head of the DAI'; on the DAI: it is 'an organization which opposes the Church, and its head is the Communist Gregorio Hernández de Alba and his gang';* on the projected native commission for the Putumayo: 'let us hope that the Minister of the Interior, a most loyal Catholic, though always surrounded by a group of freemasons, will one day restore the salary owed to the Indian Chapters, and give the Mission back the money that is simply

*Here Fray Bartolomé was using well-tried MacCarthyist methods. If there was any ideology underlying Gregorio Hernández's action, it was certainly far from being even that 'micro-communism' of the Creoles which South American reactionaries see as the greatest danger our society faces. Furthermore, when this missionary appeals to the solidarity of the senior officials of the State to support the privileges of the Roman Church against the danger of freemasonry, it is important to note that in Colombia masonry is no longer either secret or anti-Catholic, and that its influence is limited.

going to go to waste through the pointless bureaucracy of the commission . . .'[7]

Seeing his work as mediator thus under attack, the official set about gathering evidence about the problems of all the Indians of the Putumayo, especially as regards education, the missionaries' greatest subject for self-congratulation. He records the complaints of the Sibundoy, received during a 'secret meeting', that the only teachers' training school was far too expensive for their children to attend. And he adds that throughout the territory less than fifty per cent of the children enrolled actually went regularly to school; that barely two or three per cent of them went even as far as the fourth or fifth year of elementary school; that people complained of racial segregation, and of the harsh treatment and other abuses carried on in the boarding schools or 'orphanages' administered by the religious.

However, to satisfy the Catalan priests, the DAI put off the establishment of the native commission which so alarmed them, and the waiting space thus given them enabled the Capuchins to cope with two fresh problems which brought them into conflict with the civil authorities.

The first occurred in August 1962, and was caused by the Attorney General of the republic, Andrés Holguín. This important personage, a conservative and a member of one of the country's most illustrious families, actually issued a report in which he denounced the flagrantly unconstitutional nature of the Convention of the Missions. His shattering comments on the violations of the freedom of education guaranteed by the Constitution, the delegation of administrative functions to the missionaries, and finally his baldly stated demand that the government 'take adequate measures to get this convention revoked' caused a sensation.[8]

The second event that caused the missionaries to shake in their shoes was the judgement pronounced by the equally conservative Supreme Court, made public in 1962. That judgement, which had the force of law, stated definitively and permitting of no appeal that the laws of Colombia had always recognized the *resguardos* as 'fully and entirely the property of the Indians', including the missionary *Cofradías* inside them. Furthermore, it declared null all rights that might be claimed to the lands in question, by any persons not belonging to the Indian communities, whether arising from peaceful occupation, purchase, or any other means of acquisition.[9]

You may imagine the effect this declaration had on the Capuchins. They, who only a few months earlier were still assuring Father Rampón that the valley was the property of the Sibundoy before they arrived, now had to insist on the opposite – as they did in the Sibundoy *Catholic Bulletin*: 'We cannot think that the national government has ever at any time considered all the land of the valley as belonging to the natives. Had they not considered it unused land, they could not have given judgments of ownership to the settlers who have gone on to farm it.'[10]

What this was really saying was that the Mission, as 'colonist and tiller of the land', was trying to seek support from the complicity of State officials in order to cast a veil over the way in which Fidel de Montclar had declared the valley of the Inga and Sibundoy *baldío* (unused land).

Despite these first official moves against the missionaries' absolute rule, their fears proved unfounded. Neither their power nor their authority was in serious danger; no annulment of the agreements between the State and the Vatican was undertaken; and the civil authorities continued as before to respect the 'Church lands', so much so that later on a State body actually bought them back from the Mission.

So the year 1963 found the Sibundoy valley quite peaceful. Fray Bartolomé took advantage of this to put out feelers towards some agreement with the 'communist' head of the DAI. To start with he sent him a letter denying the official information he had received, and assuring him that the missionaries' sole wish was 'to be left to work for their ideal'. And, without leaving him time to reply, he sent a second letter to fill in any detail possibly missing from the first:

The fact that we are dealing with natives in general does not mean that our reasoning about them should always follow the same pattern. Natives vary, even within a given area. Here, for instance, it is not unheard of for some of those who have taken the largest pieces of communal native land to be natives themselves. You will find among them some who travel elsewhere and come back with large sums of money, acquired God knows how; they are arrogant and intractable, and the fact that money can buy anything does the rest. They bring back very advanced customs and notions, which constitute a genuine social danger. . . . That is why one must distinguish between native and native.

We missionaries ourselves have made the mistake, here and elsewhere, of believing that the great solution was to give work to the natives. However I still do this to some extent; and without its costing the nation a penny, I make up teams of joiners, carpenters and painters who compare favourably with the best-trained white workmen. But I act prudently here, for in other parts of our Mission – and in one Mission in Ecuador – problems have arisen: since it is not always possible to give employment to those trained in certain skills on the Mission lands, they move away, and will even leave wives and children, thus leading to a trail of disaster. . . . Under no circumstances must they be decolonized.

There is one people in our Mission who were at one time a hard-working race who seemed to have a great future ahead of them [the Inga of Santiago]. With the encouragement and stimulation of people who did not understand the problems involved, they set out to travel, and to live without working, thus growing accustomed to idleness. Though we missionaries issued warnings of all kinds before it was too late, we were not heeded, and now it *is* too late. . . . Who is to blame?

I would like to ask one favour of you: do not invite the Sibundoy Indians to festivals of folklore and dancing elsewhere in the country. Natives are natives – that is to say, they have weaknesses of all kinds. Some of them have described to me how people have tried to lead them astray. . . . Here the wives have complained. One of them told me only a few days ago: 'My husband does not want to be a bad man, and he told me how he saw wicked things in Cali and wanted to come home as soon as he could.'[11]

In other words, though the Catalan Mission had spent sixty years supposedly integrating the natives into the western, Christian world, Fray Bartolomé was saying that his community took particular exception to two aspects of the government's integration policy: (1) bringing the Indians into contact with the outside world 'because they brought back very advanced customs' which constituted a veritable 'social danger'; and (2) training them as artisans, because this turned them into potential emigrants, thus leading to the phenomenon of 'de-colonization'.

Such statements indicate the gulf existing between the civil and the religious authorities despite their apparently common goal: for the religious 'integration' meant keeping the Indians under their authority; whereas for the government it meant bringing them into the life of the Colombian population as a whole. In this, the Capuchin missionaries were far removed indeed from the official position of the Roman Church, and especially of its head John XXIII, who had just published his encyclical *Mater et Magistra.**

However the statements of Fray Bartolomé were no more than a pale reflection of the clerical authoritarianism prevailing in the Vicariate of Sibundoy, as the head of the national police was to discover to his cost during that same year, 1963, when his men were thrown out by another Capuchin priest. This incident took place in Yunguillo, an Inga community living in the warm lowlands beneath the Andes, which had for some years been the cure of the Capuchin Isidoro de Montclar. Life

*The whole Catholic missionary effort had, as is well known, undergone intensive modernization during the previous decades. A great many priests, like the North American anthropologist Louis J. Luzbetak, had managed to convince a large body of opinion of the need to abandon primitive methods in favour of others more in tune with the times. In this connection we may stress the enormous achievements of the Second Vatican Council, and the existence of some missionary leaders with highly developed social consciences: a notable example of these is Monsignor Gerardo Valencia Cano, the missionary head of Buenaventura in Colombia; his work for the social improvement of the underprivileged has won him tremendous praise and, alas, also much blame. Monsignor Valencia Cano was the only Colombian prelate to sign the *Pastoral from the Third World*, and belongs to the Golconda group, some of whose leaders openly supported the theories of the guerrilla priest Camilo Torres, and have consequently been suspended by their bishops.

there flowed on without much excitement until the time when the settlers, wanting to take over the unused land in the vicinity, began visiting the Indian *parcialidad*. Faced with this danger, Fray de Montclar immediately set about preventing any contact between Indians and Creoles, which so enraged the latter that the national police had to open a police station in the village to guard against possible conflicts. But, according to the head of this small detachment of police, the Capuchin father was not very cooperative:

... This region [he wrote to his superiors] is inhabited by some hundred Indian families, living under the authority of Fray Isidoro, whom they obey, and indeed they can only be described as his slaves. ... He forbids them to give shelter to the whites, or even to sell them anything at all ...

His orders are that if a white man sets foot in the district he must show a military pass or safe-conduct, since national identity cards are not recognized here. The native governor has special instructions for those who do not produce this document: they are to be tied firmly by the hands and feet, and beaten, and then taken to Mocoa ...

Fray Isidoro has told me that he would inform the police commandant that there was absolutely no need for a police station here; that he had certainly not asked for one. ... The Father also let it be understood that he did not like white people entering the territory; his motive would seem to be that they will not let themselves be ordered about and abused as the Indians are at present.[12]

And the missionary was not slow in keeping his promises: on 15 July 1963 the authorities were forced to abandon the police station in question, since those staffing it were left without any 'means of subsistence' because of the civil resistance organized by Fray Isidoro.

Yunguillo was then left with a single inspector to represent the State; and his 'activity' consisted solely in recognizing his impotence in the face of the missionary *Regulation* and the 'punitive power' exercised by the priest. Among the less serious cases he reports, we may mention 'that of Rafael Chindoy who, for having welcomed a white man into his home, was condemned to metalling thirty metres of road'.[13]

Criticism of this kind did not come kindly to Fray de Mont-clar, and he complained of the inspector to the civil authorities of the territory, who sent an on-the-spot commission of inquiry. That commission, in its report of June 1964, recognized 'that all the incidents deplored [by the inspector] had been corroborated', and added:

(1) The priest in question ignores every civil authority, and himself receives all appeals from the natives, and deals with civil problems of all kinds.

(2) He makes regular visits to the surrounding area, where every Indian family is obliged to pay him a contribution according to its economic means . . . which they pay with the gold they get from the rivers.

(3) He lets fly the most abominable abuse at the Indians, and humiliates them with all kinds of punishments, such as working on the Mission buildings, on his roads and tracks, tree-felling, etc. Such tasks are laid on men and women, and even children; he went so far as to strike a boy full on the temple for not knowing the answer to a catechism question.

(4) The Reverend Fray Isidoro has selected certain pieces of land, some on the side of the Putumayo commissionership, others by the river Caquetá, where no one is allowed to work on the grounds that they are Mission property; this has forced a great many Indians to leave for other districts.

(5) He makes the Indians do building work without any pay, telling them it is their obligation; which is especially unjust to those among them who are very poor indeed.

(6) He forces young Indian girls to marry boys of the same race without even knowing them beforehand – a proceeding which has caused a great many cases of one or other partner's leaving the home later on.

(7) When some of her neighbours told the Reverend Fray Isidoro that the widow Eulalia Becerra de Chindoy was misbehaving, he ordered her to leave the village of Yunguillo immediately; and if she did not the Indian Chapter would be ordered to burn down her house – and all this without making the slightest effort to find out whether or not the accusations against her were true!

I declare [the head of the commission says in conclusion] that the majority of the natives have personally assured me of the truth of all these statements, as have certain minor officials who have visited the area; but that none of them will speak up for fear of the possibility of reprisals by Fray Isidoro.

I also declare that I have learnt of several young Indians of both sexes who have had to leave the Yunguillo district out of fear of the insults publicly uttered against them from the pulpit by the above-mentioned priest, telling everyone all the details of their private lives.[14]

However, once this report had been handed in and filed in the appropriate place, Fray Isidoro was left to carry on with his apostolic ministry.

But this is only one aspect of the skirmishing that went on between the regional government and the Capuchin mission of the Putumayo. There were also attempts on the part of the government to put an end to the excesses resulting from the 'punitive power' of the missionaries, and the Vicariate's total control of public education.

It was the judicial authorities who took the first step by deciding to hear the case of an appeal from the governor of Sibundoy concerning the appalling lesions left on a young Indian girl by the beating administered 'on orders of the parish priest'. Unfortunately the case was withdrawn.[15]

The confrontation over public education grew out of a quite unexpected incident: the take-over of the Pius XII College by the Missionaries. It was found that despite fifty years of Capuchin ministry the territory still had only primary schools, and two teachers' training schools. The population continually made representations to the Ministry of Education but, given the 'Convention of the Missions', the minister could do nothing more than grant the Sibundoy Vicariate the sums needed for this public service, without being able either to specify how they should be spent, or to keep any check on them. As years went by like this, despite all the promises to improve matters made by the Vicar Apostolic, the regional government decided to set up a secondary school. According to the spokesman for the Minister of the Interior, all was going well until, 'by a curious coincidence, as soon as regular government aid was allocated to it' (in 1962), the Vicariate took over the school, and began to pay the teachers 'at a rate which was, among other things, lower than that established by law'.[16] When the teachers protested, the missionaries sought shelter behind the omnipotent Convention of the Missions, adding, as an extra argument, that the idea of founding the school had been theirs in the first place.

Thus the first attempt to break the monopoly of the Catholic Missions in education ended in failure.[17] Henceforth officials at every level were yet again to have to rest content with observing the activities of the Capuchins from afar, though noting that the teaching given in their schools was 'poor if not nonexistent'. It was wholly unsuited to the local way of life; Indians were only allowed four years' schooling (to prevent their advancing to further 'decolonizing' studies); there were none of the State-financed student restaurants; the Vicariate paid its teachers thirty per cent less than the salary recommended by the Ministry of Education;* and there was furthermore a discrepancy between the statistics published by the missionaries of the numbers of schools, teachers and students, and the figures appearing in their own account books.†

In his function as Inspector of Public Education the Vicar Apostolic explained this anomaly in terms both of the need to choose teachers more for their moral qualities than their professional qualifications, and of his lack of economic resources. This point of view, it must be pointed out, was not shared by the civil authorities; as against the Vicar Apostolic's second argument, they objected that the missionaries administered over a third of the territory's public monies, without control of any kind from the government.‡

---

*The monthly salary of schoolmasters authorized by the State was at that time 450 pesos. Teachers employed by Fray Plácido Crous's Vicariate received 300. And there were women teachers who got even less: these were paid out of 'Mission funds' by the Capuchins themselves.

† To take one example: during the academic year 1965–6 the Capuchins declared that they were maintaining in the Putumayo 120 schools, staffed by 180 masters. Yet their account books for that year only record 61 schools, staffed by 144 masters.

‡ If we look, for instance, at that same year 1965, the breakdown of the

The final battle between the State and the Catalan Fathers was to break out as a result of the announcement of the arrival in the Sibundoy valley of the INCORA (Colombian Institute for Agrarian Reform).*

When a study was actually made of the way the land was divided the figures we have already seen were amply confirmed: there were over 400 families owning no land at all; 169 had less than a hectare; 229 had between 1 and 3 hectares. At the other end of the scale, the Capuchin Mission, with over

---

budget for the territory appears as follows: sums paid to the Vicariate Apostolic for public education: 2,331,614 pesos; budget of the Special Commissionership in the strict sense (not excluding certain further sums paid to the Vicariate): 4,875,011 pesos.

*The establishment of this body dates back to 1962. Officially its purpose was to effect a just redistribution of the land by means of getting rid of estates that were either too small or too large – which between them made up the majority of all land-holdings. In fact the activities of this Institute were an instrument for the attempt of the property-owning classes to stifle the growing desire of the peasantry for a change in the social, economic and political structures of the country; this is clear from the following two points:

(1) Since its foundation, the INCORA has been run by a committee made up of twenty-eight members representing the government, the political parties, the large landowners, the armed forces and the Church, and two members representing the peasants.

(2) The reform in question is achieved by means of giving back to the nation all land not being cultivated by its owners (who generally receive substantial compensation), as well as by some purchases and the occasional expropriation. But the redistribution is not free: the peasants have to pay both for the land and the improvements made to it.

Despite all these safeguards, the large landowners still objected strongly to the establishment of the INCORA. The institute therefore put off until some more favourable date in the future the main objective for its existence, and chiefly set out to encourage rural credit, settlement in the virgin forest, and the reclamation of swampland and desert which it was not so hard to persuade the owners to part with, and distribute in allotments to the poor peasants.

With a policy such as this in view, the Sibundoy valley was an ideal area for experiment by the INCORA: for the socio-economic problems resulting from minifundism were specially serious there, and it had been demonstrated that, were it properly drained, it could well become an area of intensive production.

1,000 hectares, shared half the entire plain with 39 other large landed proprietors.[18]

It was then that the INCORA, in July 1964, approved a plan for draining and redistributing all the land in the Sibundoy valley.

Panic struck the large landowners. They at once set about a campaign of calumny to convince the Indians that this plan of the government's was directed particularly against them; and Fray Bartolomé de Igualada, the Mission's Bursar, declared to one government representative:

The people cannot possibly understand this plan, or all the problems it must involve . . .
The natives who own land drink it away in *chicha* . . . and the rest, who have only recently arrived, obviously have no right to any . . . !
Don't complicate their lives with a fuss about pieces of land![19]

To support their statements, the Catalan missionaries, together with sixty landowners, set up a 'Committee for the Defence of the Sibundoy Valley', which unleashed a publicity campaign playing every possible variation on the message of protest addressed to the president of the republic, for, according to them, agrarian reforms 'must only serve to prevent the establishment of centres of communist agitation'.[20] Further, with the aid of leaflets and parish loudspeakers, they set up another campaign in the valley to counter 'the danger of Castroist communism' represented by the INCORA; finally, they tried to get the Indians to rise in protest against the plan through their well-tried instrument – the Indian Chapters.

Months passed, and the tension increased. In May 1965 the Vicar Apostolic decided to reinforce the anti-government forces by composing a lengthy pastoral in support of his second-in-command. The landless Sibundoy learnt from it that their duty was to clear the virgin forest, rather than fix their hearts on the 'Mission lands'; that the INCORA was 'an autonomous official institution, in other words not a part of the national government'; and that the Mission only held on to its *haciendas* because 'one cannot give unless one has'. Having said all this, Fray Plácido went on to defend the Church's possessions in Sibundoy with the following arguments:

The Vicar Apostolic can answer for the nineteen years during which, by God's will, he has been at the head of the Vicariate . . .

If at any time irregular buying or selling had taken place, then it should have been spoken of, proved, and justice done at once . . .

The undersigned, during the forty and more years God has granted him to live in this beloved territory, has known a great many missionaries, and none of them could he believe capable of behaving unjustly in carrying out his apostolic task with all the self-denial that involves . . .

How could anyone think such missionaries would be capable of acting unjustly for material gain?[21]

Though the lies and sophistries of the Capuchins' arguments are glaring, we may pause for a moment on three particular points:

(1) Fray de Igualada's solicitude ('Don't complicate their lives with a fuss about pieces of land') gives clear indication of his determination to keep the Inga and Sibundoy in a state of serfdom, contrary to everything said by Paul VI and the Second Vatican Council.[22]

(2) When he alleges the inability of those Indians to cultivate and administer their own land, he is denying all the historical evidence, in particular the fact that the survival of these pre-Colombian races is due to the preservation of their own traditional crops – maize, potatoes and other tubers – and not to those introduced by the Europeans.*

*It must be recognized [says Jesús Idrobo, Researcher from the Colombia National University] that the Sibundoy are good farmers, and display great curiosity and equally great interest in introducing into their valley any plants that may be economically valuable. I will give just one example: the edible tubers known as *zitzes*, of which they have succeeded in acclimatizing six varieties, though the conditions of the area are far from favourable. In fact this particular achievement brings them into successful competition with the most modern techniques; England has been trying for years to grow these particular tubers in the lesser Antilles, and has only succeeded with one or two varieties. . . . This is no new phenomenon, but is characteristic of an entire tradition. We may recall that when, a few centuries back, Cieza

(3) The inadequate reasons given by the missionary leader to justify the amount of land owned by the Mission were directed to disarming the criticisms mounting against him from within the Church itself. For the Church was represented on the governing council of the INCORA by two priests, one of whom was a young sociologist moving rapidly towards an extreme radical position: Father Camilo Torres Restrepo.

So it was no coincidence that shortly after Fray Plácido's pastoral, on 21 June 1965, this young priest gave this assessment of the situation:

Sibundoy is a classic case of the Church's having yielded to the temptation of political and economic power. The problem is not so much that the Capuchin missionaries own too much land, although they do. It is my belief that their opposition to the establishment of the INCORA stems from their fear of losing the power they now have over the Indians who are subject to their present theocratic rule.[24]

Though the records of Father Camilo's activities at the INCORA are 'classified material', our knowledge of him makes it possible for us to be certain that his continued presence on the INCORA committee since its foundation was of inestimable value to him. This institution, timid though its reformism was, gave him his greatest experience of the poverty and social injustice existing in Colombia. This contact in the flesh with the sufferings of our people, combined with the powerlessness of the State and judiciary to provide any solution to their problems, were to play their part in turning this priest into the revolutionary activist he became at the end of that same year (1965). The position he then took up appeared to him as no more than the logical consequence of the immense attempt at renewal being undertaken by the Catholic Church

---

de León first caught sight of that valley, from the top of Mount Patascoy, he saw there a mass of well-planned crops. It was for that reason that the traces of terraces remained around Santiago and Colón. The comment of the Spanish chronicler is very interesting, for it proves that the Indians were past masters in such agricultural techniques well before the Spanish arrived.[23]

since the Second Vatican Council. But here Camilo's logic parted from that of the national Church which, unlike the Church in other parts of South America, remained as a whole firmly attached to its privileges and material goods, as illustrated in the story of the Sibundoy valley. That is why, early in 1966, Camilo Torres the guerrilla died in the Colombian Andes.

The Department of Native Affairs chose the moment when the campaign against agrarian reform was at its height to raise its head once more by setting up in the Sibundoy valley the 'Commission for the Assistance and Protection of the Natives' (CAPI). One is not surprised to learn that it met with the most determined opposition, especially since it made a great effort to enforce the government's policy of integration, despite the apathy of both the Inga and the Sibundoy themselves.

The poverty of its results seemed to provide a weapon for each of the opposing parties: to the head of the CAPI, its failure was due 'to the fear of the Indians that they would be punished by the Fathers, and condemned publicly from the pulpit'; to which the Vicar Apostolic retorted that 'the Indians had recognized the attitude of mistrust if not of positive hostility towards the missionaries among certain of those acting on behalf of the authorities'. The very fact that two such contradictory statements could be made indicates how deeply rooted was the subjection (or apathy) of the natives; a situation which must ultimately be favourable to the Capuchins, since they could thus keep a firm watch on the activities of all the officials. For, according to Fray Bartolomé de Igualada, the Capuchins had told their flock to let them know at once if they noticed anything in the behaviour of the officials 'which did not seem right'.[25] And among the steps taken by the CAPI there were at least two major ones which 'did not seem right' to the missionaries:

(1) The intention to return to having the native Chapters popularly elected – a custom suppressed sixty years before in the area by Fidel de Montclar. This intention had been embodied in law quite recently.[26]

(2) The wish to get rid once and for all of the 'power to punish'; this resulted from the fact that the head of the Commission himself had the occasion to see that it was still fully in force – in 1966 – as the result of one particular case which seemed to him utterly scandalous: a young woman from Santiago, found guilty of a sin of the flesh, had been publicly flogged 'on the part of her which had sinned'.*

To the first of these steps Fray Bartolomé simply replied by an outright refusal: 'Your report is not true,' he declared. As for the 'power to punish' wielded by the missionaries in their function as presidents of the native Chapters, he defended it thus:

> One must not exaggerate. Though it is true that the Chapters do sometimes use the punishment in question (without the missionary's having ordered it) . . . it is because of a tradition which the people respect. However it is not part of the normal run of punishments; if it is thought undesirable, then it can easily be stopped, though I know that such a decision would not be well received by the Indians.

And, in his own special style, he concludes: 'If they trust us, let them support us, and we shall be only too pleased to work for the good of the Indians and their country; if they do not trust us, let them send us away.'

Despite such altruistic statements, the CAPI set about convincing the Inga and Sibundoy that they should reject the candidates for the Chapters forced upon them by the *doctrineros*. And then something totally unexpected occurred: not merely

---

*She was afterwards married by force to her partner in sin, but soon left him and both later founded their own homes. I quote this detail because punishment of this kind, carried out in this way, has never been among the customs of the Indians. Corroboration of this comes from Justo Jacanamijoy, a Sibundoy in close touch with the Capuchin Mission; he said to me, 'Several governors wanted me to be the whipper, because I have a hard hand, and I had to agree. . . . In applying this punishment, there was a distinction: when given to a man, one beat him with a long whip on his thighs and legs; when it was a woman, it was the other way round – she was whipped on the back, with a short whip so as not to hurt her breasts.'

did the Inga accept this suggestion, but they were bold enough
to react angrily when, a few days later, a representative of the
Vicar Apostolic unexpectedly turned up at a pre-electoral
meeting they had organized. The first to rebuke him was one of
the Tisoys:

> What have you done for us? You began by seizing the lands of our
> ancestors, where you now have thousands of cows, giving thousands
> of bottles of milk – of which you never give a single glass to our
> children. Children die of hunger every day in this valley, but when
> have you ever given us so much as a drop of milk?

Other voices followed his:

> You preach charity, but you never practise it. We have to pay you
> for everything, even an injection – at your charity hospital an in-
> jection costs thirty centavos!
> My mother died for lack of medical care. She wasn't wanted in the
> charity hospital, because she was an Indian and poor!
> The Mission has the land which you say belongs to the Church:
> and what do you do with the income from it? The government sub-
> sidizes education, and the hospital too; so just what does the
> Mission itself do? I was one of your pupils, but I remember quite well
> that you never gave me so much as an exercise book or a
> pencil.[27]

To fill its cup of bitterness, the Mission suddenly suffered a
sudden death: Fray de Igualada, its most zealous and practised
defender of the decade. At this crucial point, therefore, the
Capuchins were left unable to protest.

This was undoubtedly the reason why all these years of
battle between the Capuchin Mission and the Colombian State
ended in two relative victories for the latter: on the one hand,
democratic elections were established for the Indian Chapters,
with the electors having a choice between free candidates and
pro-Mission candidates; on the other, corporal punishment
was limited to twelve strokes of the whip.

Relations between the civil and religious authorities now
entered a period of calm, which was further consolidated by
the advent of a quite new factor – the only thing capable of

effectively influencing the Capuchins' attitude: the beginning of an evolution in the Colombian Church. Not of the 'rebel' Indo-American Church, whose tiny voice had not yet penetrated as far as the Sibundoy valley, but of the traditional Church itself. For, despite all its conservatism and isolation, it could not go on for ever ignoring the new tendencies inherent in such documents as the Pope's *Populorum Progressio*, and the Colombian episcopate's own *Declaration on Development*.

With this new atmosphere which finally forced the Capuchins of the Putumayo to relax their intransigence somewhat, the Native Commission seized the opportunity to undertake various campaigns of social action, and the INCORA set on foot the draining of the valley, and bought back some of the larger settler estates. But none of this really brought about any fundamental change, as is clear from the following two examples:

(1) The Vicariate still keeps thirty per cent of the money paid to it by the Ministry of National Education for the payment of teachers.[28]

(2) The Catalan missionaries in the end stood out against the authority of the bishops. Although the latter agreed in principle that the INCORA could buy back land from the Church, the Capuchins refused to accept this 'unless the Holy See, which alone signed the Convention of the Missions with the national government, judges it to be acceptable'.[29]

In other words, in order to preserve the 'Mission lands', the Capuchin community in the tiny Sibundoy valley appealed directly to the Vicar of Christ on earth.

CHAPTER 17

Seventy Years On

The Indies are tempting to cupidity, and the Capuchins when they go there are in danger of forgetting the spirit of Poverty in their Rule, and starting to amass gold and silver.

(FRAY ANDRES DE CONCENTAINA, 1646)

The Catholic Church of the Putumayo is a religious, cultural and economic power.

(FATHER LINO RAMPON, 1962)

When we come to our own day, it is important to note the state of the Putumayo, the work of the Capuchin mission, and the present position of the Sibundoy whom we have been studying throughout this book. But first let me remind the reader:

(1) That a rapid survey of the life of the Sibundoy in 1970 shows to what extent the traditional elements which provide them with their *raison d'être* have stood out against the tremendous attempts over three generations to put an end to that Indian culture. This clearly demonstrates the failure of the *integrationist policy* among these 'savages'.

(2) That the conflict between Church and State over the mission lands has virtually ceased – not because one side has finally triumphed, but because of the need both see to cope with the 'nefarious' influence of the young rebel church of Colombia which understands precisely what the colonialist phenomenon really means, and which is trying to break with the traditional church and its traditions and stand alongside

the victims of its exploitation, the people. But both powers look on this as a truce rather than an alliance. It is a truce, however, which helps to reinforce the *integrationist policy* of the present government, now preparing a further, and it hopes final, assault on the last bastions of Indian culture.

(3) That in its final pages this book itself becomes evidence by showing first, how the Capuchin missionaries are still defending their 'civilizing' work in Colombia; and second, how little chance of survival there is for the Inga and Sibundoy, and indeed any other Indians, in face of the all-powerful West.

Any traveller coming to the Putumayo today, whether by land or air, can observe that the original forest is continually being pushed back, the population is increasing and, in short, that this once-forgotten land is becoming integrated into the life of the nation. This now irreversible process is especially evident in the Puerto Asís area, the centre of the North American oil companies' activities; here, in the millennial forests of the Amazon, the black gold is beginning to flow out through a pipeline which crosses the barrier of the Andes.

But, once again, the encroachment of the West brings certain consequences in its train. First, there is the new wave of land seizures and injustices of every kind which it is the custom of economic and cultural imperialism to perpetrate in order to force an entry: the Siona and Cofan tribes, which by 1965 had been reduced to 640 people in all, have been further reduced to half that number in less than five years.[1] Second, there is the vast increase in the cost of living that results from the arrival of the dollar on a large scale, and of Colombians from all over the country anxious to get their share of the manna in this new El Dorado.

The missionaries, for their part, concentrate their efforts on the villages. As in the past they leave them from time to time for sporadic evangelizing tours of the area, where they still sometimes find the same inconveniences as in the past: it was on the back of an Indian that the Vicar Apostolic visited the Yunguillo area in 1965. But since times have changed somewhat the evangelizers now accept and openly admit the in-

valuable help they get from the North American oil firms'
helicopters. Thanks to these they have managed to achieve
yearly tours among the most isolated communities, bringing to
these 'savages' the services of baptism, confirmation, confession, communion and the sacrament of marriage.[2] This assistance from modern technology has made it possible to
restore a number of old traditions. Thus, even at his age, Fray
Plácido Crous went in person to Yunguillo in 1967 in order to
receive the homage of the Inga, who restored for the occasion the traditional custom of the *camarico* of welcome, presenting the patriarch with farmyard poultry, hundreds of eggs,
and a wooden bowl full of fruit, banknotes and gold nuggets,[3]
just as in the days of the conquistadors.

But to return to the Sibundoy valley, let us consider how it
appears from the outside to the visiting traveller.

In its central and western part, the river Putumayo and its
tributaries still flood a swampy area of some thousand hectares, where the only thing that grows is *totora*, or esparto
grass, used in various Indian skills.* Towards the centre one
also sees areas of woodland, and these also appear around the
old towns of Manoy and Putumayo (now Santiago and San
Andrés). The majority of the Indians live together there, surrounding those who still have the wretched scraps of land sold
to them by the Mission. All the rest of the valley, and the
slopes of the mountains, are covered by the *haciendas* of the
missionaries and settlers, large or medium-sized estates, apart
from the occasional tiny holding that provides subsistence for
an Indian family.

In contrast with this peaceful countryside, there is a clatter
of noisy machines digging the canals around the edges whereby
the Colombian Institute for Agrarian Reform is hoping eventually to free the floor of the valley from the annual scourge of

---

Totora (*Thypha angustifolia*) – known in Peru as 'matting straw' – is
to be found all over the swampy areas in the Andes, and is used in the
same traditional ways. It is specially characteristic of Lake Titicaca,
where the Bolivian and Peruvian Indians use it both for thatching their
huts and making their *balsas*, or rafts.

flooding. The undertaking presents its own further social problems, since these mechanical monsters at times ruin the natives' tiny plots, for which destruction they have as yet received no compensation.*

As one approaches Santiago and San Andrés the numbers of men in *capisayos* and women in *sayas* to be seen indicate that these villages are still inhabited by their founders, whereas in Colón and San Francisco the presence of trousers is a sign that Creoles predominate. On the other hand, in the old village of Sibundoy Grande both ethnic groups live together, since whites have rented or bought a great many houses from Indians. One can however still see there – as in so many old engravings – women bent over their traditional work of weaving. None of these villages has any of the most elementary public services, for the small supplies of electricity and piped water put in by the missionaries only feed their own houses and those of a few of the more important landowners. Hence another special local characteristic: public wells and fountains.

The final outward aspect the visitor might note is the size of the Mission buildings in Sibundoy, the capital. They can be seen from every part of the valley, rising high above the greying limed roofs standing humbly below them, as though to remind the world of the power of the Church. The cathedral, the monasteries, the schools, and the Capuchins' office buildings make up a third of the village, the whole of which is surrounded by the missionary *hacienda* of La Granja which borders it to the north, east and south.

But beyond this outward appearance lies a complex involving economics, education, sanitation and apostolic work, and a whole daily way of life which it is essential to describe.

What strikes the practised observer first of all is the co-

* The drainage work-sites extend over an area of 8,500 hectares. The work was begun in February 1968, and was expected to be completed by August 1971. The cost was originally expected to be 2,000,000 dollars, repayable by the landowners on a scale commensurate with the improvement in the value of each one's land.

existence of large and medium-sized estates devoted to extensive stock-raising, with the mass of little allotments devoted to intensive crop-growing. This must be looked at more closely, because in an agricultural and stock-raising area like this, the way the land is distributed among its inhabitants provides the main key to an understanding of the prevailing standards of living.

If one studies the cadastral surveys (a synopsis of which will be found in Appendix 1), one comes to these conclusions:

(1) Over half of those working the land (three quarters of them Indians) have less than three hectares apiece, amounting to no more than five per cent of the entire level area of the valley.

(2) People owning less than ten hectares are in the proportion of two Indians (Inga or Sibundoy) to one settler. But since the whites have little taste for farming, the actual work falls on the Indians.

(3) Above ten hectares, the percentage of the land owned by Creoles increases with the amounts owned, and at the top of the scale they are alone, with the fourteen estates that go to make up almost half the valley.

(4) The native community (sixty per cent of the total population) owns only twenty-two per cent of the land.

(5) While 491 natives and 'poor whites' are huddled with their families on 875 hectares, the Capuchin Mission fathers have 1,092.[4]

To this must be added a fact not recorded by the survey: the presence of nearly 500 families, almost all of them Indian, who own nothing at all.

In brief, the statistics bear out the history we have been looking at. The feudal fate planned for the valley of the Inga and Sibundoy by the Great Crusader, Fidel de Montclar, has been wholly achieved: chief of all the landowners is the Church, surrounded by a small number of large proprietors and – apart from the embryonic middle class of small businessmen and officials – all the rest, the vast mass of the people in other words, is made up of people who can only be called serfs.

The fate that has befallen the Indians includes sub-proletarianization, minifundism, and destitution. For the very rich and fairly rich settlers, on the other hand, fate has allotted the preservation of the colonialist and irrational criteria by which this fertile valley and the area around it are used. Consider the following figures:

(1) Twenty per cent of the land is let out on a *métayage** system, ten per cent rented pure and simple.

(2) The large landowners graze 51,000 head of cattle and 4,000 horses on 22,000 hectares of flat or gently sloping land, while the small farmers have no more than 1,088 hectares.

(3) Poverty prevents the tiny landholders from diversifying their crops, which are limited to the basic sustenance foods – maize (thirty-eight per cent) and beans (thirty-one per cent), with potatoes and other vegetables only grown on twenty-two per cent.

(4) The small labour force needed for extensive stock-breeding results in a high level of unemployment and a low level of wages – between 25 and 50 cents (US) per day, depending on whether or not the worker also gets food.[5]

If to all these factors we add the poverty of the crops produced, and the fact that the cattle and their products (meat, butter and cheese) are all exported to the interior of the country, we can see why the people of the Sibundoy valley live in a permanent state of malnutrition. In such circumstances there would be little point in any programme of reform.

The INCORA, for its part, found itself powerless when it came to carrying out its programme for redistributing the land. First because by law it could only buy back a few *haciendas* of more than 100 hectares (and the same law permits the landlords to choose which land they keep), which made it quite impossible to allot economically viable holdings to the hundreds of people owning little or no land; and then because the price of that land, once the work of improvement was finished, was fixed at that point at 1,000 dollars a hectare,

*Land tenure in which the farmer pays part (usually half) of produce as rent to the owner, who furnishes stock and seed.

a price manifestly inaccessible to the Indian masses, for whom the indebtedness into which this would lead them could be no more than another form of serfdom.

However, let us conclude the long story of the 'Mission lands'. I do not know whether the Vicar Apostolic did in fact, as promised, appeal to the Sovereign Pontiff to arbitrate. But at the beginning of 1968 his position softened somewhat, and he began negotiating with the INCORA. But this was no simple matter. The negotiations dragged on and on, because of haggling over the sums to be paid in compensation and, even more, because the Capuchins would not let themselves be treated as a single juridical entity, declaring that the Church in the valley was a 'trinity': the Vicariate itself and the two parishes of Santiago and Sibundoy. Weary of argument, the government finally accepted this subtle distinction, which enabled the Mission, instead of keeping a hundred hectares like the other large landowners, to keep three hundred, chosen with great care: they comprised in fact the *hacienda* of La Granja, whose situation made it exceptionally profitable. As for the value of the land given up, that was fixed at 2,242,000 pesos, or 132,000 dollars.[6]

The moment the agreement was signed, as though by magic, all the rumours which had until then been flying around among the people about the danger of 'Castroist communism' represented by the INCORA ceased, giving way to an atmosphere of peaceful collaboration with the civil authorities.

Obviously these last-mentioned events would have a rapid effect in altering the destiny of the valley. That is why I should like to attempt to present a final balance sheet of the work of the Catalan missionaries, who made that valley their main centre of operations in Colombia.

The fact that so many of the events took place in our own day makes it easier to study the economics of the matter. It is of course impossible to provide an exact evaluation of the net profit to the missionaries from the *haciendas* in the most recent years. However, if we take as a basis the average production capacity per hectare of land like theirs – valued by the local office of the *Agencia Créditicia* at three head of cattle per hectare – the Mission's herds can be reckoned to be about 3,000 head. Rumour places the total nearer 5,000, a figure confirmed by the records of the official animal vaccination service. If it is true, as a lot of people say, that the missionaries moved a large part of their old herds on to land let to their friends and supporters, then this latter figure would certainly be nearer the correct one. Furthermore, the value of the produce from all these animals is equally uncertain: the only figure admitted by the Capuchins is a mere 700 litres of milk per day.[7] The second largest of the missionaries' fields of activity is that of construction. Of recent years that has slowed down, since 'definitive' modern buildings have been completed for the Mission in Sibundoy, still the seat of the Vicar Apostolic. We know what a vast contribution the natives have made to all this, both in materials and in free labour, given to honour the 'Divine Shepherdess', patroness of the Mission; such 'voluntary' contributions are still being made today towards the decoration and interior furnishings of the huge cathedral. We may note in particular that it was the natives who provided the gold needed for making decorations and the various objects used in religious ceremonies, among them a magnificent monstrance.

This does not mean that building work has been brought to a full stop. One need only visit the village of San Andrés on a Monday to realize this. The traveller will there see, as in the old days, the entire native population assembled to work for nothing on the church building site, under the orders of a Spanish Capuchin. And the Indians are immensely enthusiastic: sustained only by a small amount of powdered milk – taken by the Mission from the gifts received from Caritas – they will pick up, often with their bare hands, and carry to the village, the vast stones needed to build the new church.

This outstanding proof of the religious zeal of the natives leads us to take a closer look at the missionaries' apostolic activities. The works exclusive to their ministry are first and foremost achieved by the activity of pious societies, seminaries, and catechism classes. But there are other institutions designed to maintain the piety, submission and generosity of their parishioners:

(1) There are five special feasts: St Andrew, the Divine Shepherdess, Our Lady of Fatima, Our Lady of Las Lajas, and St James the Apostle, patron of Spain.

(2) Pilgrimages to the shrine of Las Lajas (in Nariño province) organized on its special feast, and the Carnival in Sibundoy.

(3) The daily house-to-house carrying of the Blessed Virgin and various saints, to be honoured and presented with gifts by the Indians.

(4) To this source of day-to-day revenue must be added contributions both regular and occasional for the upkeep of the church. The regular contributions come from church collections, the payment of tithes, in cash or kind, and the *camaricos*. The latter, which used traditionally to be only a voluntary offering on major feasts, are now demanded daily for ordinary services.[8] Occasional contributions are of four kinds:

(a) Begging appeals for missionary establishments* and for the support of the discalced Carmelites brought from Spain by the Capuchins to satisfy the territory's 'need for the contemplative life'.[9]

(b) The sums assessed at between 150 and 500 pesos – depending on their importance – due to be provided by the *Alférez*† for the decoration of the altar at Christmas, in Holy Week and at Corpus Christi.[10]

*The only list of such collections to be published regularly refers to the white parish of San Francisco, run by the only secular priest in the valley. We learn from it perhaps most notably that a single collection made at one feast in 1967 brought in 36,230 pesos (1,872 dollars), and the following year, 'without any ceremony at all, 22,000 pesos' (1,131 dollars) in two hours. As for the parishes served by the Capuchins we know that the 'Cathedral week' held in Sibundoy in March 1967 brought in a total of 39,316 pesos (2,081 dollars).

†In virtue of an old Spanish tradition specially respected in Colombia the *Alférez*, representing the oldest families of the nobility and middle class of the parish, were in charge of the statues and their adornment –

(c) The annual collection for the Pope.*

(d) A number of special collections, like the one organized in 1968 for the international Eucharistic Congress in Bogotá.[11]

The Indians, and especially the poorest among them, willingly give their contribution to all these. There is a link between this and their ancestral piety towards the dead – which is perhaps measured by the number of masses they pay to have said for them. Requests for masses are so numerous that the Capuchins can often only fulfil them months later, though even the simplest category, the shared mass, costs ten pesos, not including the *camarico*.

This devotion to the mass enables the Mission to retain its supremacy over the civil authorities, a state of affairs about which one official has this to say:

Without bitterness or hatred to anyone, it may be said that the delay in the acculturization we are trying to achieve is related to the wishes of the Capuchin Mission. For eighty per cent of the population persists in consulting the missionaries about whatever they are told by agricultural experts or any other kind of official.[12]

---

often a mass of genuine treasures accumulated over the centuries from legacies and gifts. On big feasts, and especially during the processions of Holy Week, the *Alférez* publicly carry round the *andas* (or stands) with the statues on them, covered in jewels and rich ornaments. The office of *alférez*, considered a most honourable one, is hereditary, and as can be seen, lucrative.

*This collection, for the purpose of adding to the Vatican's treasury, is taken up every year by the Capuchins on the 'Pope's Feast'. Here is a quotation from the editor of the Sibundoy *Catholic Bulletin* for May 1965: 'For this feast we must all ... give generously to the customary collection sent to the Holy Father every year. Last year His Holiness Paul VI sent the following message to the Vicar Apostolic of this Mission: "The Sovereign Pontiff, thanking you for the alms of 650 pesos which you have sent him, and moved by this repeated manifestation of filial devotion, sends your Excellency and his beloved sons a particular and full Apostolic Benediction, as a pledge of the heavenly favours which will finally reward them for their generosity and sacrifices." ' In the years since then nothing has changed except that the sums collected, to judge from succeeding messages of the same kind from the Vatican, reproduced in the *Catholic Bulletin*, have almost doubled.

Such realizations are an indication of how far we still have to go in freeing our compatriots from this vassalage. And they force us to consider one fundamental question, which the reader will no doubt have asked himself more than once during the course of this book: *why* do these Indians, be they Inga or Sibundoy, put up with this 'guardianship' by the Capuchins and all its excesses?

One should first recall the alienation which religious power can create in naturally simple people – the greeting given on entering a house is 'Sacramento' – and then the way in which the government, appearing to them so ineffective and distant, has simply abandoned them. But the link between these two factors, and the consequent paternalistic dependence, only becomes clear when we analyse the thinking of the Indians themselves – as for instance this monologue uttered by Diego Mavisoy, the governor of San Andrés:

One gentleman from the government will come and promise this thing, and that thing, and the other thing. He promises that it will all be for the benefit of the Indians. But he does not keep his word. Then another one comes, and the same thing happens all over again. So the Indians decide that these gentlemen only come to pull the wool over their eyes. . . . Whereas the missionaries may only promise poverty, or some tiny alms or gift – but what they promise, they keep to; yes, sir, they keep to it. . . . For instance, there are the Monday jobs (*mingas**) for the Church; all they pay for them is a little powdered milk. But they actually give it to us. What they promise they do, unlike the gentlemen from the government. . . . Oh well! That's life!

All over the Andes, Indians' conversations are interspersed with the saying 'That's life.' It reflects the fatalism into which they have been forced by the socio-cultural imperialism of the West. But, to me at least, the intention they give this statement

---

*The *mingas* (from the Quechua word *minkay*, meaning to help with work) are of Inca origin. The word means taking part for nothing in some communal work for the public good. The religious have kept alive this ancient Andean tradition to the advantage of the Church.

suggests that they see their destruction not as the result of any transcendent law, but merely as the success of the strongest.

The degree of realism which we see in Diego Mavisoy's reflections also explains the presence of malcontents – of certain Inga and Sibundoy still strong enough to stand up for themselves, and others who have been disappointed to see their land swallowed up in the *Cofradias* of the Blessed Virgin, in return for nothing but the 'poverty, or some tiny alms or gift' promised them by the missionaries.

While the Creole population of the Putumayo goes on growing steadily, the Indian population of the Sibundoy valley remains the same in some areas, and is certainly diminishing in others: with the Inga this is due to emigrations and trading trips to the interior; with the Sibundoy it is the result of an infant mortality rate up to and even sometimes surpassing fifty per cent of all births.[13]

Thus, from his entry into the world, the Indian is subject to natural selection; a fairly 'civilized' Sibundoy woman expresses it thus:

Just before the birth, you try not to work too hard. When the time comes, another woman in the family comes to help you or, if your husband is kind, he will support your shoulders as you give birth. You crouch over and – there we are! The baby is there! You see sir, if you have no money, you drop your child just like animals do.*

Another woman relative then comes to help the mother in the house for a fortnight, so that she herself may be free to do nothing but look after her child. Indian women are well aware indeed of the many risks facing new-born children, as we can see in this traditional refrain sung by little Sibundoy girls:

> All men have come
> and still come into the world crying,
> from a loving and anxious woman.

*The phrase 'like animals' is suggestive. On the one hand, it indicates that Indian women would like to have the advantages of modern gynaecological techniques, in conformity with their stage of advanced acculturization. But on the other, it shows how far they are from realizing the value of this traditional position (crouching) in childbirth, only just being rediscovered by modern medical science.

264 A State within a State

> The child sleeps in her gentle arms,
> and when he awakens,
> she thanks God,
> because he is still alive.[14]

With the protection of his mother's prayers, the baby has to
face the dangers that are ever-present to all his tribe: smallpox, gastro-enteritis, malnutrition and its consequences. Later
on he will risk dysentery, tuberculosis and the various forms of
rheumatism. In fact the children of most of the Sibundoy who
have been forced out to live in the swampy land are less robust
than their parents; by the age of twenty, they tend to have lost
all their teeth, and fall an easy prey to sickness of every kind. It
is easy to see why, when one remembers that the two schools
on the plain have no sanitation, and their water comes from
contaminated streams.

To remedy this situation medical and sanitary services have
been established by the Church and the State. But these consist
only of a dispensary – in the white village of Colón – and one
doctor for the entire valley. The natives only seek his help
rarely: he says that is because he has only the most inadequate
means at his disposal; they say because it costs more than they
can afford to consult him, and that furthermore, they come up
against a quite systematic racial discrimination.[15] For its
part, the Vicariate has set up the 'missionary hospital of
Colón', subsidized by the State, which makes up for its own
total lack of equipment and trained staff by making use of the
services of the official doctor. But, as we saw in the preceding
chapter, the Indian community barely gets any help from this:
so much so indeed that when I visited its spotless, vast, and up-
to-date wards, I only found there a single patient, one white
child; a year later (January 1968), an inspector from the Ministry of Public Health was to find the same thing.* The nuns who

*The only statistics ever given by the Mission to the Ministry of Pub-
lic Health relative to the activities of the 'missionary hospital' refer to
the first six months of 1967. In the main, they were these: Out-patient
consultations (infirmary) 272; Medical services (out-patients) 97; Sur-
gical operations 6; Maternity cases 3; In-patients 3; Pediatrics 0; Beds
available 33.

run the hospital are wholly at a loss to explain this phenomenon; but according to the Indians it is entirely due to the costs fixed by the missionaries: for instance, to have a baby in hospital costs between 500 and 600 pesos (twenty-five to thirty dollars).

However great may be the Indians' desire to receive the advantages of modern medicine, they find themselves, as in the past, forced to seek all the old traditional curative measures of their ancestors. Some even indicate a positive mistrust of white men's medicine; thus their use of their own traditional medicine, based on divination and the use of herbs, etc., has increased: far from dying out, in fact, the fame of the Inga healers and herbalists is continuing to grow, and to extend far beyond the Sibundoy valley. Similarly the use of the *yage* (a hallucinatory drink) has also come back considerably into favour, which must surely be partly due to the wish to escape from the wretchedness of this world.*

*There is a great quantity of scientific documentation of the use of the *yage*, an extract from the stalk of the plants of the *Banisteriopsis* family (*B. inebrians*, *B. caapi*, *B. quitensis*, etc.), together with that of a great many kinds of narcotics extracted from plants of the *Datura* genus, in the whole area lying between the Napo (in Ecuador and Peru) and the Putumayo (*borracheros, yerba de huaca, huanto, huantuc, chamico, tonga, peji*, etc.). It would be beyond the scope of this study to try to summarize the entire history and use of these drugs. Let me however mention that there has been a series of exhaustive studies in the Sibundoy valley during the past ten years by various North American and European researchers. Specially eminent among them is the American Melvin Lee Bristol, who published eight studies between 1964 and 1967 (in Harvard University's Botanical Museum Leaflets). This scientist, who spent three years living among the Inga, discovered nine varieties of *borracheros* in use among them, which he considers must represent generations of effort in selecting and acclimatizing the plants. The work is continuing today, for I myself saw in the garden of the best-known of the Sibundoy herbalists attempts being made to acclimatize the *yage*, a native of the warmer land of the Lower Putumayo. These narcotics and hallucinogens enable healers and others 'to be transported to the bosom of their family' when they are on a journey, 'to find lost objects' (in all the Shamanic traditions of America and Asia they are a method of finding the soul of a sick person), and in general, 'to know, perceive, experience, know more deeply, learn . . . so as to develop awareness, expecially in the domain of

So, through an unexpected turn of affairs, the lack of medical help from the colonizers brought with it the reinforcement of one of their own most specific cultural traits among a people in other ways highly acculturized – a trait which in all logic missionary action should have given priority to getting rid of, since medicine touches so closely upon the sphere of religion.

This does not mean that the Catalan missionaries did nothing for the physical health of the Indians: they maintained a first-aid post, known as a dispensary, in every parish, and it is not possible to estimate just how valuable these posts really were. There nuns would administer routine treatment, send the sick to the doctor in Colón, and give them good advice. The natives, however, do not seem convinced of the usefulness of such services: some because any free treatment is rare, and they are *sold* medical samples sent free from laboratories (even aspirin tablets);[16] others because the advice they get from the religious (men or women) seems to achieve little result. Here is one random comment from a Sibundoy woman which is most revealing:

Here we often lose a lot of blood after giving birth. I had a flux which went on for six months, and since my mother told me that though Indian remedies could cure it, I wouldn't be able to have any more children afterwards, I went to see Fray Bartolomé. He told me that what I must do was to have another child at once. I had it all right, but it was born dead.[17]

Missionary sources tell us that another form of social service was the distribution to the Indians of the food provided for the Mission by the philanthropic organization Caritas. And though some Indians knew nothing of this, and others say they only received it in exchange for work, it is certain that the missionaries do in fact carry out this charitable work, though sporadically. Indeed, on coming out of the High Mass in Sibun-

---

vision [clairvoyance]'. All of which led the American scientist to conclude: 'In this way, and perhaps others too, *yage* helps the Sibundoy to learn to live.'

doy Cathedral on 1 January 1967, I myself saw the missionaries giving an egg to each of the poorest parishioners present.

As regards education, the prime task delegated to the missionary Church by the Colombian State, the situation described in preceding chapters has not changed. The interpretation the Capuchins place on the Convention of the Missions enables the Vicariate to refrain from giving the government any information as to how public education is carried out, or how the money it receives for this purpose is spent.*

The only source of information, and that is very vague, is the *Catholic Bulletin,* from which we learn that illiteracy is down to seventeen per cent in the Sibundoy valley, and the number of classes and pupils has increased, though school attendance 'has not yet reached the legal minimum, certain parts of the province being especially behindhand'.[18] This comment from the Capuchins leads us to note that, according to the Marist Brothers, the Indian children remain the most industrious at school, even though they have only four years of elementary schooling – a step justified, according to the head of the Mission, by 'the lack of teaching establishments in which the children could start a further series of studies'. Beneath this reasoning would seem to lie the Capuchins' great principle that 'decolonization' – i.e. turning these children into artisans – must be avoided at all costs, and their conviction of the 'moral dangers' to which they would be exposed were they to pursue their studies outside the Sibundoy valley.

The quality and significance of the teaching given in these public schools, and in the two teachers' training colleges at Sibundoy, also provides food for thought. I will here mention only four aspects of it:

---

*These funds continue to be very considerable in relation to those allotted to the civil administration of the territory. The figures for 1968 show the sum allotted for education as 5,026,930 pesos, as compared with the total Putumayo budget of 7,559,153 pesos. Yet the missionaries still stress in their publications how inadequate is the aid they get from the State for education. And they constantly point out that during the year 1967, 'the Vicariate paid over 200,000 pesos out of its own funds for public education'.

(1) Because of the high cost of the teaching, the uniforms, and the other provisions demanded by the Mission rules, only three Indian girls enrolled in the female teachers' training college, and there is not one Indian student in the boys' college.

(2) The battle waged by the earlier missionaries to get the Inga and Sibundoy to wear the same clothes as white people has been replaced by a subtler campaign: for 'morality in clothing'. The propaganda for this among the young is evident from this typical letter from a group of white college girls published by the *Catholic Bulletin*:

> In our college we have begun the apostolate for decency in dress. ... We have sent a notice to every household in Santiago, asking them to help us in this campaign. We have also sent letters to Puerto Asís and Sibundoy, to get our fellow students to do the same.[19]

(3) All reference to aboriginal culture and history is being systematically eliminated, which leads to a considerable number of errors in the teaching given the children: thus, to give only one example, we read in the handbook edited by the Vicariate's under-secretary for education that the 'village of Santiago was founded in 1870'.

(4) The children are taught in a spirit of admiring respect for the congregation of Catalan Capuchins, as may be seen from these few questions and answers from a *Handbook of Geography, History and Civic Education*:

> Q: In brief, to what do we owe the progress of the Putumayo?
> A: With justice and sincerity, we may say that the general progress of the Putumayo is due to the community of Capuchin missionaries.
> Q: Are the inhabitants of the Putumayo therefore grateful to the Capuchin missionaries?
> A: Of course. Seeing the achievements of the Capuchin missionaries, both spiritual and material, the intelligent inhabitants of the Putumayo (both Indians and settlers) feel indelible gratitude to them in their hearts.[20]

Even today, the fading voices of the old people sometimes rise to speak out against this systematic alienation of the

Indian soul. Old Dominga Juajibioy, a grandmother of nearly a hundred, sometimes tells her grandchildren and great-grandchildren this story in the evenings:

One of our ancestors' stories tells how we were born in this very Sibundoy valley. There was here a cacique named Carlos Tamoabioy, who ruled from Mount Patascoy to La Tortuaga and Chinbonoca. The Sibundoy territory covered all that ground. There was a time when the people of Aponte wanted to steal it, but the Great Cacique, Carlos Tamoabioy, declared war on them, and the Sibundoy won. During that war, the lance of one of our great chiefs named Dionisio pierced the body of another chief named Juan Martín. And from then on the Sibundoy were free.*

According to one of her great-grandchildren, Dominga Juajibioy would often close her story with the 'Proclamation of the Liberator', expressed in these words:

You, Indians, have already been witness to all my efforts: liberty reigns where tyranny reigned but yesterday. In the time of Carlos Tamoabioy a great many people died fighting the men of Aponte. How sad it is to think of all those who died! That is why we must die for our beautiful valley. That is why we must be brave, and fear no one . . .

This proclamation is yet another example of Indian and Creole elements intermingling. One might at first think the term 'Liberator' referred to General Bolívar, for this is the title by which he is known all over South America. But this account has no relation to 'Bolívar's proclamation' – which we all learnt at school – except that it has a similar ring of

---

*Despite the three centuries and more of oral tradition lying between this account and the events it retails, the distortions are fairly easy to recognize. The phrase 'people of Aponte' is used here to mean Juan Martín de Fuenmayor, the first *encomendero* of the two valleys. And the war spoken of might be either the memory of confrontations with other Inca tribes before the coming of Carlos Tamoabioy, combined with the continuing opposition to the first conquistadors and *encomenderos*, or a psychological transposition into the sphere of armed fighting of verbal disputes of more recent date between the two tribes. Certainly the cacique Dionisio was a real person. He was one of the most fierce of all the defenders of the Indian heritage in the Sibundoy valley.

enthusiasm; and in the mind of Grandmother Juajibioy the term 'Liberator' suggests a combination of Bolívar and the Great Cacique Tamoabioy – a figure rich in symbolism for his descendants. Thus are the seeds of the past still being sown in the minds of the young, in the hope that they will grow up some day.

We may conclude by looking briefly at a few other aspects of everyday life as it appears today in the Sibundoy valley.

Nothing more absorbs the attention of all the inhabitants, be they Indian or Creole, than the work of the gigantic machines of the INCORA. But this sign of modernity has done little to alter the Indians' way of life, which is still very like that of their fathers and grandfathers. The first thing that strikes one is the survival of the noble families of the past, some of whom have more or less adopted the white man's styles of dress and of living. This group has four elements in it:

(1) Those outstanding figures, highly literate and well versed in the law, who fought court battles to defend their land. Of these Diego Tisoy remained the unquestioned leader until his death in May 1968.

(2) The ever-growing proportion of the Inga who live by trade, turning the profits from their long selling trips into land, houses, jewellery and other luxuries.

(3) The highly respected body of *curacas* (herbalist-healers), who earn considerable profits from their work, while preserving all the traditions of native medicine.

(4) The small minority who set a high enough value on modern education to make the effort to acquire it, whether by their own means, or by succeeding somehow in getting hold of scholarships for their children. At the head of this handful of educated men is the anthropologist Alberto Juajibioy (the only native actually practising a profession in the liberal arts), one woman teacher, a few minor officials and white-collar workers, and a few young people now receiving some form of skilled training (as nurses, etc.).

Among the others – that is to say the vast majority of the

people in the valley – daily life still bears the characteristics of the distant past.

Traditional costume, sometimes with the addition of a pair of shoes, is still always worn, and gives a splendidly bright and unusual appearance to the crowds who fill the roads and paths on Sundays, as they troop towards the villages to go to mass, to sell their produce in the market, and exchange their views, either at the Chapter or in the village square.

There is still a lively attachment to the land. Those Indians who have not been deprived of everything still build their hut, as they always did, in the middle of their piece of land (*chagra*). These huts, rectangular, with wooden walls and high roofs of carefully plaited straw, arc divided inside into two or three rooms, depending on what the individual family can afford. Comfortably-off families will have a bedroom, which no one but the family ever enters, a parlour, where friends or work-mates are welcomed from time to time, and the kitchen, which is the centre of the family's activities. This last gives one the best idea of the Indians' capacity for adapting themselves to their circumstances. On the ground, or on a bench made of clay, three stones support the cooking pot, above which hang the family's supplies of meat, from a plank of bamboo attached to the roof, on top of which salt and other provisions which must be kept dry are preserved from the damp air rising from the swampland. The proportions of these huts are so perfectly planned, and the egress for the smoke so exactly arranged, that from only a few yards away it is impossible to know whether the fire is alight or not. Such is not at all the case with the houses of brick with iron roofs built by the settlers and the more acculturized natives, where smoke and smells of all kinds pervade the entire place.

Aboriginal plants such as *zitzes* and maize still form the basis of their food. Maize beer or *chicha,* which is both food and drink to them, has never been supplanted, despite all the efforts of governments, missionaries, and modern drink manufacturers to get rid of it.

Agricultural work is still often done communally by *ua-*

chingas, groups of fifty or so people of all ages and both sexes, under the leadership of an elder of the tribe. These *uachingeros* move from one holding to another, weeding, sowing and reaping, just as they did in the days of the Incas.

Kinship structures also still retain a great deal of the past. The use of the mother's name was abolished fifty years ago, and has been replaced by that of the father of the family. But with this difference; if the wives follow the Spanish custom of keeping their maiden name and adding it with a *de* to their husband's name – e.g. Escolastica Chindoy de Mavisoy – the husbands add to their surnames the Christian names of their wives, also with a *de* – e.g. Avelino Chicunque de Maria, Salvador Chindoy de Mercedes, Angel Jacanamijoy de Filomena, and so on. Thus they have found a compromise between the matriarchal heritage and the prosaic need to differentiate among people of the same name. Of these there are many, owing to the paucity of saints' names handed out by the missionaries over the baptismal font and the profusion of Marcelinos and Marcelianos in honour of the Canyes brothers.

Apart from agricultural work, the chief concern of any family owning any land at all is to defend itself from the extortions of the settlers, and to keep the drainage canals in working order. For those who own nothing, their time is spent in looking for work, and in the illusory hope of being granted some tiny piece of the chimerical *resguardo* created in 1956, whose very existence has been ignored by the government ever since.

The Indian Chapter has indeed preserved all its old authority. Though long distorted by the influence of the missionaries, it is now returning to being what it always was before they came: it settles disputes; punishes (in a cell nowadays) the disorderly; and 'advises' with a few strokes of the whip any sons or husbands who fail to respect their family obligations – but only when asked to do so by the parents or wives involved who find themselves unable to cope with the situation.

It is noteworthy in this regard that it is the women who are the main prop of this traditional institution – an institution to which the more acculturized of the men object – because the Chapter protects them from the *machismo* so prevalent in Creole society.*

Acceptance of the authority of the missionaries is still evinced by the gifts given to the Church, and the crowds attending religious services. The men always remain apart from the women, both in processions and inside the church; the natives also find themselves left at the back, the front of of the church being reserved for whites.

Though the Carnival is not quite what it once was, it is still the one occasion in the year when the whole community together can express its common feelings. *Chicha* still has a large part to play in it, but on the other hand it is to be lamented that such traditional elements as the arches of flowers, games and dances inside the church (forbidden by 'Brother Strong-arm') have gone, and that one barely hears the violins, harps and other musical instruments which thirty years ago still gave this occasion so much of its special character.

But, above all, what one notes about the Indians is that the lack of work, and thus of money to enable them to raise their standard of living, has resulted in a kind of paralysis.

To improve matters, an artisans' cooperative was set up in 1969. But the problem of trying to sell its products – traditional belts and woven materials – combined with the very poor wages it paid (about 35 cents [US] per day) prevents its representing a very stable amelioration.

In fact, the situation of the Inga and Sibundoy would seem to be getting gradually worse and worse. For the only real ambition of the Indian is to return to the possession of his *madre-tierra*, and apart from this there seems no possible bridge between the past and the future. And the purchase of the allotments put up for sale by the government has got them

*Machismo, from *macho*, meaning 'male', refers to the distortion of the whole notion of virility into a cult of sexual prowess and strength. The word is usually used to mean masculine superiority, in the strict South American sense. It must also be pointed out that *crimes passionnels* are almost unknown among the Sibundoy. There was one in 1968, and it was the talk of the valley.

so deep into debt that a great many families have, even now in 1970, decided to give up and go away, under the leadership of their elders, to look for peace and freedom in the loneliness of the forest. A great many more are preparing to follow this example, having finally given up all hope of getting back the land of their ancestors. In other words, the Colombian state – this time in the name of technology, western productivity and 'national' integration – is preparing to achieve what seventy years of Capuchin colonialism failed to do; it is trying, once and for all, and by non-violent means, to annihilate these people who will not be 'civilized'.

The Indians are well aware of the painful consequences of such an exile. It is therefore hardly surprising that a group of the most determined of them, seeing no other solution, found a crumb of hope in the faint possibility that I might be able to find some answer to their agonizing problem. Mirage though it is, this hope came to them in 1969, shortly after the Capuchin mission in Putumayo, wounded to the core by the publication of this book in Colombia, opened the longest and most persistent campaign in its history to justify its work and to condemn this new 'detractor of religion'. A court case was brought against me on the ground of 'calumny', while every pulpit, every newspaper, every radio station, pamphlets, loudspeakers, church publications – every available means – was brought into the fray in this fresh crusade all over the south of the country. They are at it still.*

*The accusation of calumny brought against me was based on the general statement that my work denigrates the work of the Missions, and that the Vicar Apostolic has found seven 'falsehoods' in the sources; these are: (1) the missionaries never tried to change the name of the village of Sibundoy Grande; (2) they never forbade the Indians to ask for title-deeds to their lands; (3) the Mission cattle were not transported in trucks which belonged to them, but in hired trucks; (4) the Pius XII College was not 'kidnapped' by the Vicariate Apostolic, since it already held the monopoly of public education; (5) the salaries of the teachers were not cut, but only readjusted to suit the needs of the moment in order to provide better services; (6) the Mission *haciendas* belonged not to the Mission but to the Church; and (7) the Mission did not have as much as 3,000 head of cattle.

However, the scandal this aroused, and its repercussions elsewhere in the world, have left their mark. In July 1970, while the Vatican was lending a million dollars to enable a few Indians – not Inga or Sibundoy – to buy the land suggested by the INCORA,[21] the Capuchin missionaries, in obedience to orders from above, were handing over their mission to

---

Apart from this, the mass of material put out during those eighteen months – especially the dozens of articles in journals and reviews, and the hundreds of radio programmes specially intended for the Indian audience – is so vast as to defy enumeration. By way of example, here are the principal arguments and positions adopted by the review *Cultura nariñense* in Pasto between January 1969 and June 1970:

Condemnation of the book before even seeing it.

Condemnation of the weekly *El Catolicismo*, the official paper of the archdiocese of Bogotá, for praising 'the author's courage' (shortly after which the editor of *El Catolicismo* resigned).

Personal abuse of the author and all Colombian journalists guilty of having made favourable comments on the book.

Declarations that the author had 'never set foot' in Sibundoy, and that his photographs were not genuine and his quotations false.

Condemnation by the bishop in a Pastoral Letter of the Indians' 'false friends'.

Speeches in favour of the Catalan Mission given as part of public demonstrations organized in Pasto and in the Putumayo, during which thousands of leaflets were distributed bearing the title 'The Inhabitants of the Putumayo, and the Anti-clerical Book by Bonilla'.

Comparison of the author with a writer of pornography.

Articles by scholars of the Order directed to demonstrating the 'bad faith' of the author, vaguely linking him with Leibniz, Hegel, Marx, Engels, Papini, and declaring that in the 'wickedness of his thought' one 'could see comparisons only in far-off Mesopotamia in the third century'.

Hypotheses as to 'where the money came from' for the Colombian edition – identifying its source both as 'atheist communism' and 'the capitalist old guard in disguise'.

Finally, and this I mention only briefly, a racialist argument: 'The basic question,' wrote Monsignor Mejía, 'is too profound and is so vast in scope that one cannot attribute the authorship of the book to a single individual – particularly one who is quite unknown – about whom there is nothing specially transcendent. Extremely powerful group interests are trying in vain to hide behind this fragile mestizo screen which conceals nothing.'

another community, and moving back to the banks of the Amazon, the area ruled by Fray Marceliano de Vilafranca. And the national government, seized with a sudden interest, was rapidly speeding up its negotiations with Rome to alter the Convention of the Missions.*

The departure of the seraphic friars is certainly regretted by that most alienated section of the Indian population, who are now wondering what to expect from their new spiritual leaders, the Redemptorists. Others, those mentioned earlier, cling to the hope that the State will eventually hear the petitions they are still putting forward.[24] And there is also a small group of young people among whom the discovery of their people's history has reawakened feelings of nationalism and non-conformism which they would willingly carry to the ultimate extreme.

As I conclude my story, everything that happens provides food for talking in every leisure moment, for discussion around the dying fire at night. But in the whirlwind of world affairs through which we are living, such small reactions are barely noticeable. It is certain that the enforcement, more marked every day, of integration is shutting the door to any possibility of survival for what remains of this age-old Indian culture,

---

*It is still too soon to be clear about all this. But we can at least conclude the tale of the evangelizing work of the Capuchin fathers in the Putumayo by recording here the pressures they used to get the Church in Colombia to condemn this book. The Colombian hierarchy replied as follows: 'With this statement it is not our intention either to wound or to condemn anyone, but to stress the spirit of responsibility which all Catholics must have when judging the work of the missionaries for the Church and the country.'[22] The Mission's appeals to the Vatican met with no more success. This is the answer transmitted through the Apostolic Nuncio in Colombia: 'In this regard, His Excellency, Cardinal Villot, Secretary of State to His Holiness, in his official statement number 2,273, of 24 March 1970, said this: "As regards the Capuchin missionaries in the Vicariate of Sibundoy, Your Excellency will be so kind as to transmit the esteem of the Holy See to the prelate of that Vicariate, notifying him personally, as well as his brother-missionaries, of the consolation of the Apostolic Benediction which His Holiness bestows on them with all his heart . . ."'[23]

crushed in a mere seventy years by the heavy hand of the heralds of Western 'civilization'.

The future of the Inga and Sibundoy would seem bound up with the extent of the integration of their young people into the foreign society which is stifling the culture of their ancestors. The elders, who no longer believe in miracles, can only look on sadly as they note in the younger generation the disappearance of traditions dating back to what they see as the golden age when their world was governed and defended by the Great Cacique, Don Carlos Tamoabioy.

Division of Land Ownership in the Sibundoy Valley (1966)

Size (in hectares)	Natives				Settlers			
	Proprietors in number	in %	Areas in number	in %	Proprietors in number	in %	Areas in number	in %
Less than 1	123	16.8	70	0.7	46	6.3	25	0.3
1 to 3	175	23.8	315	3.3	54	7.4	109	1.2
3 to 5	55	7.5	203	2.2	38	5.1	153	1.6
5 to 10	38	5.2	261	2.8	37	5.0	258	2.8
10 to 50	38	5.2	736	7.8	83	11.3	1,888	20.0
50 to 100	5	0.7	312	3.3	26	3.7	1,830	19.4
100 to 200	1	0.1	185	1.9	12	1.7	1,743	18.6
200 to 300	—	—	—	—	1	0.1	237	2.5
Over 300	—	—	—	—	Mission	0.1	1,092	11.6
Totals	435	59.3	2,082	22.0	298	40.7	7,335	78.0

These figures are taken from the cadastral surveys of the Agustín Codazzi Institute for 1966

The Testament of Carlos Tamoabioy

PART 1

In the name of the Father, and of the Son, and of the Holy Spirit, three persons and one true God, I make this testament. Though sick in body I am sound in understanding and will, and I yield up my soul to God our Lord, who purchased and redeemed it with his most precious blood; may my soul be carried to heaven, for I trust in His Divine Majesty, and my body be laid in the ground from which it was formed to make me a man.

Item, I declare to be my own goods, belonging to myself, Don Carlos Tamoabioy, the land known as Tamoabioy; and I appoint as my testamentary executor Don Melchor Jajuanandioy, that he may do all he can for the good of my soul.

Item, I declare that I have three legitimate children, by my legitimate wife, Feliciana Jajamanchoy; their names are as follows: the eldest, Don Pedro, and the younger son Don Marcos Jajamanchoy, and my legitimate daughter is Doña María Jajamanchoy; them I declare heirs to my properties.

Item, I declare that I leave these lands to my legitimate children, Don Marcos, Don Pedro and Doña María, and to Don Melchor, my nephew and the executor of this will, that they may make use of them in a proper manner, because such is my declared wish, that they may use them without any discord, before three witnesses: Don Gaspar de León and Don Reymundo Jacanamejoy, and the commissioner Don Diego Ignacio Pérez de Suñiga; and I would also have it known that I leave this land, known as Tamoabioy, which extends for three leagues in length, from the stream at the top known as Guaraca, to the place at the bottom which we call Aponte, which lies downstream from Juanambú. And this I leave to my children and all my people, for such is my will, which is not to be disregarded, nor opposed on pain of a fine.

Item, I declare that the piece of land named Abuelapamba, extending from a milestone set up by a stream called Cungoyaco, this land I leave to my Indians belonging to the village of Santiago and the village of Sibundoy Grande, for it is my will that they use it, and defend it if they are disturbed by any ill-intentioned person.

Item, I declare that the said lands I here bequeath are mine, for they come from my ancestors; and that no person whatsoever has any claim to them, even Captain Don Salvador Ortiz, who has established his estates there; they are not his at all, and if he tries to invade them or use violence then appeal must be made before the Royal Court, for I declare that nothing I have is not legitimately mine in all law and justice; and that knowing this my Indians can even appear before His Lordship himself with this testament, and the witnesses to it.

Item, I declare that I leave another piece of land, named Jabanguana, to Pablo Chinamamboy for him to have, for that is my will, and also to his first cousin Rodrigo Chasoy, for that too is my will. Because I am near death, and to make certain that what I say in this testament is what I intend, I close it this fifteenth day of March in the year 1700; in the presence of the witnesses, Don Gaspar de León, Don Reymundo Jacanamejoy and Captain Don Diego Ignacio Pérez de Suñiga, I the testator declare this to be my true will, signing it with my name, Don Carlos Tamoabioy.

PART II

In the name of the Father, and of the Son, and of the Holy Spirit, who are three distinct persons and one true God. Amen, Jesus.

May all who see this testatory letter know that I, Don Carlos Tamoabioy, hereditary Cacique of the village of Santiago, am making this will while sick in body, but sound in understanding and with my judgement unimpaired. I declare that if God wills to transport me from this present life to the other, I place my soul in the hands of God our Lord who has bought and redeemed it with his precious blood, and may my body be put in the earth of which it was formed; and considering that death is a natural thing, I direct this, my testament, in the following way: first, I declare that, if God Our Lord wishes to take me from this life, my body be buried in the chapel of the Blessed Virgin of the Rosary, for I belonged to her confraternity, and that the priest-in-charge of this village of Santiago should accompany my body with the Great Cross as usual, and that a mass be sung in the presence of my body with its bearers; for such is my will . . .

Item, I declare that no harm must be done to the vassals and governors of the said village of Sibundoy Grande, for the lands we possess, known as those of Pujatamuy, where there is a great cross, have been recognized as ours from time immemorial; and these lands are also ours by the judgment of the Señor Visitor Don Luis de Quiñones during his visit, limited and marked out by Visitors who left them to us with sanction and orders to defend them; and the other lands, of Chesnivijoy [the Visitor] also decreed a ban and an order that it should be known that they belonged to the native Indians, and that the vassals of these lands should keep them.

Item, I declare and say that the parts of the Putumayo, which cause no harm to the said governors, such as Don Francisco Criollo, on the Jansasoy land, and other lands known as Maboychoy, and others named Guanvicatanjanoy, and yet others named La Ensillada, that all these belong to the Lords Caciques and governors of the village of Putumayo, because they were so adjudged by the Señor Visitor Don Luis de Quiñones, and all of us, and all the other Visitors who had the royal command and authority to decree boundaries.

Item, I declare that another land named Jujuapanchoy, in

between and above the two other pieces of land, is for my Indians who belong to the village of Santiago.

Item, I declare that it is my will that my executors should execute as good Christians all this I lay upon them, and all that I have arranged in this my testament, since because of the state of my health I am unburdening my conscience and setting free my soul for the life to come, and that the executors of this will are the said witnesses Don Gaspar de León, and the Commissioners, Don Diego Ignacio Pérez de Suñiga and Don Reymundo Jacanamejoy. And because this is my true will I am making it, this fifteenth of March in the year 1700, before Don Gaspar de León, Don Reymundo Jacanamejoy, and Don Diego Ignacio Pérez de Suñiga, the present witnesses. This will, I the testator, sign with my name, Don Carlos Tamoabioy.

Bibliography

Texts quoted

Aguado, Fray Pedro, *Recopilación historial*, Bogotá, 1916.

Alcácer, O.F.M. Cap., Antonio de, *Las misiones capuchinas en el nuevo reino de Granada hoy Colombia* (1648–1820), *Seminario seráfico misional capuchina*, No. 7, Bogotá, 1959.

Amazonia Colombiana Americanista, official organ of the CILEAC, editor Marcelino de Castellví O.F.M.Cap., four issues published between 1940 and 1945, a fifth in 1953, and the sixth in 1962 under the title *Censo indolingüistico de Colombia*.

Anales de la Cámara de Representantes, Bogotá, Biblioteca del Congreso Nacional, dating back to 1898.

Arango, Rev. José, 'El Capellán de la policía nacional visita las regiones del Putumayo', from the weekly *El Catolicismo*, No. 119, Bogotá, 16 February, 1945.

Arcila Robledo, O.F.M., Gregorio, *Apuntes históricos de la Provincia franciscana de Colombia*, Bogotá, 1953.

Boletin de la Junta de Inmigración, Pasto, 1914.

Boletin Católico, official organ of the Vicariate Apostolic of the Caquetá from March 1938 to April 1969 (No. 374).

Bristol, Melvin Lee, *Botanical Museum Leaflets*, Harvard University, 1964–7.

Cabot Lodge, John, in the weekly *La Calle*, No. 63, Bogotá, 12 December 1958.

Caicedo Hidalgo, Luis, *Geografía, historia e instrucción cívica de la Comisaría del Putumayo*, Sibundoy, 1965.

Camacho Leyva, Ernesto, *La policía en los Territorios nacionales*, Biblioteca de la escuela de policía General Santander, Vol. VII, Bogotá, 1947.

Canet de Mar, O.F.M.Cap., Benigo de, *Relaciones interesantes y datos históricos sobre las Misiones católicas del Caquetá y Putu-mayo desde el año 1632, hasta el presente,* Bogotá, 1924.

Carabantes, O.F.M.Cap., Josepho, *Práctica de misiones, remedio de pecadores,* León, 1674.

Castellanos, Rev. Juan de, *Elegías de varones ilustres de Indias,* Madrid, 1926.

Castellví, O.F.M.Cap., Marcelino de, 'Ethnografía de los indios subun-doyes en relación con la del resto de Colombia', lecture given at the Javeriana Pontifical University, 22 October 1938.

——*Historia eclesiástica de la Amazonia Colombiana,* Medellín, 1944.

Cieza de León, Pedro, *Crónica general del Perú,* Madrid, 1941.

Concordato and Convenios de Misiones, *Intendencias y Comisarias,* Bogotá, 1937.

Crous, O.F.M.Cap., Plácido, *Los Misioneros y el valle de Sibundoy* (pastoral letter), Sibundoy, 27 May 1965.

Cultura Nariñense, Nos. 7–25 (the monthly review of the Casa Mariana de Pasto), Pasto, January 1969–July 1970.

Diario Jurídico, Bogotá, M.G. Archives.

Diario Oficial, Bogotá, M.G. Archives.

Eco Liberal, Pasto, from September 1898 onwards.

Escandón, General Joaquín, *Informe sobre la terminación del cam-ino de Mocoa,* Pasto, 1912;

——*Resolución,* No. 7, Pasto, 15 November 1913.

Fals Borda, Orlando, 'El vinculo con la tierra y su evolución en el departamento de Nariño', in the review of the Colombian Acad-emy of Sciences, Vol. X, No. 41, Bogotá, 1959.

Friede, Juan 'Leyendas de nuestro señor de Sibundoy y el santo Carlos Tamoabioy', *Boletin de arqueología,* Vol. 1. Bogotá, 1945;

——*El Indio en lucha por la tierra,* Bogotá, 1944.

Groot, José Manuel, *Historia eclesiástica y civil de la Nueva Granada,* Biblioteca de autores colombianís, Bogotá, 1953.

Guama Poma de Ayala, Felipe, *Nueva crónica y buen gobierno,* illustrated Peruvian codex, *Travaux et mémoires de l'Institut d'Ethnologie,* No. XXIII, Paris, 1936.

Gutiérrez, Rufino, *Informe rendido por el procurador de hacienda al Ministro de instrucción pública sobre el territorio escolar del Caquetá y Putumayo,* No. 2786, Popayán, 1912.

Hardenburg, W. E., *The Putumayo, Devil's Paradise,* London, 1913.

Hernández de Alba, Gregorio, *Religiosos e indios en los siglos XVI y XVII,* duplicated, 1966.

Hispano, Cornelio, *Los fieras del Putumayo o de París al Amazonas*, Paris.

Holguín, Andrés, *Informe rendido al presidente de la República doctor Alberto Lleras Camargo por el procurador general de la Nación*, Bogotá, 1962.

Igualada, O.F.M.Cap., Francisco de, 'Estado de la Misión del Caquetá en 1940', in *Amazonia colombiana americanista*, Vol. 1, No. 2, Pasto, 1940.

INCORA, *Informe del proyecto de adecuación de tierras en el valle de Sibundoy*, 1963.

Informes

The various reports referred to at different times in the text may be conveniently listed under this one heading:

Informe presentado al Excelentísimo Señor Doctor Don Francisco Ragonesi, Arzobispo de Mira, y Delegado Apostólico en Colombia, Bogotá, 1911.

Obra de los misioneros capuchinos de la delegación apostólica, del Gobierno y de la Junta Arquidiocesana Nacional en el Caquetá y Putumayo, Bogotá, 1912.

Misiones Católicas del Putumayo, Documentos oficiales relativos a esta comisaría, official illustrated edition, Bogotá, 1913.

Informe sobre la Misión del Putumayo, Bogotá, 1916.

Informes sobre las Misiones del Caquetá, Putumayo, Goajira, Casanare, Meta, Vichada, Vaupes, y Arauca, Bogotá, 1917.

Informes que rinden el Vicario Apostólico de la Goajira y el Prefecto Apostólico del Caquetá y Putumayo al Ilustrísimo y Reverendísimo Señor Arzobispo Primado, Presidente de la Junta Arqidiocesana de Misiones en Colombia, sobre los trabajos realizados por los misioneros en los respectivos territorios de su jurisdicción, 1917–1918, Bogotá, 1918.

Las Misiones Católicas en Colombia. Labor de los misioneros en el Caquetá y Putumayo, Magdalena y Arauca – Informes 1918–1919, Bogotá, 1919.

Las Misiones Católicas en Colombia, Informes, años 1919, 1920, 1921, Bogotá, 1921.

La Misión del Caquetá: Recopilación de datos y documentos ordenados por M.S.F. y C., Pasto, 1923.

Un viaje por el Putumayo y el Amazonas. Ensayo de Navegación, Bogotá, 1924.

Informes de las Misiones Católicas de Colombia relativos a los años de 1925 y 1926 publicados por orden del Gobierno Nacional, Bogotá, 1926.

Informe anual a la Honorable Junta Arquidiocesana Nacional de Misiones: Labores de la Misión del Caquetá en 1930 y 1931, Bogotá, 1932.

Iza, O.F.M.Cap., Delfín, *Asuntos de actualidad relativos al Putumayo,* Bogotá, 1924.

——*Viva el Caquetá y Putumayo,* Pasto, 1927.

——*¡Alerta Católicos!,* No. 292, Pasto.

John XXIII, Pope, *Mater et Magistra,* encyclical, 1961.

Juajibioy Chindóy, Alberto, 'Breve estudio preliminar del grupo aborígen de Sibundoy y su lengua Kamsá en el sur de Colombia', *Boletín del Instituto de Antropología de la Universidad de Antioquia,* Medellín, August 1962.

Liévano Aguirre, Indalecio, *El proceso de Mosquera ante el senado,* populibro No. 3, Bogotá, 1966.

——*Los grandes conflictos sociales y económicos de nuestra historia,* Bogotá, 1966.

Luzbetak S. V. D., Louis, *The Church and Cultures,* Techny, Illinois, 1963.

Medina, Mgr Leonidas, *Conferencia sobre las Misiones del Caquetá y Putumayo,* given in Bogotá Cathedral, on 12 October 1914.

——*Decreto no 16 por el cual se condena una hoja volante,* tract, Pasto, 1914.

——*Carta abierta del obispo de Pasto al Ilustrísimo y Reverendísimo Señor Doctor D. Bernardo Herrera Restrepo* (Archbishop of Bogotá), Pasto, 1914.

Mirador Amazónico, from the Prefecture Apostolic of Leticia, Amazonia, Colombia, from June 1953 onwards.

Misiones Capuchinas, a bulletin, starting January 1959.

Moncayo, Julio, *Mensaje del gobernador de Nariño a la Asamblea de 1916: Sobre los baldíos del valle de Sibundoy,* Pasto, 1916.

Monroy, Pablo, *Informe del intendente y jefe militar del Putumayo* No. 1, Mocoa, 1 October 1907.

Montclar, O.F.M.Cap., Fidel de (see too Delfín Iza, and under *Informes*):

——*Contestación a la "Carta abierta" del señor Rafael Villota,* Pasto, January 1911.

——*Inocentado y relación de los sucesos que tuvieron lugar en Santiago al dia de Navidad,* Santiago del Putumayo, 6 January 1911.

——*En los tribunales. El Caquetá, los capuchinos y sus detractores*, Pasto, 20 January 1911.

——*Lo que opinan de la labor de los misioneros en el Putumayo los generales Lucio Velasco y Ernesto Borrero*, Pasto, 10 April 1913.

——*El Octavo. No levantar falso testimonio ni mentir*, Pasto, 19 November 1913.

——*Defensa de los Reverendos Padres Misioneros Capuchinos y contestación a un Informe calumnioso de don Julio Tomás, publicado en el Diario Oficial y reproducido en la Gaceta Departamental de Nariño*, Pasto, 1913.

——*Ay de aquel hombre por quien viniera el escándalo*, Pasto, 6 January 1914.

——'Obras son amores y no buenas razones', in the paper *La Defensa*, Pasto, 10 January 1914.

——*Emigración de Antioqueños al Putumayo*, Sonsón, 27 May 1925.

——*¡A Sucre!*, Pasto, 12 October 1916.

——*La legalidad del embudo*, Pasto, 28 October 1916.

——*Circular del reverendisimo prefecto apostólico del Caquetá sobre elecciones*, Sibundoy, 8 January 1918.

——*Todo por la patria y la patria por la fe*, Sibundoy, 13 January 1918.

——*Los gatos escrupulosos*, Sibundoy, 27 January 1918.

——*Los misioneros del Putumayo y las mentiras de "Orientación liberal"*, Pasto, 1918.

——*Conferencia en el teatro Faenza de Bogotá*, Bogotá, 1924.

——*Los misioneros capuchinos al público de Nariño y del Putumayo* (a public notice), Pasto, 27 June 1927.

——*Carta Pastoral*, Barcelona, 30 May 1929.

Moreno, Mgr Ezequiel, *Los buenos católicos*, Pasto, 21 April 1903.

Orientacion Liberal, editor Nicolás Hurtado, Pasto, 1918–30, from a private collection.

Ortiz, Sergio Elías, 'Capellanía del Santo crucifijo de Sibundoy', *Boletín de Estudios históricos*, Pasto, Vol. 1, No. 1, 1928.

——'Antiguallas históricas', ibid., Vol. I, No. 9, 1928.

——'El pleito de Hachinchoy y Abuelapamba', ibid., Vol. VI, No. 68, 1935.

Pabón Núñez, Lucio, *La cuestión de las religiones acatolicas en Colombia*, Bogotá, 1956.

Paul VI, Pope, *Populorum Progressio*, encyclical, 1967.

Pérez, Felipe, *Geografía física y política del territorio del Caquetá, perteneciente al Estado del Cauca*, Bogotá, 1862.

Pinell, O.F.M.Cap., Gaspar Monconill de, *Excursión apostólica por los ríos Putumayo, San Miguel de Sucumbíos, Cuyabeno, Caquetá y Caguán,* Bogotá, 1929.

——*Primera carta pastoral del Excelentísimo y Reverendísimo Vicario Apostólico del Caquetá a sus misioneros y fieles,* Bogotá, 26 October 1930.

——*Octava carta pastoral del Exelentísimo y Reverendísimo Señor Vicario Apostólico del Caquetá a sus misioneros y fieles,* Sibundoy, 1938.

Pius X, Pope, *Lacrimabili Statu,* encyclical, 1912.

Plaza, José Antonio, *Compendio de la Nueva Granada desde antes de su descubrimiento hasta el 17 de noviembre de 1850,* Bogotá, 1850.

Procuraduria general de los territorios, *Misiones y Misioneros en Colombia,* Bogotá, 1964.

Propaganda Fide, *La obra de las misiones católicas en Colombia,* Bogotá, 1934.

'Puerto Asís Ayer y Hoy', *Boletín católico,* Sibundoy, 1961.

Quito, O.F.M.Cap., Jacinto de, *Relación de viaje en los ríos Putumayo, Caraparaná y Caquetá entre las tribus huitotas,* Bogotá, 1908.

——*Miscelánea de mis treinta y cinco años de misionero del Caquetá y Putumayo,* Bogotá, 1938.

——*Historia de la fundación del pueblo de San Francisco en el valle de Sibundoy,* Pasto, 1952.

Restrepo Posada, Rev. José, *Arquidiócesis de Bogotá,* Bogotá, 1961.

Reyes, General Rafael, *Conferencia en la Sorbona,* Paris, 1914.

Romero, Adolfo, 'El problema agrario en la comisaría especial del Putumayo', in *Tierras y Aguas,* No. 15, Bogotá, 1939.

Romero, O.F.M.Cap., Francisco, *Llanto sagrado de la América meridional,* Bogotá, 1955.

Rosero, Rev. Dario Alcides, *Gira Apostólica del Excelentísimo y Reverendísimo Señor Fray Gaspar, Obispo titular de Cadosia y Vicario Apostólico del Caquetá a San José de la Victoria,* Ipiales, 19 May 1930.

Santa Gertrudis, O.F.M.Cap., Juan de, *Maravillas de la naturaleza,* Biblioteca de la Presidencia de la República, Bogotá, 1956.

Sañudo, José Rafael, *Apuntes sobre la historia de Pasto,* Pasto, 1897.

Thomson, N., *El libro rojo del Putumayo,* Bogotá, 1913.

Tisoy, Francisco, Diego y Domingo, *¿Y Qué?,* Pasto, 1 December 1913.

Tisoy family, *La verdad en su punto*, Pasto, 11 April 1914.

Triana, Miguel, *Por el sur de Colombia*, Paris, 1907.

Ulloa, Antonio de and Juan, Jorge, *Noticias secretas de América sobre el estado naval, militar y político de los reynos del Perú y provincias de Quito, costas de Nueva Granada y Chile. Gobierno y régimen particular de los pueblos de indios. Cruel opresión y extorsiones de sus corregidores y curas. Abusos escandalosos introducidos entre estos habitantes por los misioneros. Causas de su origen y motivos de su continuación por el espacio de tres siglos. Escritas fielmente según las instrucciones del Excelentísimo Señor Marqués de la Ensenada, primer secretario de Estado, y presentadas en informe secreto a Su Majestad Católica el Señor Don Fernando VI. Sacadas a luz para el verdadero conocimiento del gobierno de los españoles en la América meridional por don David Barry; en dos partes,* first published in London, 1826.

Uribe Uribe, General Rafael, *Por la América del sur*, Bogotá, 1955.

Velasco, Rev. Juan de, *Historia del reino de Quito en la América meridional*, Quito, 1841–4.

Vicariato Apostolico de Sibundoy, see *Boletín Católico, Informes, Puerto Asís ayer y hoy;* also pastoral letters, 1949–69.

Vilafranca, O.F.M.Cap., Marceliano de, *Los terrenos de la Misión y los indígenas en el Valle de Sibundoy (Putumayo): Conferencia pronunciada ante un numeroso grupo de colonos del Valle de Sibundoy,* Pasto, 29 December 1946.

Vilanova, O.F.M.Cap., Pacífico de, *Capuchinos catalanes en el sur de Colombia,* 2 vols., Barcelona, 1947.

Villava, O.F.M.Cap., Angel de, *Una visita al Caquetá por un misionero capuchino de la Custodia de la Santísima Madre de Dios del Ecuador-Colombia,* Barcelona, 1895.

Zarama, Daniel, *Obra de los misioneros capuchinos, de la delegación apostólica, del gobierno y de la junta arquidiocesana en el Caquetá y Putumayo,* Bogotá, 1912.

Zarama, Rafael, *Reseña histórica,* Pasto, 1942.

Suggested further reading

Cooper, John M., 'Stimulants and narcotics', in *Handbook of South American Indians*, Vol. V, 'The Comparative Ethnology of South American Indians', Bureau of American Ethnology, Washington, 1949.

Gheerbrant, Alain, *L'Église rebelle d'Amérique Latine,* Paris, 1969.

Guzman Campos, Germán, *Camilo Torres*, New York, 1969.

Lelong, Bernard, and Lancrey-Laval, Jean-Luc, *Cordillère magique*, Paris, 1955.

Gerassi, John (ed.). *Revolutionary Priest: The Complete Writings and Messages of Camilo Torres*, New York and London, 1971.

Notes

The titles of all books and publications referred to in these notes is given in abridged form wherever they have already appeared in the Bibliography.

Most commonly used abbreviations:

Arch.	Archives
C.C.	Central archives of the Cauca
M.G.	Government Ministry
N.C.	National Archives of Colombia
C.C.A.	*Caja de Crédito Agrario* (Agrarian Credit Bank)
C.A.P.I.	*Comisión de asistencia y protección indígenas* (Commission for the aid and protection of the natives)
D.A.I.	*División de asuntos indígenas* (Department of Native Affairs)
Rev.	Review
Informes	Official reports from the Apostolic Mission for the Putumayo, addressed to the Church and State of Colombia, and published by the government
	Boletín católico (The official Catholic Bulletin of Sibundoy)

Chapter 1

1. Alberto Juajibioy Chindoy, *Breve estudio*.
2. Rafael Zarama, *Reseña histórica*, Part 1, p. 15; Juan de Castellanos, *Elegías . . .*, p. 437.
3. Alberto Juajibioy Chindoy, *art. cit.*
4. Fray Pedro Aguado, *Recopilación historial*, pp. 242–8.
5. Sergio Elías Ortiz, *Antiguallas históricas*, p. 278.
6. Fray Juan de Santa Gertrudis, *Maravillas de la Naturaleza*, Vol. I.

7. Sergio Elías Ortiz, *Capellanía*, pp. 307–9.
8. José Rafael Sañudo, *Apuntes*.
9. Report from Captain Diego de Ospina, quoted in Indalecio Liévano Aguirre, *Los grandes conflictos*, pp. 220–21.
10. Fray Francisco Romero, *Llanto sagrado*, pp. 114–67.
11. Gregorio Hernández de Alba, the anthropologist, studies and partially translates this document in his statement *Religiosos e indios en los siglos XVI y XVII*, presented before the first Congress of National Territories held in Bogotá in May 1966. (Exists in duplicated form only.)

Chapter 2

1. J. R. Sañudo, *Apuntes*, p. 93.
2. There are eleven *cedulas reales* on the subject in the C.C. (Col. C. II–11 T).
3. J. R. Sañudo, *Apuntes*, p. 96.
4. N. C. Arch. (Miscelánea, Vol. 116, folios 408–17).
5. Sergio Elías Ortiz, *El pleito*.
6. Request presented to the Pasto government on 11 February 1676 (C.C. no 2119, Col. C I–7 Gob).
7. Accounts of such efforts, and of the taxes due to the sovereign, are to be found in the C.C., *cedulas* 2230 (Col. C I–24 En) and 770 (Col. C I–17 T).
8. C.C., no 3064 (Col. I–17 T), and the Testament of Carlos Tamoabioy, see Appendix 2.
9. C.C., no 3064 (Col. CI–17 T).
10. C.C., nos. 3061, 3062, 3064 (Col. C. I–17 T).
11. Decree signed 8 April 1722. C.C. no 3027 (Col. C I–17 T).
12. All the quotations and statements referring to the Jachinchoy and Abuelapamba lawsuit are taken from the highly detailed study by the historian Sergio Elías Ortiz.
13. Madrid, 28 April and 20 May respectively. C.C. no 2581 (Col. C I–24 En).
14. January and May 1711. C.C. no 8346 (Col. C III–23 En).
15. C.C. no 5040 (Col. C II–11 T).
16. Evidence collected by Fray Marcos de Castellví, in 1939. *Notas etnográficas y geografía del pueblo de Santiago*, unpublished manuscript of which the author has a photocopy.
17. Evidence collected by the Marist Brother Genaro; rev. *Amazonia*, Nos. 4–8, p. 82.
18. From the journal *Orientación Liberal*, No. 251, Pasto, 25 December 1927.
19. Felipe Pérez, *Geografía . . .*, Vol. I, p. 327.
20. Pérez, ibid. p. 271 ff.

21. Quoted by Pérez, ibid., p. 317.
22. ibid., p. 321.
23. Jacinto de Quito, *Miscelánea*, Chap. XIX.
24. Augustín Codazzi, quoted by Felipe Pérez, *Geografía*, p. 325.
25. Juan Friede, *Leyendas*.

Chapter 3

1. Jorge Juan and Antonio de Ulloa, *Noticias secretas*, pp. 231–68.
2. See Indalecio Liévano Aguirre, *Los grandes conflictos*, Chap XV.
3. José Rafael Sañudo, *Apuntes*, Part 2, p. 95.
4. This is said by, among others, the Capuchin chroniclers Benigno de Canet de Mar (*Relaciones interesantes*), and Pacífico de Vilanova (*Capuchinos*).
5. José Antonio Plaza, *Memorias para la historia*, p. 349.
6. Fray Gregorio Arcila Robledo, quoted in Plaza, op. cit.
7. C.C. nos 4740 and 5428 (Col E I–11 Ms).
8. Jorge Juan and Antonio de Ulloa, op. cit., pp. 334–490.
9. Letter from Don Antonio Manso y Maldonado, president of the Court of Nueva Granada, 1729. Quoted by Indalecio Liévano Aguirre, *El proceso de Mosquera*, p. 50.
10. Antonio de Alcácer, *Las misiones*, p. 27.
11. ibid., p. 167; also Chap IV.
12. Ibid., p. 238.
13. ibid., p. 243.
14. José Restrepo Posada, *Arquidiócesis de Bogotá*, p. 377.
15. Law of 28 July 1824.
16. Indalecio Liévano Aguirre, *El proceso de Mosquera*, p. 45. Decree of 9 September 1861.
17. Decree of the Archdiocese of Bogotá, 15 March 1871.
18. Law No. 153, 1887.
19. Law No. 35, 1888.
20. 24 September 1888. Further agreements were signed in 1898, 1902, 1908, 1918, 1928 and 1953.
21. Indalecio Liévano Aguirre, *Biografía de Rafael Núñez*.
22. Fidel de Montclar, *Los misioneros capuchinos al público de Nariño y Putumayo*; a public notice of which the author has a copy.
23. Law of 11 October 1821.
24. Decree of 15 October 1828.
25. Cf. Juan Friede, *El indio en lucha por la tierra*; Indalecio Liévano Aguirre, *Los grandes conflictos*; and Orlando Fals Borda, *El vínculo con la tierra*.
26. Law No. 66, 1874.
27. Law No. 72, 1892.
28. Decree No. 74, 1898.

Chapter 4

1. Angel M. de Villava, *Una visita*, p. 10.
2. Pacífico de Vilanova, *Capuchinos*, Vol. I, pp. 39–41.
3. Angel M. de Villava, op. cit., p. 37.
4. Benigno de Canet de Mar, *Relaciones*, pp. 24–5.
5. Jacinto de Quito, *Miscelánea*, p. 25.
6. Jacinto de Quito, *Historia*, p. 5.
7. Decree of the Prefecture Apostolic given in 1889, and ratified by the governor of Popayán the following year.
8. See among others the issues of *Eco Liberal* from 20 November 1897 to 30 January 1898.
9. Up until 1938, 'concubinage, an illegitimate and reprehensible union' was subject to punishment by the courts.
10. For more details on the state of the Sibundoy valley at that moment, in addition to the books listed, it is also worth studying the *Informes*, or reports, published by the Apostolic Mission of the Caquetá and Putumayo from 1911 onwards.
11. Accounts by Jacinto de Quito and the Bishop of Pasto, Ezequiel Moreno, quoted by Pacífico de Vilanova, op. cit., Vol. 1, p. 89.
12. Evidence from Jacinto de Quito quoted by Pacífico de Vilanova, op. cit. Vol. 1, p. 89.
13. Jacinto de Quito, *Historia*, passim.
14. Fidel de Montclar, *Los misioneros* (see Chap. 3, note 22).
15. Pacífico de Vilanova, op. cit., Vol. 1, p. 98.
16. Decree No. 104 of the Cauca government, 1 April 1903, the whole of which is quoted in Pacífico de Vilanova, op. cit., Vol. 1, pp. 92–5.
17. Ezequiel Moreno, *Los buenos católicos*, a pamphlet.

Chapter 5

1. Jacinto de Quito, *Biografía*, pp. 29–30.
2. Quoted by Pacífico de Vilanova, op. cit., Vol. 1, p. 127.
3. 'Inventario general de todos los bienes muebles e inmuebles de la iglesia de Santiago,' taken from the book of *La Cofradía de San Pedro*, p. 31. Santiago parish arch., 1906.
4. Marceliano de Vilafranca, *Los terrenos*, p. 2.
5. Bartolomé de Igualada, quoted by Father Lino Rampón, *Problemas sociales*, p. 33.
6. Rufino Gutiérrez, *Informe*, p. 26; quoted in Vilanova, op. cit., Vol. 1, p. 310.
7. W. E. Hardenburg, *The Putumayo*.
8. Jacinto de Quito, *Miscelánea*, p. 72.
9. 19 October 1906; quoted by Vilanova, op. cit., Vol. 1, p. 171.
10. January 1907, quoted ibid., p. 172.

11. ibid.

12. Quoted by Francisco de Igualada, '*Estado*', pp. 26 and 26 *bis*.

13. ibid.

14. ibid.

15. Sibundoy, 5 August 1908, quoted by Vilanova, op cit., vol. 1, p. 173.

16. Jacinto de Quito, *Miscelánea*, p. 42.

17. ibid., p. 38.

18. Interview of 4 January 1967 in Sibundoy.

19. Cf. *Informes*; also Jacinto de Quito, *Miscelánea*.

20. Estanislao de las Corts, quoted in Vilanova, op. cit., Vol. 1, p. 178.

21. Cf. ibid., pp. 304–11.

22. Cf. *Informes*, especially that for 1918–19, pp. 11–12.

23. Vilanova, op. cit., Vol. 1, p. 173.

24. Estanislao de las Corts, quoted ibid., p. 179.

25. Letters of 6 and 30 October 1908, quoted ibid. pp. 225–6.

26. ibid.

27. Letter of 3 November 1909, quoted ibid., p. 226.

28. Salt was of major importance in preventing the formation of goitre.

29. Jacinto de Quito, *Miscelánea*, pp. 89–90.

Chapter 6

1. Vilanova, op. cit., Vol. 1, pp. 129 and 54.

2. Fidel de Montclar, quoted ibid., p. 240.

3. ibid. pp. 255–9.

4. Villava, op. cit.

5. Vilanova, op. cit., Vol. 1, p. 145.

6. There is a large bibliography. Cf. Rafael Uribe Uribe, *Por la América del Sur*; Cornelio Hispano, *Las fieras del Putumayo*; N. Thomson, *El libro rojo de Putumayo*; W. E. Hardenburg, *The Putumayo*; Sir Roger Casement, *The Blue Book*.

7. 'Los Bárbaros de la civilización', *Jornal do Comercio*, Manaos, 18 October 1912.

8. Vilanova, op. cit., Vol. 1, p. 249.

9. ibid. p. 261.

10. Journal, *La Sociedad*; quoted ibid., p. 235.

11. Vilanova, ibid., p. 21.

12. *Boletín del ministerio de relaciones exteriores*, Bogotá, July–September 1912, p. 565.

13. Statements repeated in the *Informes* for 1916 to 1924.

14. Letter to Fidel de Montclar, 16 February 1912. Quoted Vilanova, Vol. 1, p. 281.

15. Letter of 10 April 1912. Quoted ibid., p. 281.

16. Letter to Fidel de Montclar, 7 May 1912. Quoted ibid., p. 282.

17. ibid., p. 280.

18. Cf. *Informes*; Vilanova; and the pamphlet *Puerto Asís, Ayer y Hoy*.
19. Joaquín Escandón, *Informe sobre la terminación*.
20. *Relación del viaje*, pp. 12–13.
21. Fidel de Montclar, *Defensa de los reverendos padres*, p. 2.
22. Cf. the defenders of the Capuchins: Rufino Gutiérrez, *Informe*; and Daniel Zarama, *Obra de los misioneros capuchinos*.
23. Vilanova, Vol. 2, p. 71.
24. *Informe* for 1918–19, p. 23.

Chapter 7

1. *Informe* for 1911.
2. Fidel de Montclar, Letter to the Minister of Foreign Affairs, *Misiones Católicas*, 15 August 1911.
3. Law No. 52, 1911 for 20,000, and No. 14, 1912 for 100,000 pesos.
4. *Semanario Comercial*, Pasto, 12 April 1912.
5. *Bol. Cat.*, September 1965. Cf. Lino Rampón.
6. Fidel de Montclar, *Informe* for 1916, p. 26.
7. *Anales de la Cámara de representantes*, Bogotá, 23 August 1911.
8. ibid., 13 November 1911.
9. ibid., 20 September 1911.
10. Fidel de Montclar, *La legalidad del embudo*.
11. Juan Friede, *Leyendas*.
12. Fidel de Montclar, *Informe* for 1916, p. 14.
13. Vilanova, Vol. 2, p. 51.
14. Daily paper, *La Epoca*.

Chapter 8

1. Fidel de Montclar, *Inocentada* (in the author's possession).
2. Fidel de Montclar, *En los tribunales*.
3. Statement of the special commissioner, No. 7, 15 November 1913.
4. Francisco, Domingo and Diego Tisoy; *¿Y Que?* (booklet in the author's possession).
5. Fidel de Montclar, *El octavo*; *Ay de aquel hombre*; *Obras*.
6. Fidel de Montclar, *El octavo*.
7. Fidel de Montclar, *Ay de aquel hombre*.
8. Fidel de Montclar. Cf. *Informe*, 1918–19, p. 87.
9. Weekly paper, *Orientación Liberal*, Pasto, 24 November 1918.
10. The evidence of his son, José Rafael Escandón.
11. *Informe* for 1913.
12. Juan, Nicolás, Manuel and Diego Tisoy and others, *La verdad en su punto*.
13. Fidel de Montclar, *Informe* for 1913.
14. *Orientación Liberal*, Nos. 34, 38 and 39, 1919.
15. Mgr. Leonidas Medina, *Carta abierta*, Pasto, 30 March 1914.

Chapter 9

1. Fidel de Montclar, *Informe* for 1916. Also see Gutiérrez and Vilanova.
2. Jacinto de Quito, *Miscelánea*, Chaps. 10 and 11.
3. ibid., p. 22.
4. ibid., Chap. 13.
5. Fidel de Montclar, *Informe* for 1911, p. 103.
6. *Informe* for 1918.
7. Vilanova, Vol. 2, p. 145.
8. Interview with Diego Mavisoy, 20 September 1969.
9. *Informe* for 1918-19, p. 26.
10. Jacinto de Quito, *Miscelánea*, p. 35. The second statement was made to the author.
11. *Informe* for 1918-19, p. 27.
12. ibid., pp. 11-12.
13. *Obra de los misioneros*, 1912, pp. 125-7.
14. Rufino Gutiérrez, *Informe*, p. 6.
15. *Informe* for 1911, pp. 33-4.
16. *Misiones Católicas*, 1913, p. 63.
17. *Informe* for 1918, pp. 180-81.
18. Jacinto de Quito, *Miscelánea*, p. 31.
19. Rufino Gutiérrez, op. cit., p. 16.
20. Father Louis Luzbetak, *The Church and Cultures*, pp. 116-42.
21. Rev. *Amazonia*, Vol. 2, p. 84.
22. Bautista Juajibioy; interview of 7 April 1970.
23. Vilanova, Vol. 1, p. 176.
24. ibid., p. 178.
25. *Informe del Intendente y Jefe Militar del Putumayo*, Mocoa, 1907.
26. Gutiérrez, op. cit., p. 29.
27. Letter of 29 December 1915; quoted Vilanova, Vol. 1, p. 178.
28. Fidel de Montclar, *Lo que opinan*.

Chapter 10

1. Decree by the Departmental Assembly of Nariño, No. 47, 20 July 1914.
2. *Boletín de la Junta de Immigración*, No. 1, Pasto, 27 May, 1914.
3. Fidel de Montclar, *Informe* for 1916, pp. 14-15.
4. Fidel de Montclar, *¡A Sucre!*
5. Fidel de Montclar, *La legalidad*.
6. Vilanova, Vol. 2, pp. 51 and 54.
7. ibid.
8. Fidel de Montclar, *Los misioneros capuchinos al público*.
9. Letter from Fray Querubín de la Piña to the Prefect Apostolic, 12 June 1917, quoted in the *Informe* for 1917, p. 79.
10. *Informe* for 1917-18, p. 150.

11. Report from the Governor, Francisco Albán, quoted in the *Informe* for 1917–18, pp. 150–52. The version given in the *Anales de la Cámara de Representantes*, No. 79, 1918, is somewhat different.
12. Ramón M. Tabarez, Pedro Luis Vélez, A. and Emiliano Toro, *Orientación Liberal*, Nos. 39 and 40, February–March 1919.
13. *Orientación Liberal*, No. 31, 24 November 1918.
14. Fidel de Montclar, *Los misioneros del Putumayo y las mentiras*.
15. Vilanova, Vol. 2, pp. 188 and 189.
16. *Diario Oficial*, No. 15,546, Bogotá, 20 July 1915.
17. For an account of the tumultuous debates of 22 to 25 August, see *Anales de la Cámara de representantes*, No. 76, Bogotá, 1917.
18. *Informe* for 1917–18, pp. 129–30.
19. Proceedings in the Chamber of Representatives. Cf. *Nuevo Tiempo*, Nos. 5,666 ff., Bogotá, 7 October 1919.
20. *Informe* for 1917, p. 10.
21. *Informe* for 1916, p. 7.

Chapter 11

1. Fidel de Montclar, *Informe* for 1917–18, pp. 155–6.
2. Fidel de Montclar, *¡A Sucre!*
3. Fidel de Montclar, *La Legalidad del embudo*, quoted in the *Informe* for 1917, p. 40.
4. Benigno de Canet de Mar, *Relaciones*, p. 114.
5. This map is based on that of Brother Pedro Claver, made in March 1922. Cf. rev. *Amazonia*, Vol. 2, p. 8.
6. Among others, cf. *Orientación Liberal*, 12 November 1922.
7. Decree by the higher court of Pasto, 20 August 1921.
8. The author has a map of the period giving the names and positions of the settlers.
9. Judgment of the higher court of Pasto, report in *Foro Nariñense*, No. 66, Pasto, 1917.
10. ibid.
11. *Informe* for 1917–18, p. 124.

Chapter 12

1. Vilanova, Vol. 2, pp. 155–6.
2. *Informe* for 1917, p. 51.
3. *Informe* for 1917–18, pp. 135–9.
4. Quoted in *Informe* for 1917, pp. 54–8.
5. *Informe* for 1917–18, pp. 188–9.
6. Ignacio de Barcelona, letter to the Prefect Apostolic, 20 April 1918. Quoted in *Informe* for 1917–18, p. 138.
7. Paulino de Barcelona, letter quoted in *Informe* for 1917–18, p. 116.

8. Ignacio de Barcelona, letter to the Prefect Apostolic, 12 March 1919. Quoted in *Informe* for 1918–19, p. 117.
9. Document in the author's collection.
10. *Informe* for 1921, pp. 49–55.
11. Vilanova, Vol. 2, Chap. 1.
12. *Informe* for 1925–6, p. 53. Cf. Vilanova, Vol. 2, Chap. 13.
13. Gaspar de Pinell, *Excursión apostólica*.
14. Duplicated. A photocopy is in the author's collection.
15. *La Misión del Caquetá*, 1923.
16. *Informe* for 1927, pp. 291 ff.
17. Gaspar de Pinell, op. cit.

Chapter 13

1. *Informe* for 1916, p. 25; Vilanova, Vol. 2, p. 257.
2. Cf. *Informes*, Vilanova, and *Bol. Cat.*, Nos. 202–3.
3. Cf. Vilanova, Vol. 2, Chap. 6; *Orientación Liberal* for 20 November 1921.
4. Notebook of the Mission's accounts, in the author's collection.
5. Figures taken from a Mission notebook with the full list of settlers involved in the affair. Six of those names have beside them the phrases, 'He is dead', 'he was drowned', or 'he was killed'. Document in the author's collection.
6. Ecclesiastical condemnation of the liberal papers *Orientación Liberal*, and *Juanambú*, reproduced by Benigno de Canet de Mar, Circular No. 6, 2 April 1923 (a tract).
7. Benigno de Canet de Mar, *Relaciones*, pp. 114 ff.
8. Colombian national budget for 1923.
9. Delfín Iza, *Viva el Caquetá*.
10. Interview of 21 November 1969; evidence signed in April 1970.
11. Marceliano de Vilafranca, *Los terrenos*, pp. 3–5.
12. This was no new rule. Cf. the law of 6 March 1932, and that of 23 June 1843. It was repeated in Decree No. 74 of 1898, and law No. 19 of 1927.
13. Vilafranca, op. cit.
14. Fidel de Montclar, *Los Misioneros capuchinos al público*.
15. Statement No. 12 from the palace of the governor of Nariño, 22 June 1922.
16. More information will be found in Vilanova, Vol. 2, Chap. 17.
17. Francisco de Igualada, *Estado de la Misión*, p. 29.
18. Jacinto de Quito, *Miscelánea*, p. 91.

Chapter 14

1. Gaspar de Pinell, *Primera carta pastoral*, Bogotá, 26 October 1930.
2. Amadeo Rodríguez, *Relación completa de la conferencia privada que*

hoy, 22 de junio de 1932, tuvo el jefe de la frontera del Amazonas con el Ilustrísimo Señor Obispo Gaspar de Pinell. M.G.Arch.

3. Extracts from the evidence recorded in the Sibundoy valley in November 1969. In the author's collection.
4. *Propaganda Fide: La Obra.*
5. Transcription by Father Lino Rampón p. 32. M.G.Arch.
6. Photocopy in the author's collection.
7. Francisco de Igualada, *Estado de la Misión,* p. 19.
8. Petition to the Minister of Industry, 11 June 1934. M.G.Arch.
9. Note to the Minister of the Economy, 20 October 1938. M.G.Arch.
10. Letter from the commissioner of the Putumayo to the Minister of Industry, 5 March 1934, M.G.Arch.
11. Marceliano de Vilafranca, *Los terrenos,* p. 4.
12. Note to the Minister of the Economy, 22 November 1937, M.G.Arch.
13. Marceliano de Vilafranca, *Los terrenos,* p. 6.
14. Gaspar de Pinell, *Eighth Pastoral Letter,* Sibundoy, 1938.
15. Requests from several Indians to the Senate, the Attorney General and various ministers, 1940–42. Photocopy in the author's collection.
16. Evidence of the commissioner's sons, Pasto, February 1967.
17. Marceliano de Vilafranca, *Los terrenos,* pp. 6–7.
18. Marcos de Castellví, typescript, *Notas etnográficas y etnografía del pueblo de Santiago,* 1939. Photocopy in the author's collection.
19. *Informe presentado por el Dr. Adolfo Romero B. sobre el resultado de la comisión que le fue confiada al municipio Colón (Putumayo), por Resolución 307 de 7 de junio último,* Bogotá, 27 July 1939, p. 5, M.G.Arch.
20. Instance from the commentaries in a single paper, *El Espectador,* in Bogotá: *Misiones de capuchinos dan baldíos en arrendamiento* (2 November 1939), *El caso de Sibundoy* (3 November) and a letter from the lawyer, Romero (20 November).
21. Cf. the letters from Marceliano de Vilafranca to Adolfo Romero, 2 and 5 July 1939, and one from the Vicar Apostolic to the Minister of the Economy, February 1940, M.G. Arch. The other rectifications are to be found in *El Espectador* (9 November 1939), *Los misioneros niegan que esten alquilando baldíos,* and in the review *Orden y Trabajo* (November 1939), 'Una importante aclaración sobre el caso Sibundoy'.
22. Decrees No. 2,575 of 28 October, and No. 2,104 of 2 November 1939.
23. Request from Benjamín Caipe to the (national) Minister of the Economy, Photocopy in the author's collection.
24. Father Lino Rampón, op. cit., p. 36. M.G.Arch.
25. Marceliano de Vilafranca, *Los terrenos,* pp. 7–10.
26. Request to the senator, Julio Cesar Enríquez, signed by Ramón Mavisoy, Lisandro Mavisoy, José Pajajoy, Bautista Chicunque and Benjamin Caipe, Sibundoy, 10 June 1943. Photocopy in the author's collection.

27. Request to the Minister of the Economy, photocopy in the author's collection.
28. José Pajajoy to the Minister of the Economy, Sibundoy, 26 January, 1940.
29. Resolution No. 100 of the Ministry of Agriculture, 1946.
30. Resolution No. 140 of the Ministry of Agriculture, 1946.
31. Marceliano de Vilafranca, *Los terrenos*, p. 12.
32. ibid.
33. Request from Salvador Chindoy de Mercedes and his son Andrés to the head of the CAPI, 6 March 1968, M.G. Arch.
34. Interview with Avelino Chicunque, November 1969. In the author's collection.

Chapter 15

1. The classification of Fray de Castellví's "Americanist studies" can can be found in the review *Amazonia*, No. 3, Sibundoy, 1945, p. 4.
2. The first figures appear in the 27 obituaries which appeared in various papers and reviews in Colombia and elsewhere at the death of Marcelino de Castellví; several of them are signed by Capuchins. Rev. *Amazonia*, No. 5, pp. 167–209, Sibundoy, 1953. Marceliano de Vilafranca's own review was called *Mirador amazónico*, and the reference in question appears in its first issue, p. 14, Bogotá, June 1953.
3. Juan Friede, letter handed to Marcelino de Castellví, Bogotá, 30 April 1946. Copy in the author's collection.
4. Fr Gustavo Huertas, 'Retrato psicográfico del Padre Marcelino de Castellví', *Miscelánea del Padre Castellví*, a CILEAC publication. Sibundoy, 1953.
5. J. Arango, *El capellán*.
6. Juan Manuel Chindoy, evidence received on 20 November 1969 in Sibundoy, and confirmed by a great many other Sibundoy. In the author's collection.
7. Interview with Diego Mavisoy, November 1969, confirmed by the majority of the population. In the author's collection.
8. *Bol. Cat.*, Nos. 201–2, p. 19, Sibundoy, December 1954.
9. Lucio Pabón Núñez, prime minister, pamphlet *La cuestión*.
10. *La Calle* (a weekly), No. 63, Bogotá, 12 December 1958.
11. Information drawn from the report made by the Bogotá board of Cicolac–Nestlé for the General Manager in New York, and from the conclusions of the Congress of Agronomists in Pasto. Both are dated April 1954.
12. Report to the Minister of Agriculture in December 1953, M.G. Arch.
13. Resolution No. 37 of the Ministry of Agriculture, 12 January 1954.
14. Such irregularities were nothing new. On 18 April 1959, the commission for national territories, sent to Sibundoy, registered as

examples, six judgements given in 1928, and a number of others made after the 'national reserve' had been established.

15. Evidence of Jesus Idrobo, Professor in the Institute of Natural Sciences of the National University of Colombia.
16. This information received by the author has been confirmed by the head of the commission for the *resguardos* in Southern Colombia.
17. Cf. the population census of 1957, and *Misiones Capuchinas*, Nos. 20–21, Bogotá, September 1960.

Chapter 16

1. Bartolomé de Igualada, letter of 3 July 1960. M.G. Arch.
2. Report from the head of the commission for colonization and *baldíos*, Mocoa, November 1969. M.G. Arch.
3. Various requests from Indian chapters to the Ministry of the Interior. Cf. Lino Rampón, *Problemas*, p. 35.
4. Exchange of letters, May–June 1961. M.G. Arch.
5. Plácido Crous, interview reported by Fr Lino Rampón, *Problemas*, M.G. Arch.
6. Lino Rampón, op. cit., pp. 62 ff.
7. Jorge Osorio Silva, *Observación y análisis de los diversos aspectos indígenas en el Putumayo*, typed original, 20 April 1962, M.G. Arch.
8. Andrés Holguín, *Informe rendido*.
9. *Corte Suprema de Justicia: Régimen*, pp. 102–3.
10. *Bol. Cat.*, No. 331, Sibundoy, September 1965.
11. Bartolomé de Igualada, letters of 9 and 15 February 1963, M.G. Arch.
12. Report quoted by the senior staff of the 5th police district to the Commissioner of the Putumayo, 17 July 1963. M.G. Arch.
13. From the office of the inspector of Yunguillo to the commissioner of Putumayo, 1963. M.G. Arch.
14. Report to the Commissioner of the Putumayo, 18 February 1964. Copy in M.G. Arch.
15. Case heard before the municipal judge of Mocoa.
16. Communication from the Ministry of the Interior to the Ministry of National Education, 6 November 1963. M.G. Arch.
17. Report from the commissioner's office to the Ministry of the Interior, Mocoa, 8 February 1962, M.G. Arch.
18. Instituto Geográfico Militar Agustín Codazzi. *Levantamiento predial del valle de Sibundoy*. Cadastral Arch.
19. Didier Martínez, report of March 1965, INCORA Arch.
20. Messages and statements published in the Colombian press between 22 March and 29 July 1965.
21. Plácido Crous, *Los misioneros*, pastoral letter.
22. Second Vatican Council, Constitution on the Church in the World Today (trans. William Purdy, D.D., S.T.L.), London 1966, p. 71.

23. Jesus Idrobo, researcher from the National University of Colombia. Information given December 1967. In the author's collection.
24. Camilo Torres Restrepo, report appearing in *La República*, 21 June 1965.
25. Bartolomé de Igualada, to the head of the CAPI, letter of 13 May 1966. M.G. Arch.
26. Law No. 81 of 1958.
27. Report from the CAPI to the head of the DAI, 24 November 1966. M.G. Arch.
28. According to the Ministry of National Education, the minimum salary of teachers, as fixed and paid by the government since November 1965 was 920 pesos per month. However, the Sibundoy Vicariate, on behalf of the State, paid no more than a maximum of 600 pesos.
29. *Bol. Cat.*, No. 354, Sibundoy, August 1957, p. 3.

Chapter 17

1. The Indian tribes living at the foot of the Andes were so concentrated and so few in number as to make it easy for the DAI to make a census of them. On the other hand, figures for the Inga and Sibundoy are less reliable, both because of their scattered way of living and their frequent journeys. According to Father Massana, between 1948 and 1964 their numbers were reduced from 6,591 to 5,405. But the CAPI indicates an increase from 7,550 to 8,152 between 1966 and 1968; this figure seems hard to accept given the high rate of infant mortality.
2. *Bol. Cat.*, No. 354, August 1967, p. 6.
3. Account by the head of the CAPI in evidence.
4. Instituto Geográfico-Militar Agustín Codazzi, *Empadronamiento predial del valle de Sibundoy*, 1966.
5. Analysis of the six-monthly report of the Sibundoy CCA, July–December 1967, CCA Arch.
6. Cf. written note No. 144 from the notary's office of Santiago, 14 July 1969.
7. Father Massana, *Informe confidencial sobre la Misión capuchina del Putumayo*, 1965. Missionary Arch. of Sibundoy.
8. This was witnessed by the author and others in the church of Santiago.
9. *Bol. Cat.*, No. 337, Sibundoy, March 1966.
10. Evidence of the head of the CAPI, confirmed by Indians, June 1968.
11. *Bol. Cat.*, No. 356, Sibundoy, October 1967. The international Eucharistic Congress in Bogotá received a sum of thirty million pesos from the State.
12. Report of the head of the CAPI, 8 March 1968, M.G.Arch.
13. Report of the DAI to the first Congress of National Territories, 1966, M.G.Arch.

14. Traditional song for night vigils, sung at the end of the year 1962 by the little girls from the Las Cochas school.

15. The Indian woman L.J. gives this example of the situation: 'I once asked the sister at the Sibundoy dispensary if the doctor would be so kind as to examine me because my breasts were dreadfully inflamed. He made me pay five pesos, and I had to buy medications – which did no good at all.'

16. Another example: 'With a recommendation from Fray Pio, I walked from Sibundoy to Santiago (10 km.) thinking that the sisters there would give me medicines for my little sick daughter. They would not give them, but only sell them to me. I have never been to get a recommendation since; what's the use?'

17. Evidence of D.J., Sibundoy, September 1969.

18. *Bol. Cat.*, No. 355, p. 9, Sibundoy, September 1967.

19. *Bol. Cat.*, No. 356, Sibundoy, October 1967.

20. Luis Caicedo Hidalgo, official of the Vicariate Apostolic, *Geografía, Historia – Instrucción cívica de la Comisaria del Putumayo*, Sibundoy, February 1965. (Duplicated).

21. The *Populorum Progressio* fund was established on 26 May 1969 by Pope Paul VI with a million dollars; its administration was entrusted to an international credit agency. That fund, allowing for loans with a term of fifty years, was granted to Colombia for the fulfilment of its social programmes among the peasants. Later it was devoted to financing programmes of agrarian reform, especially among the Paez Indians in the Cauca district.

22. Statement by the permanent Committee of the Colombian Episcopate at its 25th conference. Cf. *El Catolicismo*, Bogotá, 17 March 1969.

23. Mgr Angel Palmas, Apostolic Nuncio in Colombia. Cf. *Cultura Nariñense*, No. 23, p. 71, Pasto, May 1970.

24. The inalienable right of the Inga and Sibundoy to their ancestral lands confirmed by Colombian law, came up against the practical problems involved in undertaking thousands of legal claims, which would last for years, and mean the removal of the settlers now totally established in their valley. With the help of the author, they set about asking the State to let the Institute for Agrarian Reform grant them the privilege of not paying for the land the Institute had bought back from the Capuchin Mission, given their own previous title to that land. A petition to this effect, signed by a great many of the Indians in the Sibundoy Valley, was handed to the President of the Republic in December 1969. In November 1971 it had still not been answered. It seems probable that the government does not want to solve the Sibundoy problem, for fear of establishing a precedent affecting all the land which used to belong to Indians (and of whose ownership they have proof) now in the possession of the (white) large landowners.